MW00988477

VINYL

THE ART OF MAKING RECORDS

VINYL

THE ART OF MAKING RECORDS

MIKE EVANS

STERLING

New York

STERLING
New York

An Imprint of Sterling Publishing, Co., Inc.
1166 Avenue of the Americas
New York, NY 10036

STERLING and the distinctive Sterling logo are registered trademarks of
Sterling Publishing Co., Inc.

Copyright © 2015 Quintessence Editions Ltd.

Reprinted in 2017,2018

All rights reserved. No part of this publication may be reproduced, stored
in a retrieval system, or transmitted in any form or by any means (including
electronic, mechanical, photocopying, recording, or otherwise) without
prior written permission from the copyright holder.

ISBN 978-1-4549-1781-6

This book is an independent publication and is not associated with or
authorized, licensed, sponsored, or endorsed by any person or entity
affiliated with the well-known artists, performers, labels, or companies
referenced in this book. All trademarks are the property of their
respective owners. Such trademarks are used for editorial purposes
only, and the publisher makes no claim of ownership and shall acquire
no right, title, or interest in such trademarks by virtue of this publication.

Distributed in Canada by Sterling Publishing
c/o Canadian Manda Group, 664 Annette Street
Toronto, Ontario, M6S 2C8, Canada

For information about custom editions, special sales, and premium
and corporate purchases, please contact Sterling Special Sales at
800-805-5489 or specialsales@sterlingpublishing.com.

Manufactured in China

10 9 8 7 6 5 4 3

www.sterlingpublishing.com

MIX
Paper from
responsible sources
FSC® C008047

Contents

Introduction

By Mike Evans

In an age when music is available instantly at the tap of a button, the continuing appeal of vinyl might seem anachronistic to say the least. But the very invisibility of digitized delivery systems might be the key to the endurance of vinyl, a format that has played a major role in the way we listen to music for nearly seventy years.

When rock 'n' roll first emerged in the mid-1950s, the fragile 78 rpm shellac single—black, brittle, and very breakable—was still part of the cultural currency. Cornerstones of modern pop music, such as Elvis's "Heartbreak Hotel" and "Tutti Frutti" by Little Richard, were released as ten-inch 78s and also as seven-inch 45 rpm vinyls. But by the end of the decade the heavy old 78 had all but disappeared, with the virtually unbreakable 45 having taken its place in jukeboxes, radio stations, and domestic record players around the globe.

While the move from shellac to vinyl in the singles market was largely a question of portability and convenience, where the new plastic caused a genuine revolution was with the birth of the long player. Ever since recorded sound was first captured on disc at the end of the nineteenth century, popular music had been defined by the three-minute duration of a ten-inch 78. From show tunes and ragtime to jazz, blues, and hillbilly music, every genre evolved within the confines of the single, and every song was written with the economy and discipline of the three-minute rule in mind. As a musician once stated, "If you can't say everything you need to in three minutes, then it's not worth saying."

There was, of course, much that was worth saying that couldn't be accommodated in a three-minute time span. The biggest immediate breakthrough that came with the vinyl long-player was in the field of classical music. Where previously works of twenty minutes or so had to be played on both sides of four 78s, they could now be heard seamlessly on one side of an LP. In popular music, it enabled a string of single-length tunes to be made available on one record, whether a greatest hits compilation or a collection of new material specifically recorded as an album.

It was jazz musicians (and their pioneering producers) who first recognized the luxury of being able to indulge in longer performances in the recording studio, often capturing the magic of the improvised jam session in the process. Live concert recording also became possible for the first time, an innovation that preserved many milestone events in classical, jazz, and rock music over the years that followed.

Rock and pop was still dominated by singles well into the 1960s, at which point artists like The Beatles began to view the long-player as an end in itself. By the end of the decade, via the success of such groundbreaking albums as *Sgt. Pepper's Lonely Hearts Club Band* by The Beatles and *Pet Sounds* by the Beach Boys, album-oriented rock had arrived. Double and even triple albums turned the long-player into a vehicle for seemingly unlimited explorations (and indulgences) on the part of writers, producers, and musicians.

The other great leap forward that came with the vinyl record was the quality of the sound. The microgroove technology that made it possible to fit more material on a ten-inch or twelve-inch disc also delivered much less surface noise than on 78s. More importantly, it paved the way for the introduction of stereophonic recording in 1958.

As any collector of vinyl will tell you, the sheer tangibility of the format is what triumphs definitively over its successor, the compact disc. (Never mind recent innovations in downloading and streaming music via the internet.) Vinyl is something you can hold in your hand and enjoy as a physical product. Sleevenotes, printed lyrics, and other facts and information are usually miniscule in a five-inch CD jewel case, and the potential for imaginative artwork, compared to the twelve-inch canvas of a vinyl LP sleeve, doesn't bear thinking about. The graphic artists, designers, and photographers whose work has featured on record covers over the past six decades have produced some of the most iconic images in popular culture.

Vinyl champion Jack White, whose Third Man label has stood at the forefront of the vinyl revival, said in an interview in September 2014, "When you listen to music on an iPod . . . you're like, 'This is the song, but this isn't really the record. The record is the vinyl record.' What's great about it is that things have gotten so invisible with music on a listening level, that the demand for [vinyl] over the last decade has just risen and risen and risen."

For there to be a revival, there had to be a demise, and for vinyl that started in the 1980s with the rapid boom in CDs. But even plummeting sales, which hit an all-time low in the mid-2000s, didn't mean that vinyl actually disappeared. Most radio stations were still playing stacks of seven-inch and twelve-inch singles, thousands of jukeboxes around the world never converted to CD, and for club DJs it remained the format of choice. What had changed was the balance—vinyl's popularity persisted for singles rather than albums, which suffered the biggest damage in the face of the CD. According to the Recording Industry of America, US record companies shipped over ten million vinyl singles in 1995, alongside two million LPs and EPs. By 2005, that latter figure had plunged to fewer than 900,000.

Over the next decade, however, things turned around in spectacular fashion, with vinyl album sales rising to nine million in 2014. This has to be seen in perspective, of course, with CD sales still topping 165 million and non-physical digital albums totaling 117 million. But whereas in previous eras music buyers were generally limited to the dominant format of the time, the resurgence of vinyl has resulted from an active choice made by its growing army of devotees.

To service that choice, a vinyl-dedicated industry developed. Central to this were the independent record labels specializing in high quality pressings of both classics from the past and new releases, which kept vinyl alive before the mainstream labels once again began featuring it as a regular format in their catalogs. Similarly, many record pressing plants that struggled to survive as demand for vinyl diminished are now enjoying a sharp increase in business as a result of the current boom around the world. And at the customer interface are the record stores, dedicated retailers across the planet who have been at the vanguard of vinyl availability over the years, who are now enjoying a healthy return for their commitment. Few are vinyl-only outlets, but all welcome the high fidelity fans who head straight for the racks of twelve-inch and seven-inch plastic as soon as they enter the shop.

In the UK, the increase in vinyl sales from a tiny 0.1 percent of record sales in 2007 to 1.5 percent in 2015 inspired the Official Charts Company to launch a separate vinyl chart for albums and singles. With music virtually free via digital services such as Spotify, and CD sales falling off as a consequence, vinyl has now emerged as the prestigious format among discerning music buyers. Serious collectors may purchase only a few albums a year, but, like treasured books, they can be a lifetime acquisition.

And the vinyl revival has not just been down to diehard fans buying re-releases of music recorded for vinyl in the first place. An increasing number of vinyl sales are by contemporary artists, such as Jack White, who actively promote vinyl as their format of choice.

First launched in 2007, the annual Record Store Day brings together fans, artists, and thousands of independent record shops around the world, signaling the new interest in vinyl on a global scale. Additionally, a number of non-record retailers are selling vinyl as a must-have, fashionable item. Indeed, many contemporary vinyl fans are too young to remember when it was the primary music format.

The aim of this book isn't to persuade readers to ditch one mode of listening for another, but to celebrate vinyl in all its aspects. From the launch of stereo to gatefold sleeves, concept albums to twelve-inch singles, and album art to DJ sampling, vinyl helped define popular music as we know it. Today, it offers a wealth of discoveries for a new generation of listeners.

The Early Years

Over half a century of recording history paved the way for the advent of vinyl. During this time the length of a single disc was restricted to a mere three minutes, defining popular music of every kind. This period also saw the first appearance of the album and the packaging art that went with it. It began as a collection of four or five double-sided singles, bound together like a photograph album.

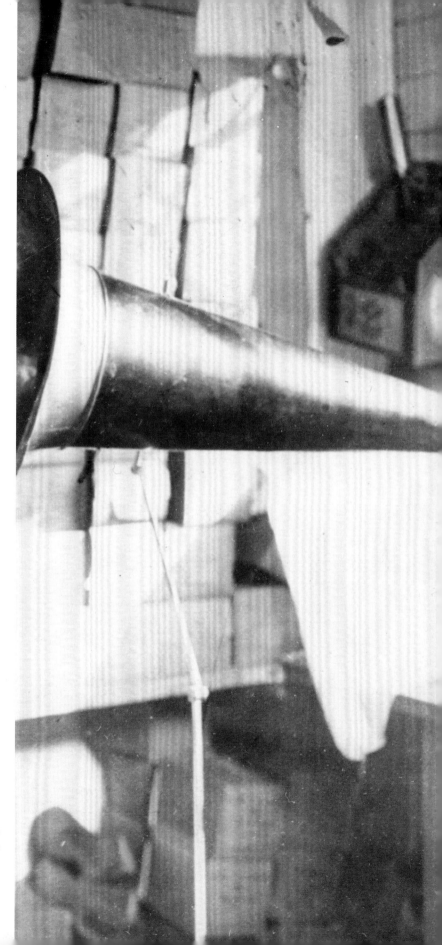

US inventor Thomas Edison with one of his phonographs in circa 1885. It became one of his favorite inventions and he continued to work on the design throughout his career.

Evolution of the Record

Nearly fifty years elapsed from the very first "talking machines" to the introduction of electrical recordings in the mid-1920s. The technological developments in this time paved the way for the vinyl revolution another quarter of a century later.

Thomas Edison develops the phonograph. A stylus reads a groove on a wax cylinder and converts it into sound via a diaphragm.

Charles Sumner Tainter and Chichester Bell patent an improved phonograph called the Graphophone.

The trademark for the Graphophone is acquired by Columbia. *(Picture from 1913.)*

1877   1878   1886   1888

Edison's invention is patented as the phonograph.

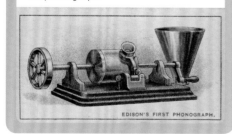

Edison perfects his phonograph with hollow wax cylinders, holding sound that lasts for two minutes.

German-American Emile Berliner produces a player using five-inch flat discs (made of wax on a zinc base), with a needle vibrating from side to side.

Berliner visits Germany to demonstrate his invention to a firm of toy makers, which produces a commercial Gramophone, marketed first in Europe.

Edison develops three versions of the Phonograph, which remain in production until 1913.

The Gramophone Company purchases the trademark "His Master's Voice" to produce a new clockwork Gramophone.

1889 **1896** **1898** **1899** **1900**

New Jersey engineer Eldridge R. Johnson builds an improved clockwork motor for the Gramophone.

Berliner opens a London branch of his Gramophone Company.

Berliner employee Fred Gaisberg starts to use shellac to make 78 rpm (revolutions per minute) flat discs. Their surfaces are laced with slate so the disc wears down the needle instead of the needle wearing down the disc.

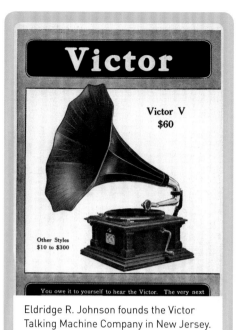

Eldridge R. Johnson founds the Victor Talking Machine Company in New Jersey.

Italian opera star Enrico Caruso makes his first acoustic recordings for the Gramophone Company.

Caruso's recording of "Vesti la giubba" ("On With the Motley") becomes the first million-copy seller in recording history.

1901 **1902** **1903** **1904** **1906**

Ten-inch shellac discs are introduced.

Twelve-inch shellac discs are introduced.

The French company Pathé Frères develops a system of flat discs of vulcanized rubber, with a jeweled stylus that plays at 95 rpm moving from the center of the disc outward.

By the outbreak of World War I, production of both the Pathé disc machine and Edison's cylinder machines has come to an end, leaving the field open for Berliner's Gramophone.

Victor and Columbia begin producing electrically recorded discs, using a microphone, instead of the previous system of capturing sound acoustically.

Victor releases the first electrical classical recording: Chopin impromptus and Schubert's "Litanei," performed by Alfred Cortot.

1914

1925

Victor launches the Orthophonic Victrola record player, representing a huge step forward in record reproduction.

In February, the first electrical recording, using the Western Electric System, is released by Columbia: Art Gillham, billed as "The Whispering Pianist," performed "You May Be Lonesome."

The first commercially successful electrical record is "Let it Rain, Let it Pour," a fox-trot dance tune by Meyer Davis's Le Paradis Band, released in May by Columbia.

First Albums

Once the shellac 78 rpm disc had become established as the standard format for mass-marketed recorded music (usually in a ten-inch size, though occasionally twelve-inch), an ever-growing army of consumers wanted somewhere to keep them. By 1910, bound collections of empty record sleeves were sold as "record albums" in the manner of photograph albums, for customers to store their easily broken shellac discs.

In the 1930s, record companies began issuing collections of 78s by one performer or one type of music—or, in the case of classical music, long works split over several 78s—and marketing them as "albums," albeit for a time in plain covers. Then, in 1940, Columbia's newly appointed in-house designer Alex Steinweiss persuaded the company to release an album of four 78s (containing eight two-song medleys) called Smash Song Hits by Rodgers & Hart, with a pictorial front cover and notes on the music on the inside and back. The art of the album cover was born.

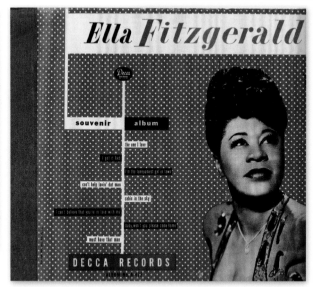

≪ The Ella Fitzgerald *Souvenir Album* rereleased as a ten-inch long-playing record in 1949, when Decca adopted the microgroove vinyl system.

‹ The *Souvenir Album* (1947), an album of 78s by Ella Fitzgerald on the Decca label. The binding making up the "album" can clearly be seen on the left-hand edge.

⌃ Artist Jim Flora worked under the pioneering Alex Steinweiss at Columbia Records. The artwork for this 1947 set of 78s by Louis Armstrong (reissues of eight of his classics sides with the Hot Five, recorded between 1925 and 1928) is typical of Flora's effervescent, humorous style.

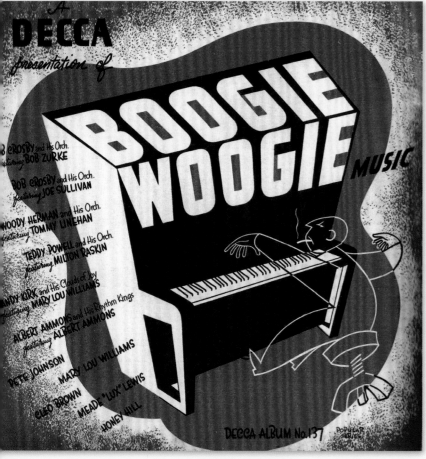

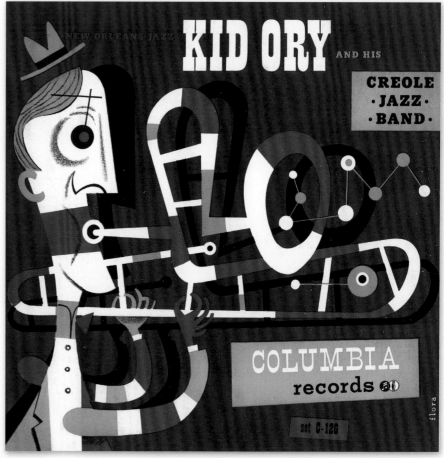

⟨ Jim Flora's cover for *Mambo For Cats* (1955).

∟ From the early 1940s, when the boogie-woogie craze was in full swing, a Decca 78 collection of boogie-woogie and boogie-related recordings.

∨ Another playful Jim Flora artwork from 1947, depicting jazz trombonist Edward "Kid" Ory.

Record sales boomed throughout the 1940s, with big band leaders, such as Benny Goodman and Woody Herman, jazz stars, such as Louis Armstrong, and fashionable crooners, such as Bing Crosby and Frank Sinatra, all releasing multiple albums of their music. Equally popular were themed albums of various styles, such as boogie woogie and Latin American, as well as collections of songs from Broadway shows. Most popular of all were pieces of classical music.

With the advent of the microgroove long-playing record (LP) in 1948, many of the album collections of 78s were simply reissued in their entirety on LPs. A typical ten-inch album accommodated the equivalent of both sides of four or five singles. And the artwork pioneered on the 78 albums, by artists such as Steinweiss, Jim Flora, and Bob Jones, would lay the foundations for the design innovations accompanying the vinyl revolution.

« Frank Sinatra's classic collection *The Voice of Frank Sinatra* (1946) became the first popular release on long-playing vinyl, when Columbia rereleased it after their launch of the LP in 1948.

⌐ Louis Armstrong released scores of records with his jazz band the All Stars.

‹ Volume III of Victor's "Hot Jazz" series, a mid-1940s set of four 78s by vibraphone star Lionel Hampton.

⌃ By the mid-1940s, Decca had a wealth of jazz in their back catalog, such as this reissue of eight of Jimmie Lunceford's biggest hits from the 1930s, *For Dancers Only*.

After Emile Berliner introduced the first disc-playing Gramophone (as distinct from Thomas Edison's Phonograph cylinder machine) in 1889, the records themselves were initially pressed in various materials, including hard rubber. But from the late 1890s, a shellac-based compound was beginning to be used, and in 1900 one of Berliner's employees, Fred Gaisberg, introduced a shellac formula that included a mineral filler of pulverized slate, which gave the disc a surface strength against the continuous grinding pressure of the metal needle during playing. (Gaisberg's meticulous diaries include often entertaining comments on the artists he committed to disc: "Today we made records of more bum artists," "Grand Opera choruses with orchestra accompaniments, solos with orchestra accompaniment…the most pretentious yet attempted on a talking machine.")

Pressing Matters

With variations to the exact composition of the compound, shellac became the standard material for 78 rpm discs up until their demise in the 1950s. Nevertheless, early record manufacturing is littered with instances of "unbreakable" discs being introduced to challenge the brittle and easily shattered shellac. In 1904, Nicole records, made of cardboard with celluloid lamination and a "label" printed on the disc, debuted in the UK. While certainly unbreakable in normal use, the pressings suffered from very high surface noise.

The Columbia Phonograph Company introduced an unbreakable disc in 1907. Purporting to have been invented by Italian radio pioneer Guglielmo Marconi—of whom there was a picture on the label, although his link was tenuous, having merely been hired by the company as "consultant physicist"—the new, flexible disc was called the Marconi

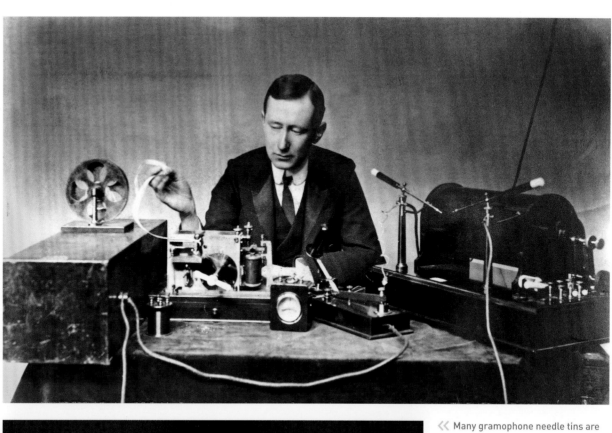

≪ Many gramophone needle tins are now desirable collector's items.

∧ Italian physicist Guglielmo Marconi is famous for his pioneering work on long-distance radio transmission.

< Marconi Velvet Tone records were marketed by Columbia as being as "Wonderful as Wireless."

Velvet Tone. Made of strong paper laminated with two sheets of celluloid, it delivered remarkable surface quality, but at the cost of listeners having to purchase special gold-plated Marconi needles in order to play it. Production ceased within a year, and, by 1910, a New York department store was selling off the 75¢ discs at 17¢ a piece, with gold needles thrown in for free.

Innovations that suffered similar fates included British flexible discs: one by Goodson Records, marketed in the 1930s; the other by Filmophone, made of transparent celluloid in various bright colors, available from 1930 to 1932.

The most imaginative enterprise involving unbreakable

PRESSING MATTERS THE EARLY YEARS

《 American singer Gene Austin, one of the first "crooners," circa 1930.

⌐ An Italian needle tin bearing the "His Master's Voice" trademark.

⋀ A label for a release by the short-lived flexible disc company Filmophone.

⟨ Actor, singer, and comedian Eddie Cantor during a recording session for RCA Victor, circa 1935.

The most imaginative enterprise involving unbreakable discs was Hit of the Week, a series of plastic records published weekly like a magazine. Made of a blend of paper and resin called Durium, they could be bought on newsstands across the United States. The project was a direct result of the Great Depression, during which fans had less disposable income; at 15¢ a copy, they were the cheapest records available. Among popular artists of the period who appeared on Hit of the Week were Eddie Cantor, Gene Austin, Rudy Vallee, and Duke Ellington's Orchestra (billed as the Harlem Hot Chocolates).

Those one-sided records appeared from February 1930 until the final edition in June 1932, but records made of Durium continued to be released in the UK and sold on the same basis for a year or so more. They were also exported to other European countries, including Sweden and Denmark.

∧ Singer Rudy Vaellee, performing at a night club.

❭ Pop singer Pearl Bailey during a recording session for Columbia Records, circa 1945.

❭❭ Duke Ellington released two Hit of the Week records with his orchestra, as the Harlem Hot Chocolates.

Although perfected with improved technology over seven decades, the basic process of making vinyl records remains similar to when it was first introduced in the 1940s.

First of all a recording is made—usually in a studio, but sometimes in a mobile setup in the case of live recordings at concerts and such. At this point, the producer and engineers perfect the sound that will end up on the record. Then the first step in the manufacturing process takes place, when the taped or digitally recorded sound is transferred to what is known as a "lacquer." This is an aluminum disc coated in acetate lacquer, into which the electric analog signals of the original recording are cut via a record-cutting machine,

Making a Record

called a lathe, with a heated diamond stylus or needle. (Glass was used instead of aluminum during the war years.)

This first stage often takes place in the same studio where the original recording is made, after which the imprinted lacquer is sent to a production plant. There, the black disc is cleaned—using distilled water to make sure any grease is removed before being coated in a thin layer of silver—to make it electrically conductive.

The disc is placed in an electroplating bath for three or four hours, where individual nickel molecules attach themselves

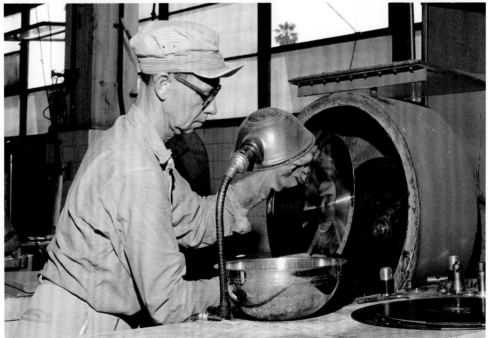

Employees demonstrating different
stages of the record making process
at the Columbia Records Hollywood
pressing plant in.1963.

to the silver. This creates what is known as the metal master. When it is separated from the original lacquer, this master is now a negative with ridges instead of grooves, so a positive nickel copy is made from that, called the mother. The mother copy is played and checked for any faults, then used in turn to make negative nickel stampers—which, as the name implies, are the versions from which the final run of records is pressed. It's at this stage that the actual vinyl comes into play.

《 A machine cuts grooves onto the surface of a copper plate to create a metal master disc.

⌐ The metal master disc is placed in the metalwork bath to be electroplated.

∧ A row of electroplating baths.

⟨ The master disc and a matrix copy. The matrix copy is used to create the mother copy.

< The copper master disc (left) is separated from a nickel stamper disc in the electroplating bath.

∧ An engraving machine is used to apply matrix numbers onto a master copper disc.

The word "vinyl" is an abbreviation of polyvinyl chloride (or PVC), which comes in the form of black pellets (or other shades if a colored disc is being manufactured). These pellets are sucked into a hydraulic press and melted at high temperature before being squirted out as vinyl biscuits, which are sandwiched and flattened between two stampers representing each side of the finished record. Any excess PVC is trimmed off, and the disc is stiffened using cold water. Multiple stampers are used to allow for large quantities to be pressed, and fresh stampers are utilized at each run of records. It's at this pressing stage that the labels are also introduced, so what comes off the press is the finished article—the glistening symbol of recording technology familiar to generations as the vinyl disc.

⌃ Paper labels before being attached to the records.

⌐ The vinyl "biscuit" from which the discs are sliced.

⌐ A machine applies the finishing touches to a disc.

> The polyvinyl pellets that are melted to create the discs.

≫ A stack of vinyl discs emerge from a press.

1940s

After early forays into long-playing vinyl technology, the LP format was finally launched by Columbia Records in 1948. It was soon taken up by all the major labels, including Decca, Capitol, and, after some reluctance, Columbia's archrival RCA. It also ushered in the era of memorable sleeve art, pioneered by men like Alex Steinweiss and Jim Flora, who had cut their teeth on the bound albums of 78s over the preceding years.

< English conductor and impresario
Sir Thomas Beecham examines a
pair of turntables and some vinyl.

V for Victory

The first use of vinyl in record-making came nearly two decades before the spread of the microgroove long playing record. In 1931, RCA Victor launched the first commercially available vinyl long-playing records, known as program-transcription discs: twelve-inch discs that played at 33⅓ rpm and featured about ten minutes on each side. They were discontinued by early 1933 due to financial pressure on the company and consumers during the Great Depression. Around the same time, Columbia introduced ten-inch longer-playing vinyl discs, but these too were phased out in mid-1932.

Vinyl was used regularly when shellac, used to make 78s, was in short supply during World War II. The United States entered the war in December 1941, and the troops needed morale boosters from home, but no music was released to fulfill the demand, because of a strike called in July 1942 by the American Federation of Musicians (AFM) union that lasted nearly two-and-a-half years. To fill the gap, sound engineer G. Robert Vincent, assigned to the radio section of the Army Special Services Division, approached the War Department with the idea of recording music especially for the forces serving overseas.

With Washington's approval, Vincent assured record companies and the AFM that recordings would be for only military personnel and would be destroyed, along with the masters, when no longer needed. Commercial recordings, radio broadcasts, rehearsals for radio shows, and film soundtracks were plundered for content.

The results were dubbed V Discs, the V standing for "victory" and "Vincent." Due to the shortage of shellac, they were pressed in vinyl, as twelve-inch instead of ten-inch discs, with as many as 136 grooves per inch. Accommodating more than six minutes of music per side, they weren't exactly microgroove, but they were certainly a breakthrough.

The first discs shipped on October 1, 1943, from the RCA pressing plant in New Jersey. The shipment of 1,780 boxes, each containing thirty records, went just to Army personnel (the Navy and Air Force were added later), and they featured music by the likes of Bing Crosby, Artie Shaw, Duke Ellington, and Frank Sinatra.

The project ran until May 1949. During that time, more than 3,000 recordings were shipped all over the world via more than eight million discs. Most were subsequently destroyed as agreed with the music industry, meaning that surviving discs are now collectors' items.

Military precision: Sound engineer
G. Robert Vincent. As well as launching
V Discs, Vincent helped establish
Armed Forces Radio, and in 1945 he
was Sound Recording Officer for the
United Nations at the Nuremburg trials.

PUT YOUR ARMS AROUND ME ...
BEA WAIN

Frank Sinatra appeared on the B side of V Disc #1, singing "Blue Skies" with the Tommy Dorsey Orchestra. The A side of the historic recording consisted of two songs by Bea Wain, an equally big name at the time.

PRELUDE TO A KISS
DUKE ELLINGTON

By the end of the 1930s, bandleader Duke Ellington was a huge star, making his presence on a V Disc a real coup. As a bonus, "Prelude to a Kiss" is an example of the classical flourishes that he brought to swing music.

BOY MEETS HORN
CHRIS GRIFFIN

Chris Griffin, trumpeter in Benny Goodman's orchestra, clashed with his demanding boss. Yet each time he tried to resign, Goodman upped his salary. And as a gesture of conciliation, he was awarded his own showcase, "Boy Meets Horn."

I NEVER FELT THIS WAY BEFORE
DUKE ELLINGTON

A songwriter as well as a bandleader, Ellington benefited from the additional income from the former when the AFM strike ended in a deal that increased royalties for musicians: a huge financial cost to big bands, such as the Duke's.

Columbia chief Edward Wallerstein's ambition was to have a single disc that could contain at least seventeen minutes of music per side, enabling, as he put it, "About ninety percent of all classical music to be put on two sides of a record."

The development of the long-playing record had been filled with delays—not least the effect on research budgets of the economic depression in the 1930s, followed by World War II in the first half of the 1940s—and technical difficulties. The latter, which included pickups that were too heavy, grooves that were too wide, and disc material that was too soft, were addressed from 1945 by a research team at Columbia, headed by engineer Peter Goldmark. By 1947, they had met Wallerstein's target: an LP that played at 33⅓ rpm for a full twenty-two-and-a-half minutes per side, capable of holding 224 to 300 microgrooves per inch (about 1,500 feet [457 meters] of continuous groove), compared to around ninety on a 78.

Key to this development was the evolution of the stylus. Replacing the metal needle used to pick up the signals embedded in the grooves of shellac 78s, the tiny crystal of sapphire or diamond was designed to vibrate in the groove.

Into the Microgroove

This movement was transmitted to an electromagnetic cartridge, which generated an electric signal. This, in turn, was transmitted as sound via an amplifier.

Columbia unveiled their new innovation at a press conference in the Waldorf-Astoria hotel in New York City on June 18, 1948. In front of an assembly of journalists, many of them skeptical, Wallerstein, Goldmark, and other company bigwigs put on a spectacular demonstration. On one side of the stage was an eight-foot (nearly two-and-a-half-meter) pile of 78s; on the other, 101 long-playing records that stood just 15 inches (38 centimeters). The reporters were told the two stacks of records represented the same amount of music, after which Wallerstein proceeded to play one 78. After four minutes the disc came to an abrupt end. The executive then put on an LP containing the same work—all on one side, lasting for more than twenty-two minutes. The newspapermen were astounded, and the long-playing record (or LP, as Columbia had dubbed its innovation) was launched.

The debut releases followed immediately, totaling 132 albums: 84 classical LPs on twelve-inch discs, 26 classical on ten-inch, 18 pop discs on ten-inch, and four children's

‹‹ Inventor Peter Goldmark standing next to a storage tower of 78s that hold the same amount of music as the stack of LPs he is holding under his arm.

⌐ The long-playing microgroove revolutionized the vinyl format.

⌃ Columbia Records president Edward Wallerstein with baseball players Pee Wee Reese (left) and Jackie Robinson (right).

‹ Columbia Records were at the forefront of the microgroove revolution.

releases on ten-inch. In terms of cataloging, the official first LP, issued on June 28, 1948, with the number ML 4001, was the Mendelssohn Violin Concerto in E minor, performed by Nathan Milstein, with Bruno Walter conducting the Philharmonic Symphony Orchestra of New York. The first popular music release was CL 6001, *The Voice of Frank Sinatra* (flagged on the cover as "Nonbreakable Vinylite"), previously released in 1946 as an album of four 78s.

Well aware that their competitors would jump on the technological bandwagon, Columbia had made contingency plans to stay ahead of the game. "I insisted," Wallerstein explained, "that our setup be built so that everything that was recorded at 78 rpm was also done at 33 rpm on sixteen-inch blanks. This gave Columbia a tremendous advantage over its competitors, who, when the LP finally appeared, were

These new records play full half hour, reproducing entire symphony or vaudeville act. Insert shows special turn-table which slows speed from 75 r.p.m. down to 33⅓ revolutions.

⌃ American socialite, fashion designer, actress, writer, and artist Gloria Vanderbilt with a Decca LP by Richard Tauber entitled *Songs of Old Vienna* (1954).

⌃ An advertisement highlighting the extended listening times made possible by the long-playing record.

⌐ The introduction of a sapphire or diamond stylus to play the records was a key component of the LP's success.

≫ The Voice of Frank Sinatra was the first pop album to be issued as an LP.

⌐ The first LP: The Mendelssohn Violin Concerto in E minor, performed by Nathan Milstein.

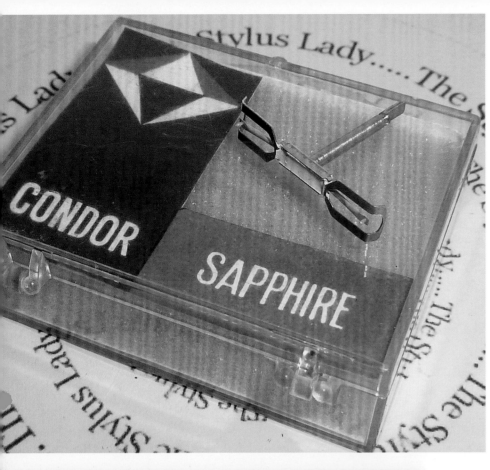

forced to make copies from their old, noisy shellac records for any material predating tape. RCA issued many of these old records with words of apology for their poor quality printed on the jackets. Columbia had masters of good quality going back almost ten years, and this made a great deal of difference in our early technical superiority."

At first, archrival RCA seemed to ignore the LP format, instead launching its rival seven-inch 45 rpm disc in 1949 for what became, for a time, the "War of the Speeds." Meanwhile, Capitol and Decca both adopted the LP format in 1949. RCA finally relented, issuing a twenty-five-strong batch of 33s in March 1950. (Most were reissues of catalog items, bar a triple-disc set of Robert Shaw conducting Bach's *Mass in B Minor* and a Wanda Landowska recording of the same composer's *Well-Tempered Clavier, Book I*.) The LP had truly arrived and soon became *the* classic vinyl format.

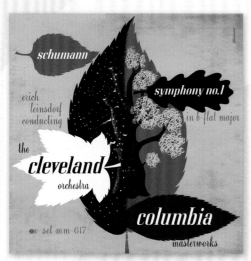

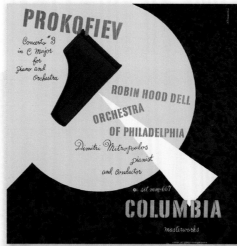

SCHUMANN SYMPHONY NO.1
ERICH LEINSDORF (1946)

As *The Shellackophile* notes, this cover omits the symphony's nickname ["Spring"], even though it originated with the composer, but the cover does "graphically portray the transition from winter to spring."

PROKOFIEV PIANO CONCERTO
DIMITRI MITROPOULOS (1946)

"The great Greek conductor and pianist, Dimitri Mitropoulos," notes *The Shellackophile*, leads "the Robin Hood Dell Orchestra . . . (essentially the Philadelphia Orchestra) in a couple of their earliest recordings under that name."

DEBUSSY SONATA NO. 2
L. NEWELL, M. KATIMS, J. WUMMER (1947)

Like the Cole Porter sleeve above, this features examples of the cover designer's spontaneous yet calligraphic writing—nicknamed the "Steinweiss Scrawl"—that was immortalized as the font Steinweiss Script.

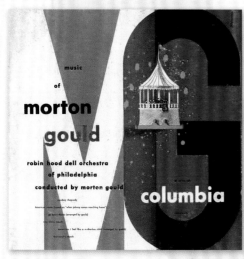

MUSIC OF MORTON GOULD
MORTON GOULD (1947)

"A smattering of each of Gould's talents— composer, pianist, conductor, arranger," noted *Billboard*. "'Cowboy Rhapsody' and 'American Salute' are Gould compositions . . . The remaining items are his arrangements of familiar works."

BEETHOVEN SYMPHONY NO. 6
BRUNO WALTER (1947)

Bruno Walter conducts the Philadelphia Orchestra in the "Pastorale" symphony. Steinweiss's cover reflects the title of the first of the five movements: "Awakening of Cheerful Feelings on Arriving in the Country."

MUSIC OF COLE PORTER
ANDRÉ KOSTELANETZ (1948)

Russian conductor Kostelanetz's orchestra presents the songwriter supreme's hits "In the Still of the Night," "Blow, Gabriel, Blow," "All Through the Night," "I've Got You under My Skin," "I Concentrate on You," and "I Love You."

Alex Steinweiss

Alex Steinweiss is a founding father of album cover art. He made his mark in the previnyl era, when albums consisted of bound volumes of three or four 78s, but subsequently pioneered the design of LP sleeves when they first appeared in the late 1940s.

Born in Brooklyn in 1917, he graduated from New York's Parsons School of Design, worked for poster designer Joseph Binder, then was appointed Columbia's art director in 1940. His job was to design point-of-sale material, posters, and catalogs, but when he turned his eye to albums, history was about to happen.

Sets of 78s were often packaged in plain, faux-leather covers with embossed lettering on the spine, like the photograph albums on which the design was based. Steinweiss realized each album could be better promoted with

an attractive cover that reflected the music inside, and he persuaded company boss Edward Wallerstein to try his idea.

His first cover was a Broadway show tunes collection, *Smash Song Hits by Rodgers & Hart*, on which the title appeared in the neon lights of a theater marquee. Sales of Steinweiss's albums promptly outstripped those in plain packaging. Within a year, Columbia's rivals Decca and RCA Victor were releasing albums in individually designed covers.

After World War II, during which he worked for the US Navy in New York, Steinweiss returned to Columbia as a consultant. In 1948, Wallerstein asked him to help develop packaging for the soon-to-launch vinyl long-playing records. He came up with what became the industry standard: a thin board sleeve lined with printed

paper, with a narrow spine just thick enough to present the album title on view when stacked upright on a shelf. The back cover bore details that came to be known as liner notes.

Steinweiss's work was characterized by a flamboyant, graphic, hand-drawn style that until the mid-1950s rarely used photographic imagery and was influenced by artists such as Paul Klee and Piet Mondrian. His "Steinweiss scrawl"—handwritten logos and cover text—became a signature element. Through the 1950s he completed hundreds of design projects for major labels, including—as well as Columbia—Decca, RCA, Remington, London, and Everest Records, which he helped launch in 1958. In a career that lasted until 1973, he designed around 2,500 covers before retiring to devote his time to painting. He died in 2011.

Alex Steinweiss working at his desk at Columbia Records in New York City, 1947. Artworks on his desk include albums by Louis Armstrong and Earl Hines (center) and a boogie-woogie compilation (right).

DECCA

Unlike its major competitors, Columbia and RCA Victor, Decca Records began as a British label, established by former stockbroker Edward Lewis. The name originated with the Decca Gramophone Company—makers of a portable gramophone called the Decca Dulcephone, patented in 1914—which Lewis bought in 1929. Within a few years of its launch, Decca was one of the world's leading record labels and is now recognized for its crucial role in both the classical and popular music fields.

Its classical list began modestly in 1929 with the release of three 78s covering a new work by Delius, *Sea Drift*. But from the late 1940s, under the guidance of producer John Culshaw, the label pioneered technical innovation with "ffrr"—full frequency range recording—and early stereophonic recording. In tandem with the advent of the long-playing record, Decca broke new ground in recording classical music, with the bonus of star names, such as singer Kathleen Ferrier and conductor Ernest Ansermet. The latter conducted the first stereo recording of Tchaikovsky's *The Nutcracker*, issued by Decca in 1959.

Decca's US arm initially released classical music recorded by British Decca until the early 1950s, when it struck a distribution deal with the German label Deutsche Grammophon. When the US company began making its own recordings, big names graced the "Gold Label" series, including Hungarian pianist Lili Kraus, conductors Max Rudolf and Leroy Anderson, and Spanish guitarist Andrés Segovia.

The American and British arms effectively operated as separate labels. American Decca pioneered the idea of the original cast recording, when it released a set of six 78s featuring songs from the musical *Oklahoma!* (1943) by the Broadway production's cast and orchestra.

The set's success prompted Decca to do the same with *Carousel* and *Annie Get Your Gun*, paving the way for complete recordings made possible by the advent of long-playing records.

Decca's pop and jazz roster included such stars as the Boswell Sisters, Louis Armstrong, Billie Holiday, the Andrews Sisters, Judy Garland, Count Basie, and Bing Crosby, the most popular vocalist of the day. In 1942, Crosby sang what became one of the biggest-selling singles of all-time, "White Christmas."

Under its first executive director, Jack Kapp, Decca also developed an enviable country music list with the Sons of the Pioneers and movie star Roy Rogers among early signings. By the 1950s, it had become RCA's main rival in the country stakes, with Kitty Wells, Patsy Cline, and Loretta Lynn gracing its catalog.

Decca paved the way for rock 'n' roll, thanks to a rich catalog of blues and rhythm-and-blues records going back to the 1930s. (The biggest R&B star of the 1940s, Louis Jordan, was signed to the label). In 1954, the company unleashed a song that truly launched rock 'n' roll: Bill Haley and His Comets entered Decca's studios in the Pythian Temple building in New York City and cut "Rock Around the Clock." The first rock 'n' roll record to top the US charts, it went on to sell a reported 25 million copies.

In Britain, Decca signed homegrown rock 'n' rollers, including Tommy Steele, Terry Dene, and Billy Fury, but miscalculated in 1962 when it turned down The Beatles, who auditioned at the company's London studios. (Nearly fifty years later, Decca partnered with Paul McCartney to release his 2011 ballet score *Ocean's Kingdom*.) Eager to avoid repeating that error, Decca signed The Rolling Stones in 1963.

Today, part of the Universal Music Group, Decca still thrives. Its catalog of legends is complemented by contemporary artists as varied as Alison Kraus, Imelda May, Katherine Jenkins, Elvis Costello, and Susan Tedeschi. But it is as one of the building blocks of the recording industry, flourishing in the years when vinyl established itself, that Decca earned its place in music history.

↱ English pop idol Tommy Steele
listens to his Ferguson Radiogram
at his parents' London home in 1957.

❯ American singer and cowboy actor
Roy Rogers playing an acoustic
guitar, circa 1940.

❯❯ Bing Crosby examines the
soundtrack to his musical *The
Emperor Waltz* (1948).

∨ The Rolling Stones pose at the
Decca pressing plant in 1964.

DECCA PRESENTS...
E.T. MENSAH (1952)

This calypso collection from the Ghanaian bandleader known as the "King of Highlife" was part of Decca's West African Series. Other entries in the series included *Dance Nights in Nigeria*, *Black Beat Rhythms*, *Ghana on Parade*, *Come to Kumasi—Ashanti High Lifes*, and *Juju Music of I.K. Dairo*.

THE ROLLING STONES
THE ROLLING STONES (1964)

This EP (on the sleevenotes for which Bill Wyman is credited for "base guitar") features four covers: Chuck Berry's "Bye Bye Johnny," Barrett Strong's Motown classic "Money" (also recorded around the same time by The Beatles), Arthur Alexander's "You Better Move On," and Leiber and Stoller's "Poison Ivy," previously a hit for The Coasters. This was typical of the Stones' cover-based repertoire of the time, in the days before wily manager Andrew Loog Oldham persuaded Mick Jagger and Keith Richard (as he was then known) that they needed to write hit songs of their own.

INTO THE FORTIES
VARIOUS ARTISTS (1959)

This collection was one of a series of six LPs, bookended by *The Late Thirties* and *The Late Fifties*. "Nothing short of S-E-N-S-A-T-I-O-N-A-L," claimed an advertisement for the set in *Billboard*. "That's the dealer reaction to the music goes 'round and around series of six of the hottest albums of all time! . . . Every hitmaker on the Decca label is represented here: Crosby, the Mills Brothers, Ted Weems, the Weavers, Bill Haley, and many more . . . This should be a solid seller, from a nostalgic or a historical side, as well as mighty good listening."

HEART OF STONE
THE ROLLING STONES (1965)

A US hit in its own right, *Heart of Stone* was issued in Europe as an EP. Of its three other originals, "The Last Time" became one of the Stones' most enduring songs— thanks in part to an orchestral version being the bedrock of The Verve's "Bitter Sweet Symphony."

OUT IN THE STREET
THE WHO (1966)

This Japanese single couples Pete Townshend's "Out in the Street" (the opener on 1965's *My Generation*) with his band's cover of James Brown's "Please, Please, Please." The Who's discography also features records on the Brunswick and Track imprints, both distributed by Decca.

THE HI-FI NIGHTINGALE
CATERINA VALENTE (1956)

This first US set by Italian singer, guitarist, and dancer Caterina Valente includes "The Breeze and I" (based on Ernesto Lecuona's "Andalucia") and "Malagueña" (also by Lecuona). "Miss Valente is well known throughout the European continent," explain the sleeve notes. "A true international star possessing beauty and personality that match her sparkling vocal technique . . . To make this offering more distinguished, [her] amazing voice is accompanied by the symphonic-sounding orchestras of Werner Müller, Kurt Edelhagen, Paul Durand, and Monaco Bell."

FFSS • FULL FREQUENCY STEREO SOUND
STEREO DEMONSTRATION RECORD (1958)

This 1958 EP showcased Decca's trademark "full frequency stereo sound." This was the result of the "Decca tree"—an innovative system of microphones used from 1954 onward to record orchestras, developed by the company's chief engineer Arthur Haddy, with his colleagues Roy Wallace and Kenneth Wilkinson. However, with stereo then regarded as a luxury, Decca and other labels continued to issue most of their records in mono until well into the 1960s. Hi-fi buffs customarily used demonstration records to gauge the effectiveness of their configurations.

ORIGINAL EVERGREEN TUNES
KING ONYINA (circa 1970)

This early 1970s gem is another example of Decca's commitment to African music—in this case, highlife (Ghanaian music full of horns and guitars) by the highly regarded Kwabena Onyina, nicknamed "King" after he won a guitar band competition in 1961.

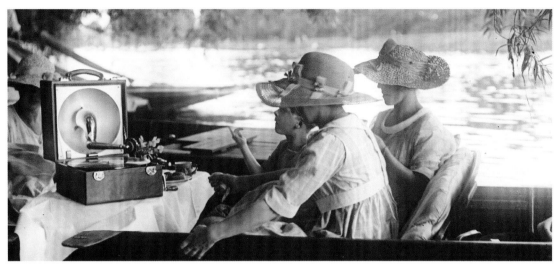

The Decca gramophone company provide the entertainment for a music-loving boating party.

Billie Holiday at a Decca recording session, circa 1946.

Decca Records producer and A&R man Dick Rowe—who turned down The Beatles—circa 1965.

∧ Patsy Cline displays her Billboard award with Decca Nashville executive Harry Silverstein.

⌐ Hungarian pianist Lili Kraus, one of the classical stars featured in Decca's "Gold Label" series.

⟩ Louis Jordan (third from left with sax) and his Tympany Five pose for a portrait, circa 1955.

1950s

During the 1950s, the long-playing record came into its own, with classical music and jazz particularly benefiting from the extended playing time. Specialist album-dominated labels such as Blue Note, Verve, and Folkways emerged, while the birth of rock 'n' roll coincided with the spread of the seven-inch vinyl single, which replaced the bulky 78 in jukeboxes and domestic record players around the world.

‹ Italian actress Claudia Cardinale
(later featured on the artwork of
Bob Dylan's *Blonde on Blonde*)
listens to Ella Fitzgerald vinyls
in Rome, 1959.

When records were restricted to the 78 rpm format, classical music enthusiasts eager to own complete works had to contend with multiple discs. The pieces, intended to be heard in concert halls, or via radio broadcasts, lasted longer than individual 78s could accommodate. The revolution that ushered in the long-playing record, therefore, had a bigger initial impact on the classics than on any other genre.

Indeed, when RCA executive and Columbia boss Edward Wallerstein announced the development of microgroove technology, his stated ambition was to make classical works available on both sides of a single disc. When Columbia launched the LP in 1948, classical records outnumbered popular and children's discs by a ratio of five to one.

Consumers weren't swayed overnight, not least because the quality of the first releases wasn't necessarily a given. "Early LPs tended to be hard, dull, and wiry in sound," wrote

Marketing the Classics

Roland Gelatt in *The Fabulous Phonograph*. "Sustained notes were wont to waver ever so slightly (producing an unpleasant effect called 'wow'); and loud passages sometimes made a faint and untimely appearance ahead of the beat—through an annoying phenomenon known as 'pre-echo'."

However, among Columbia's first successes in the new format were performances by conductors and orchestras, including Eugene Ormandy and the Philadelphia Orchestra, Bruno Walter with the New York Philharmonic, and Sir Thomas Beecham and the Royal Philharmonic Orchestra.

Following in Columbia's footsteps, Decca's roster was enhanced by distribution deals with the German label Deutsche Grammophon and Britain's Parlophone. When Decca began issuing its own classical LPs, best sellers included the "light classical" composer/conductor

COR DE GROOT,

KLAVIER,

LEITUNG:

WILLEM VAN OTTERLOO

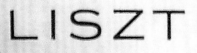

FAVORITEN-SERIE PHILIPS S 04001 L

LISZT

KLAVIERKONZERTE NR. 1 UND 2

PHILIPS
Minigroove 33⅓

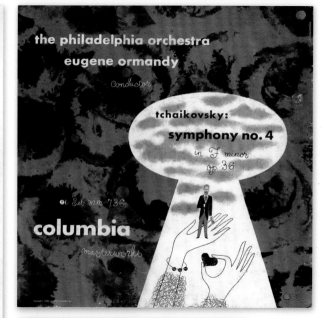

the philadelphia orchestra
eugene ormandy
conductor

tchaikovsky:
symphony no. 4
in F minor
op 36

Set MM-736

columbia
masterworks

ML 4788

Lotte Lehmann
SOPRANO

Bruno Walter
PIANO

SCHUMANN

FRAUENLIEBE UND LEBEN

DICHTERLIEBE

COLUMBIA MASTERWORKS

⟨ *Liszt: Piano Concertos Nos. 1 and 2* (1954), illustrated by fashion photographer Paul Huf.

⋀ A more formal design approach was adopted for *Schumann: Frauenliebe Und Leben Op. 42. and Dichterliebe Op. 48*, performed by soprano Lotte Lehmann.

⋀ An Alex Steinweiss cover for *Tchaikovsky: Symphony No. 4 in F Minor, Op. 36*, performed by the Philadelphia Orchestra and conducted by Eugene Ormandy (1947).

Leroy Anderson, Max Rudolf conducting the Cincinnati Symphony Orchestra, and the Spanish guitarist Andrés Segovia.

When RCA Victor began issuing 33s in early 1950, among its first releases was Offenbach's *Gâîté Parisienne*, performed by Arthur Fiedler with the Boston Pops Orchestra. Other regulars in the RCA catalog included the NBC Symphony Orchestra conducted by Arturo Toscanini, the Chicago Symphony Orchestra, and the Boston Symphony.

Competition in the seemingly genteel classical music world was fierce, and labels vied for customers' attention with imaginative artwork that ranged from the elegantly classic to the contemporary designs of artists, including Steinweiss, Bob Jones, Erik Nitsche, and, specifically for the European market, Dutch fashion photographer Paul Huf. The latter's use of professional models on albums of highbrow music demonstrated how willing the companies were to promote their lists vigorously in the marketplace, making the music more popularly accessible in the process.

∧ One of Decca's early releases in the classical LP market, *Mozart: String Quartet No. 17* (1945).

⌐ Prokofiev's *Symphony No. 6*, designed by Alex Steinweiss (1950).

> *Leroy Anderson Conducts His Own Compositions Vol. 2* (1951).

>> A photograph by Paul Huf on a cover for *Beethoven: Violin Concerto*, designed by fellow Dutchman Herry van Borssum Waalkes (1956).

FAVOURITES SERIES · PHILIPS · S 04000 L

BEETHOVEN VIOLINCONCERTO

HERMAN KREBBERS

THE HAGUE PHILHARMONIC

ORCHESTRA CONDUCTOR

WILLEM VAN OTTERLOO

PHILIPS
Minigroove 33⅓

Cult 45s

RCA Victor's immediate response to the challenge of Columbia's vinyl long-playing record was to launch a rival format: the "45." It never beat the 33 rpm LP in what was briefly dubbed the "War of the Speeds," but marked an equally significant phase in the vinyl revolution and signaled the final demise of the shellac 78.

After Columbia's launch of the LP, RCA initially remained silent, despite their rival's eagerness to share its system so that it would become the industry standard. (RCA had its fingers burned in 1931 when it launched 33⅓ LPs of its own. After a promising debut, the format sank amid poor sonics, flimsy pressings, and prohibitively expensive "radio-phonographs.")

In February 1949, RCA introduced seven-inch discs, pressed in vinyl and playing at 45 rpm. Its first US releases were on color-coded vinyl, according to genre: popular music was pressed on black vinyl, Broadway musicals on blue, classical music on red, country music on green, rhythm and blues on cerise, childrens' records on yellow, and international music on teal.

The 45s boasted the same playing time as a 78 and were marketed as an unbreakable, neatly sized alternative. The company also issued extended play (EP) records, which typically carried two single tracks, or seven minutes of music, per side. These were promoted as an alternative to the LP for classical music, with sets of three or four EPs carrying a complete work. At the same time, RCA launched a record player that included a mechanism whereby a number of discs could be stacked and played in sequence, in the manner that jukeboxes had

stacked 78s. But to hear a complete symphony, listeners still had to endure the interruptions that had plagued their enjoyment on 78s, albeit via a smoother,

automatic mechanism. However, the immediate reaction from the industry and record-buying public was more bewilderment than elation. Suddenly, there were three formats whereas, less than a year earlier, there had been only the familiar 78.

Now consumers faced the prospect of having three separate items of equipment to play their music. Soon manufacturers introduced three-speed players, but the 45 never posed a challenge to the long-playing record, and in

January 1950 RCA succumbed and released their first LP.

But it wasn't going to admit defeat after an expensive campaign to launch the 45 and spent a further $5 million publicizing the format as the preferred speed and size for popular music. The campaign worked, with pop record buyers ditching the 78 in favor of the 45 in increasing numbers. By 1954, more than 200 million had been sold, with all the major companies adopting the format for their single releases—albeit initially in tandem with 78s.

The first 45 ever issued, by RCA on March 31, 1949, was "Texarkana Baby" by US country singer Eddy Arnold. In the first batch of 45s, the rhythm and blues offering was "That's All Right, Mama" by veteran bluesman Arthur "Big Boy" Crudup. The song had been released previously on an RCA 78 in 1946 as "That's All Right" and entered history when Elvis Presley covered it in 1954 as his debut single, on the Memphis-based Sun label.

The importance of the seven-inch 45 and four-track EP coinciding with the birth of rock 'n' roll cannot be overstated. The music of Elvis, Little Richard, Buddy Holly, and other pioneers catered to a new teenage market that had pocket money for the first time, but in most cases not enough to indulge in expensive long-playing records.

Durable and compact compared to old-fashioned 78s, these new commodities—ultimately dubbed "singles"—helped trigger a boom that guaranteed their success as the standard vehicle for pop for four decades.

> An advertisement for RCA Victor's 45 rpm record player, launched in response to Columbia's new LP.

⌐ The HMV Model 2107 45 rpm record player, produced in Britain by HMV under licence from RCA Victor.

⌄ Arthur "Big Boy" Crudup, the Mississippi delta blues singer and guitarist known as "The Father of Rock and Roll" for his influence on Elvis Presley.

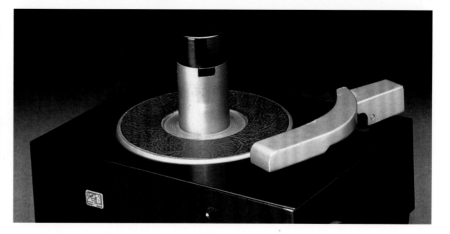

Recorded only in the distortion-free *quality zone*, music "comes alive" on RCA Victor 45-rpm records.

*What **magic number** makes music mirror-clear?*

Now, for more than a year, music-lovers have had—and acclaimed—RCA Victor's remarkable 45-rpm record-playing system. Already, millions know "45" as the magic number that makes music mirror-clear.

As the American Society of Industrial Engineers said when presenting RCA Victor with its 1950 Merit Award, "We are moved to admiration by your bold departure from past practices in developing a completely integrated record and record-player system."

Research leading to "45"—confirmed at RCA Laboratories—covered 11 years . . . and resulted in small, non-breakable records which can be stored by hundreds in ordinary bookshelves, yet play as long as conventional 12-inch records. The automatic record-changer, fastest ever built, changes records in less than 3 seconds—plays up to 50 minutes of glorious music at the touch of a button! Every advantage of convenience, compactness and cost, marks "45" as the ideal record-playing system!

See the latest wonders of radio, television, and electronics at RCA Exhibition Hall, 36 West 49th St., New York. Admission is free. Radio Corporation of America, Radio City, New York 20, N. Y.

Fully automatic RCA Victor 45-rpm record player and records—small enough to hold in one hand . . . inexpensive enough for any purse.

 RADIO CORPORATION of AMERICA
World Leader in Radio — First in Television

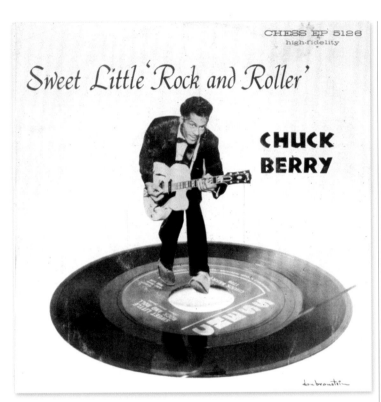

CHESS EP 5126
high-fidelity

Sweet Little 'Rock and Roller'

CHUCK BERRY

SWEET LITTLE ROCK AND ROLLER
CHUCK BERRY (1958)

This EP from a founding father of rock 'n' roll features "Jo Jo Gun" and "Sweet Little Rock and Roller" on the first side and "Johnny B. Goode" and "Around and Around" on the second. (All four reappeared on 1959's *Chuck Berry Is On Top*, a de facto greatest hits.) The imaginative sleeve is by Don Bronstein, who began as a photographer for *Playboy* before working for the Chess label. "He had his own studio and *Playboy* was just beginning," recalled founder Marshall Chess, "so he wasn't that busy. He became basically our company photographer, but he was also a music lover."

LITTLE RICHARD AND HIS BAND
LITTLE RICHARD (1957)

Little Richard could claim to have invented rock 'n' roll with 1955's "Tutti Frutti." This EP repackaged four of his other hits from 1956 and 1957: "Lucille" and "Send Me Some Lovin'" on the A side, "The Girl Can't Help It" and "Jenny, Jenny" on the flip.

TEXARKANA BABY
EDDY ARNOLD (1949)

"Texarkana Baby" was a hit for Eddy Arnold long before it became RCA's first seven-inch single in 1949. It was initially released on 78—by RCA in the United States and EMI in Great Britain—as the flipside of the number one "Bouquet of Roses," but also hit the top in its own right in 1948.

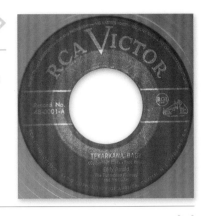

JIMMY YANCEY
JIMMY YANCEY (1955)

Amid the advent of rock 'n' roll, older forms of popular music remained highly popular. This EP collected four tracks by Chicago's influential boogie-woogie pianist and songwriter Jimmy Yancey: "Yancey Stomp," State Street Special," "Tell 'Em About Me," and "Five O'Clock Blues." The songs were originally recorded in 1939, during Yancey's first solo sessions. Although the recordings from these sessions received praise from critics, they did not sell well. It was not until after his death in 1951 that many of the tracks were finally released.

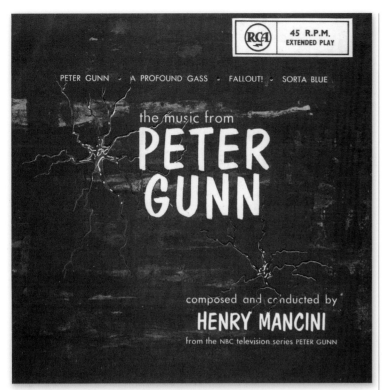

THE MUSIC FROM PETER GUNN
HENRY MANCINI (1959)

The Emmy and Grammy-winning "The Peter Gunn Theme" was written by Henry Mancini for NBC's private eye TV show of the same name. "As creator of the show, I naturally insisted on using live music throughout," writes Blake Edwards in the EP's sleevenotes. "The fact that many of the nation's greatest jazz musicians are in the Hollywood area gave us an ideal opportunity to handpick the most creative jazzmen. We also needed a composer . . . who could interpret dramatic action in the language of modern jazz. Henry Mancini is that composer."

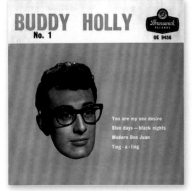

BUDDY HOLLY NO. 1
BUDDY HOLLY (1959)

Buddy Holly's death in February 1959 did little to diminish his output. This EP was one of two issued in 1959 by Brunswick Records, a subsidiary of Holly's label Coral. Brunswick and Coral were both owned by Decca, a label Holly had battled in 1957 over its proposed changes to "That'll Be the Day."

BLUES FOR LOVE
FATS DOMINO (1957)

Best known for the rock 'n' rolling likes of "Blueberry Hill" and "Blue Monday," New Orleans pianist and singer Antoine "Fats" Domino's more romantic side is showcased on this 1957 EP, featuring "My Blue Heaven," "I'm in Love Again," "So Long," and "When My Dreamboat Comes Home."

HOUND DOG / DON'T BE CRUEL
ELVIS PRESLEY (1956)

"Heartbreak Hotel" made Elvis internationally famous at the start of 1956. In the summer, he cemented his celebrity with a single twinning Leiber and Stoller's "Hound Dog" and Otis Blackwell's "Don't Be Cruel" (RCA's label boasted, in "'New Orthophonic' High Fidelity"). The version below is the seven-inch single, but it was also issued on ten-inch shellac by RCA in the United States and His Master's Voice in Great Britain. As Discogs.com notes, "Two versions of the picture sleeve were manufactured, one listing 'Hound Dog' first and one listing 'Don't Be Cruel' first."

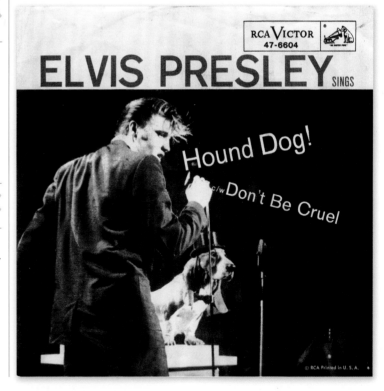

Rock 'n' Roll is Here to Stay

The birth of rock 'n' roll in the mid-1950s was driven by the sales of singles, with the vinyl 45 leading the way. But as it became clear that many of the big names weren't just one-hit wonders, the record companies soon began releasing their music on albums. These often compiled previous hits—the days of rock stars going into the studio to record an album being very much in their formative stages. (Soundtracks proved the most reliable best sellers in the long-playing market, notably RCA's blockbusting *South Pacific*.) But by the end of the decade, the evolution of rock 'n' roll had delivered some memorable albums with equally iconic sleeve art.

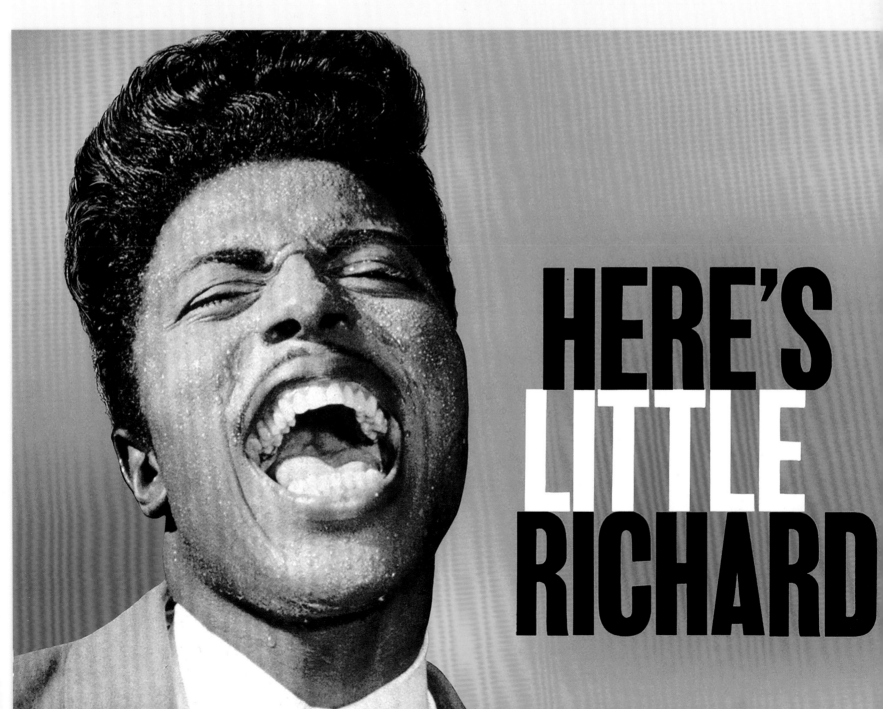

HERE'S LITTLE RICHARD

« Arguably the most explosive debut album to come out of the early rock 'n' roll era, *Here's Little Richard* (1957) featured a dozen classics.

‹ Chuck Berry's debut album *After School Session* (1957) was the second LP to be released by Chess Records.

∨ The cover for African-American girl group The Chantels' 1958 album.

∨ Carl Perkins's *Dance Album* (1958) was rushed out by Sam Phillips of Sun Records after Perkins left the label for Columbia.

∨ Imperial Records released this Fats Domino collection to cash in on his 1957 hit "I'm Walkin'."

⌊ *Elvis* was the second studio album to be released by Elvis Presley in 1956.

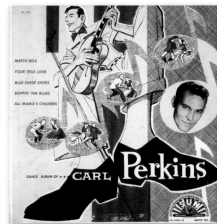

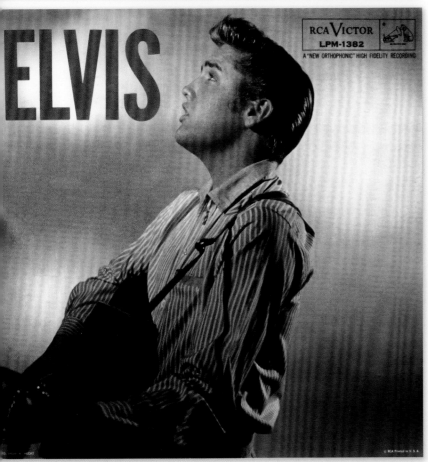

The Norman Granz Jam Sessions

Just as most classical music couldn't be captured satisfactorily on single sides of 78s, so jazz jam sessions were also captured for posterity only with the advent of vinyl long-playing records.

The jam session, in which groups of players who didn't regularly perform together as a band would improvise, was as old as jazz itself. The pioneer of preserving them on record was impresario and producer Norman Granz, born in 1918. In the early 1940s, Granz began organizing desegregated jam sessions at the Trouville Club in his home city of Los Angeles, before moving on to promote a landmark session at the Philharmonic Auditorium in Los Angeles on July 2, 1944. Billed as "Jazz at the Philharmonic"— after the printer had shortened ads from "A Jazz Concert at the Philharmonic Auditorium"—the all-star concert featured singer Nat "King" Cole,

sax giant Illinois Jacquet, guitarist Les Paul, and many other big names. It became a template for Granz's legendary Jazz at the Philharmonic promotions over the next thirty years.

After more concerts in Los Angeles, Granz began producing JATP (as it was often known) tours, covering the United States and Canada from 1945 and Europe from 1952. The greatest names in contemporary jazz took part, including Charlie Parker, Coleman Hawkins, Dizzy Gillespie, Lester Young, and Ella Fitzgerald. Granz realized he had an unprecedented opportunity to record the spontaneous magic of classic jam sessions for the first time in jazz history.

Beginning in 1944, the first recordings of individual numbers were issued as 78s in the old album format. But with the introduction of the vinyl long-playing record by Columbia in 1948,

Granz could release recordings of the extended performances for which the JATP shows were renowned. From 1950 onward, a series of sensational jam sessions were released—on ten-inch, then twelve-inch vinyl—under the Jazz at the Philharmonic banner; from 1951, on Granz's own Clef label, which he had launched in 1946. In 1956, Granz founded Verve, combining the catalogs of Clef and his other label, Norgran.

As well as jams taped at JATP shows, Granz established the notion of in-studio sessions that were extended "blows" on blues riffs or medleys of familiar tunes. A classic of the genre was 1952's two-volume *Jam Session*, in which the great alto saxophonist Charlie Parker jammed with other jazz giants, including sax players Johnny Hodges and Ben Webster and pianist Oscar Peterson, who Granz managed for years.

Norman Granz, jazz producer and impresario, who did much to promote jazz (including, crucially, unsegregated performances) via the then-new medium of the vinyl long-playing record.

JAM SESSION #1
CHARLIE PARKER ET AL. (1952)

The first of the two Charlie Parker-led *Jam Session* albums, this LP features—like many Granz-related records on his Norgran, Clef, and Verve labels—a distinctive cover illustration by David Stone Martin.

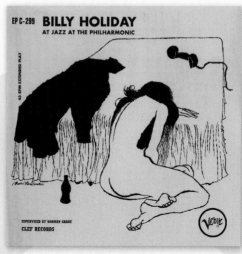

JAZZ AT THE PHILHARMONIC
BILLIE HOLIDAY (1954)

This EP features four tracks recorded under the supervision of Granz in Los Angeles in 1946: "The Man I Love," "Gee Baby Ain't I Good to You," "All of Me," and "Billie's Blues." Other editions of this spell the star's name correctly.

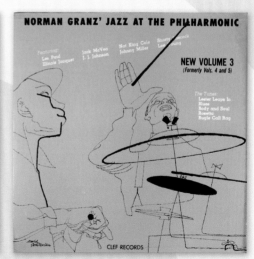

PERSONALITY JAZZ
VARIOUS ARTISTS (circa 1957)

An astonishing lineup—Nat King Cole, Les Paul, Johnny Miller, Buddy Rich, Illinois Jacquet, Jack McVea, J. J. Johnson, Red Callender, and Shorty Sherock—unleash on cuts including "Body and Soul," "Rosetta," and "Bugle Call Rag."

THE DRUM BATTLE
GENE KRUPA AND BUDDY RICH (1960)

Recorded at New York's Carnegie Hall in 1952, this features six cuts, of which the highlight is the nine-minute title track. This is the only one that features both drum legends, the rest being by Krupa with Hank Jones and Willie Smith.

JAZZ AT THE PHILHARMONIC
VARIOUS ARTISTS (1963)

Willie Smith, Red Callender, Charlie Ventura, Illinois Jacquet, Garland Finney, Chicago Flash, Ulysses Livingston, Howard McGhee, and Joe Guy bust loose on "How High the Moon" and "Lady Be Good" in Los Angeles in February 1945.

JAZZ AT THE PHILHARMONIC
PHILLIPS, YOUNG, RICH (1983)

This Verve LP compiles four cuts from Carnegie Hall in September 1950: "Norgran Blues," "Lady Be Good," "Ghost of a Chance," and "Indiana." Hank Jones, Ray Brown, "Sweets" Edison, and Bill Harris feature alongside the top-billed trio.

With long-playing vinyl in its infancy, Frank Sinatra's *In the Wee Small Hours* (1955) broke new ground by presenting a series of songs on related themes—loneliness, failed love, and despair—leading it to be hailed as the first concept album.

Sinatra had been developing the idea since his 78 rpm Columbia debut *The Voice of Frank Sinatra* (1946), which became pop's first LP in 1948. But his career had taken a downturn at the end of the 1940s, when his teenage bobby-soxer audience began to lose interest. He divorced his wife Nancy in 1951 to marry Hollywood star Ava Gardner, and in 1952 Columbia dropped him.

In March 1953, however, Capitol Records took a gamble and signed Sinatra to a seven-year contract. It was the start of a golden era for both the label and Sinatra. Later that year he appeared in the movie *From Here to Eternity*, for which he won an Oscar, and in 1954 his first two Capitol LPs appeared:

In the Wee Small Hours

Songs for Young Lovers and *Swing Easy!* Both made it to the US top three, while *Swing Easy!* also hit the UK's top five.

His marriage to Gardner began to fall apart while he was recording *Songs for Young Lovers* at the end of 1953 (the couple eventually divorced in 1957). Against this background of renewed popularity and personal trauma, in February 1955 Sinatra embarked on recording the angst-ridden songs that later constituted *In the Wee Small Hours*.

The first set of songs that Sinatra had recorded specifically for an LP evoked the melancholy and desolation of lost love in numbers such as "When Your Lover Has Gone," "I'll Never Be the Same," and the newly written title track. The recording sessions—at the KHJ Studios in Hollywood, through February and March—were with an orchestra conducted by Nelson Riddle, who also had written the arrangements and had worked similarly on Sinatra's previous two albums. The pair's relationship continued, creating some of the singer's finest work over the next few years.

Released in April 1955, the album became an instant hit. It peaked at number two on the US chart, where it stayed for eighteen weeks. It has since become a classic.

« The moody cover for *In the Wee Small Hours* (1955) said much about the theme of the music inside.

‹ Frank Sinatra at Capitol's KHJ Studios during the recording of the album.

∟ Ava Gardner and Frank Sinatra in the front row at White City Stadium to watch Randolph Turpin fight Charles Homez for the World Middleweight Boxing title in 1953.

⌄ *Songs for Young Lovers* (1954) was Frank Sinatra's first release after joining Capitol Records in 1953.

Got Live If You Want It

As Norman Granz realized when committing his *Jazz at the Philharmonic* shows to vinyl in the 1940s, the advent of the LP meant concerts could be properly captured on disc. Hundreds of memorable shows would have been lost had the format not taken off. Although live LPs came to be regarded as stopgaps and contractual obligations, in the early decades of vinyl—before studio overdubs on in-concert recordings became the norm—they provided an authentic record of the best in jazz, R&B, and folk, as in the selection of gems illustrated here.

JAZZ AT MASSEY HALL
THE QUINTET (1956)

"The greatest jazz concert ever" —in Toronto on May 15, 1953—starred five bop pioneers: Dizzy Gillespie, Charlie Parker (as "Charlie Chan"), Bud Powell, Charles Mingus, and Max Roach.

... FROM THE ROUNDHOUSE
ALEXIS KORNER (1957)

Only ninety-nine copies were issued of this LP, capturing "Alex" Korner's Breakdown Group—including Korner's fellow electric blues pioneer Cyril Davies—in London on February 13, 1957.

IN SAN FRANCISCO
CANNONBALL ADDERLEY (1959)

Recorded at San Francisco's Jazz Workshop in October 1959, this finds the alto saxophonist accompanied by his brother Nat on the cornet and the cover, and Bobby Timmons on the piano.

AT CARNEGIE HALL
THE WEAVERS (1957)

Taped on Christmas Eve in 1955, this found the folk giants reunited after the three-year hiatus and commercial fallout that resulted from Pete Seeger being accused of being a Communist.

... THE VILLAGE VANGUARD
SONNY ROLLINS (1958)

"Impressive always, fun in passing," enthused Robert Christgau of this LP (taped at afternoon and evening shows on November 3, 1957), "his improvisations are what avant-garde jazz is for."

AT NEWPORT
RAY CHARLES (1959)

"It is evident from the applause," the sleevenotes observe, "that Ray Charles was well received"— despite this 1958 show dating from before his R&B success crossed over to the jazz crowd.

BLUES FROM THE ROUNDHOUSE

ALEX KORNER'S BREAKDOWN GROUP

FEATURING

CYRIL DAVIS

77 RECORDS

THE **CANNONBALL ADDERLEY** QUINTET IN SAN FRANCISCO FEATURING **NAT ADDERLEY**

RECORDED LIVE AT THE JAZZ WORKSHOP

MELVIN SOKOLSKY — PAUL BACON

311 RIVERSIDE

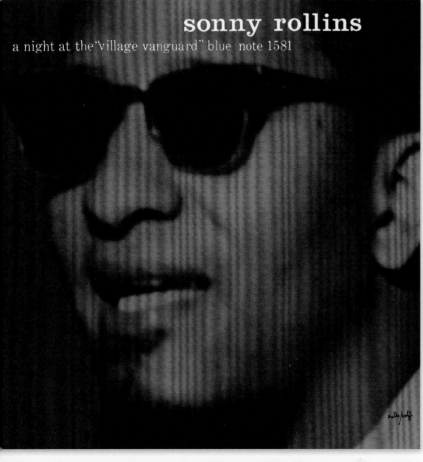

sonny rollins

a night at the "village vanguard" blue note 1581

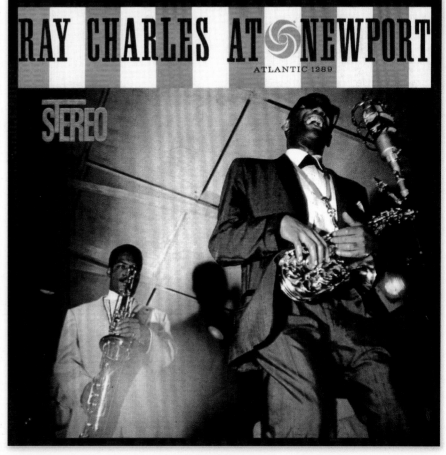

RAY CHARLES AT NEWPORT

ATLANTIC 1289

STEREO

Atlantic was ideally positioned for the revolution triggered by Columbia debuting vinyl long-playing records in 1948. Founded in 1947, the independent label was, by the mid-1950s, at the cutting edge of jazz—with album covers to match. Ten years later, it stood at the forefront of the move from singles to albums in rock 'n' roll.

Initially, Atlantic was a rhythm and blues label, issuing 78 rpm singles. Its first foray into albums, in March 1949, was a ten-inch LP of spoken-word poetry by Walter Benton: the text of his best-selling book *This Is My Beloved,* read by John Dall, with an orchestral backing by Vernon Duke.

Founders Ahmet Ertegun and Herb Abramson realized that while their R&B catalog was defined by singles, there was a market for jazz LPs. The label's next two 33⅓ releases, in May 1949, were ten-inch LPs by Joe Bushkin and Erroll Garner. Although their first twelve-inch LP, in 1951, was another spoken word release (scenes from *Romeo and Juliet*), Atlantic's jazz catalog made it a major name through the first half of the 1950s.

The label prospered with R&B—making Ruth Brown, the Clovers, and Ray Charles into stars—while jazz releases by Dizzy Gillespie, Don Byas, and Lennie Tristano assured its place in the increasingly competitive album market.

In 1955, Ertegun's brother Nesuhi took charge of the jazz catalog and the label's album releases, initiating a period in which Atlantic was at jazz's cutting edge, with major names including Charles Mingus, John Coltrane, and the Modern Jazz Quartet. Nesuhi deleted all ten-inch albums from the catalog, confirming the twelve-inch LP as the format for 33 rpm vinyl.

Atlantic's jazz LPs made a mark visually as well as musically, with designers including Robert Guidi and Burt Goldblatt, and the stunning photography of Goldblatt, Hugh Bell, and William Claxton. In the second half of the 1950s, under the art direction of Marvin Israel, the label adopted a coherent style: bold typefaces, occasional abstracts, and color photography by Lee Friedlander and others.

In the singles-driven R&B market, Atlantic followed RCA's lead with seven-inch 45 rpm singles, their first two releases in 1951 being by Joe Turner and Ruth Brown. Until the middle of the decade, vinyl 45s usually were released alongside the old shellac 78s, as new record players capable of playing microgroove records at varying speeds took over from the old gramophones and phonographs. One of the first rock 'n' roll singles to hit the charts—Joe Turner's banner-carrying 'Shake Rattle and Roll,' in 1954—was released as a 78 before also being pressed in seven-inch vinyl.

In the first half of the 1960s, the company was the market leader in soul, with landmark singles and million-selling albums by Solomon Burke, Aretha Franklin, and Otis Redding on Atlantic and its subsidiaries Stax and Atco. At the close of the decade, under producer Jerry Wexler, it released a soul album by Great Britain's Dusty Springfield, now considered an all-time classic. *Dusty in Memphis* wasn't a smash at the time, but it yielded a hit in "Son of a Preacher Man."

Singles dominated pop through the mid-1960s, when albums began to have a stronger presence. Atlantic was again at the forefront, signing new US acts, such as Buffalo Springfield, who flourished in response to the British Invasion spearheaded by The Beatles. As the move to albums documented rock 'n' roll's evolution into hard rock, Atlantic rode the wave, signing homegrown talent, such as the Young Rascals, Vanilla Fudge, and Crosby, Stills, Nash & Young and album-oriented British musicians, including Cream, Led Zeppelin, and Blind Faith.

Atlantic's vinyl catalog embraced the best in rock (including King Crimson, Genesis, Phil Collins, and Foreigner) and soul (Donny Hathaway, Sister Sledge, and Chic). Today, it thrives as part of the Time Warner group, but it was as a major player in the vinyl revolution that the label has ensured its place in music history.

⌐ Buffalo Springfield pose for a
portrait sitting on a car in 1966 in
Los Angeles, California.

» Nesuhi Ertegun (center), president
of Atlantic Records, with vice
presidents Jerry Wexler (left) and
Ahmet Ertegun (right).

› An Atlantic Records publicity still
portrait of Aretha Franklin taken
in 1967.

⌄ Led Zeppelin in 1969: (left-right)
John Bonham, Robert Plant, Jimmy
Page, and John Paul Jones.

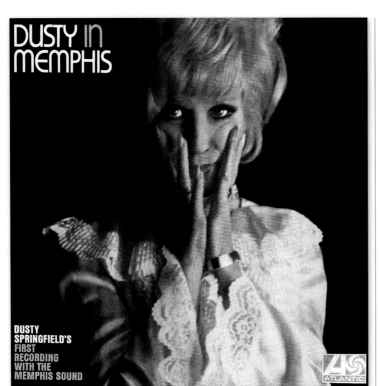

DUSTY SPRINGFIELD'S FIRST RECORDING WITH THE MEMPHIS SOUND

DUSTY IN MEMPHIS
DUSTY SPRINGFIELD (1969)

"I hated it at first," recalled the British singer of her classic to *Mojo* magazine. "If only people like [producer] Jerry Wexler could realize what a deflating thing it is to say, Otis Redding stood there. Or, That's where Aretha sang. Whatever you do, it's not going to be good enough. Added to the natural critic in me, it was a paralyzing experience . . . I wanted to fill every space. I didn't understand that the sparseness gave it an atmosphere. When I got free of that I finally liked it, but it took me a long time. I wouldn't play it for a year."

PRAIRIE DOG
DUKE PEARSON (1966)

Pianist Pearson had been one of the pioneers of hard bop (a hybrid of jazz, R&B, gospel, and blues) on the Blue Note label. But he also issued a brace of acclaimed albums on Atlantic, of which this is the second. Also issued in mono, it concludes with a five-minute take on the jazz standard "Angel Eyes."

HALLELUJAH I LOVE HER SO!
RAY CHARLES (1956)

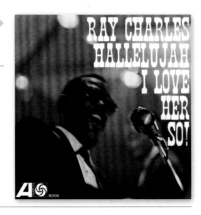

Throughout the 1950s, before his pop crossover hit "What'd I Say," Ray Charles was among Atlantic's biggest hitters on *Billboard*'s R&B chart. This gospel-based top-five smash, produced by Jerry Wexler, featured on the genius's self-titled debut album for the label in 1957.

MORE SOUL
HANK CRAWFORD (1961)

Ray Charles's music director established a parallel solo career on Atlantic, beginning with this excellent 1961 set, produced by Nesuhi Ertegun. Over a modest thirty-eight minutes—of which five are Erroll Garner's beautiful standard "Misty"—Crawford delivered a resounding lesson in swinging yet soulful jazz. Sleevenotes by *Billboard*-writer-turned-Atlantic-staffer Gary Kramer concluded: "'In order to appreciate soul (if I may quote [jazz composer] Bobby Timmons once more), you must have some of your own.' To you fellow 'soul' listeners, I strongly commend this debut album."

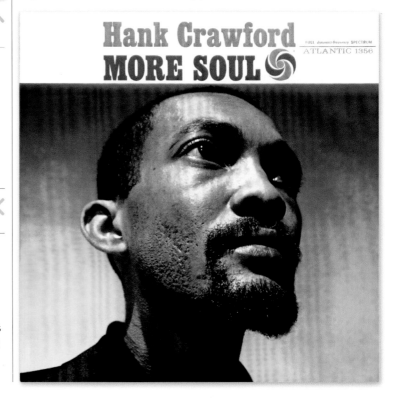

WORKIN' ON A GROOVY THING
BARBARA LEWIS (1968)

"I never felt like a big star," reflected Barbara Lewis, forty years after the release of her final Atlantic album. When her career wound down, she said, "I went back to Michigan and I never told a soul." Her first hit, 1963's self-penned "Hello Stranger," set a benchmark that, unfortunately, she could never match. But she remains an intriguing figure in the history of smooth soul, providing an early outlet for songwriter and future disco pioneer Van McCoy. Britain's Arctic Monkeys covered her McCoy-penned hit, "Baby I'm Yours."

VANILLA FUDGE
VANILLA FUDGE (1967)

Bookended by covers of "Ticket to Ride" and "Eleanor Rigby," this slab of Shadow Morton-produced heavy psychedelia also includes the quartet's druggy takes on Curtis Mayfield's "People Get Ready," The Zombies' "She's Not There," Cher's "Bang Bang," and The Supremes' "You Keep Me Hangin' On."

GROOVE FUNK SOUL
JOE CASTRO (1960)

Long before R&B laid claim to the term, jazz musicians were bringing the funk. In this instance, it was bebop pianist Joe Castro, lauded by the likes of Dave Brubeck before signing to Atlantic for two albums, of which this is the second. Castro founded the Clover Records label with Duke Ellington.

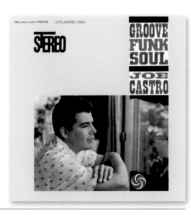

OLÉ COLTRANE
JOHN COLTRANE (1961)

Newly signed to the Impulse label, trailblazing saxophonist John Coltrane needed to deliver a final album for Atlantic. With producer Nesuhi Ertegun and a star-studded cast—including trumpeter Freddie Hubbard, flautist/saxophonist Eric Dolphy (credited as George Lane), pianist McCoy Tyner, and drummer Elvin Jones—he cut *Olé Coltrane* in a single day in 1961. Biographer Lewis Porter speculates that the side-long title piece was prompted by Coltrane's former associate Miles Davis's classic *Sketches of Spain* (1960), which also features the bold colors of the Spanish flag.

Turntable Treasures

With the move from 78s to vinyl LPs, EPs, and singles, the 1950s saw a new generation of domestic record players come into their own. The models available ranged from highly portable 45 rpm-only machines aimed at the teenage market, to extravagant entertainment systems that combined radio, TV, and multi-disc record player in one cabinet.

« The deluxe Kuba Komet television cabinet, with integrated television set, radio, record player, magnetophone, and audio tape, made in Wolfenbuettel, Munich, Germany, 1959.

‹ Designed by Dieter Rams and Hans Gugelot in 1956, Braun's SK4 record player was nicknamed "Snow White's Coffin" because of its radical transparent plastic lid.

└ The Braun combi—a portable radio and record player designed in 1955 by Wilhelm Wagenfeld—helpfully included a storage space for records in the lid of the machine.

⌄ An advertisement for the innovative new home entertainment system released by Admiral in 1949, which combined a television, record player, and radio in a single unit.

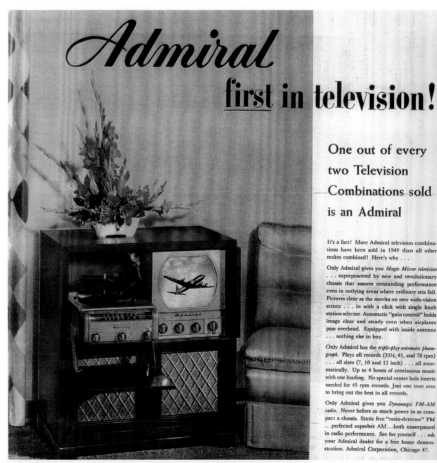

Admiral first in television!

One out of every two Television Combinations sold is an Admiral

It's a fact! More Admiral television combinations have been sold in 1949 than all other makes combined! Here's why . . .

Only Admiral gives you *Magic Mirror television* . . . superpowered by new and revolutionary chassis that assures outstanding performance even in outlying areas where ordinary sets fail. Pictures clear as the movies on new wide-vision screen . . . in with a click with single knob station selector. Automatic "gain control" holds image clear and steady even when airplanes pass overhead. Equipped with inside antenna . . . nothing else to buy.

Only Admiral has the *triple-play automatic phonograph.* Plays all records (33⅓, 45, and 78 rpm) . . . all sizes (7, 10 and 12 inch) . . . all automatically. Up to 4 hours of continuous music with one loading. No special center hole inserts needed for 45 rpm records. Just one tone arm to bring out the best in all records.

Only Admiral gives you *Dynamagic FM-AM radio.* Never before so much power in so compact a chassis. Static free "ratio-detector" FM . . . perfected superhet AM . . . both unsurpassed in radio performance. See for yourself . . . ask your Admiral dealer for a free home demonstration. Admiral Corporation, Chicago 47.

Audio Fidelity

Audio Fidelity's fame crystallized in March 1958 when it released the first-ever commercial recordings in stereophonic two-channel sound.

The label was already renowned for attention to quality, from the time of its first album—*Merry Go Round Music*, in 1954—but its place at the cutting edge came almost by default. Several labels were vying for pole position as pioneers of stereo, but while they experimented with a disc-cutting system supplied by Westrex, Audio Fidelity founder and president Sidney Frey took his rivals by surprise by asking the same company to cut a full stereo long-playing record.

The disc Westrex produced was introduced at an event held at the Times Auditorium in New York on December 13, 1957. It featured the Dukes of Dixieland jazz band (who already had LPs released on the label) on one side, and

railroad sound effects on the other. Initially, just 500 were pressed, with the label advertising in *Billboard* that it would send free copies to anyone in the industry who requested one.

The launch was a sensation, so when Frey entered the commercial market in March 1958, his label was way ahead of the game. Indeed, Frey was known as Mr. Stereo in the industry. The first four LPs—*Johnny Puleo and His Harmonica Gang, Railroad: The Sounds of a Vanishing Era,* Lionel Hampton's *Lionel,* and *Marching Along with the Phenomenal Dukes of Dixieland Vol. 3*—were in keeping with Audio Fidelity's popular approach. In the summer of 1958, it began releasing classical music, with thirteen albums specially recorded in London.

The LPs were expensive to produce and were priced accordingly. Special equipment was

required to play them, so they were a luxury item. But until Frey's competitors caught up, stores selling stereo record players had only Audio Fidelity discs with which to demonstrate them.

Naturally, however, the competition was quick to catch up. By the end of 1958 all major labels were releasing records in stereo, albeit in parallel with mono ones to suit the equipment owned by most listeners. Only after hi-fi manufacturers standardized their products to play stereo did mono gradually phase out.

Audio Fidelity issued high-quality recordings of classical, jazz, and middle-of-the-road pop. Big names included Louis Armstrong, Larry Adler, and the Clancy Brothers. But it was as an architect of the move from mono to stereophonic recording that the label secured its reputation among leaders of the vinyl revolution.

Records featuring train sounds, such as this one released by Audio Fidelity in 1958, became so common in the late 1950s that *Billboard* described the "train record" as its own subgenre.

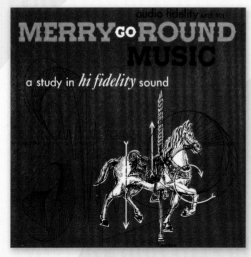

MERRY GO ROUND MUSIC
(1954)

This uncredited collection of carousel music was Audio Fidelity's long-playing debut. "Taken in reasonably small doses," advise the admirably candid sleevenotes, "carousel music is refreshingly pleasant, particularly for children."

JOHNNY PULEO AND HIS HARMONICA GANG (1958)

Diminutive harmonica player and actor Johnny Puleo led one of the label's flagship acts. Their Audio Fidelity debut, above, was followed by four further volumes, climaxing with *Western Songs* and *Encore Italiano!* in 1960.

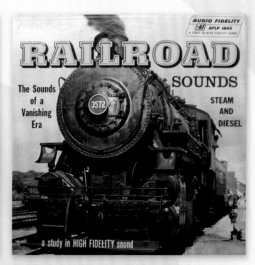

RAILROAD: THE SOUNDS OF A VANISHING ERA (1958)

Previously issued in mono, *Railroad* made its stereo debut in 1958, so enthusiasts might enjoy "Steam Locomotives and Some Diesel Locomotives" and "Diesel Locomotives and Some Steam Locomotives" in all their glory.

SATCHMO PLAYS KING OLIVER
LOUIS ARMSTRONG (1960)

With his All Stars backing band, Louis "Satchmo" Armstrong pays tribute to his late teacher and mentor, jazz bandleader Joe "King" Oliver. "If it had not been for Joe Oliver," he enthused, "jazz would not be what it was today."

MR. KISS KISS BANG BANG
GLENDA GRAINGER (1965)

Shirley Bassey and Dionne Warwick's versions of this James Bond movie theme were dropped, and nightclub singer Glenda Grainger's failed to chart. John Barry and Don Black quickly wrote "Thunderball" for Tom Jones instead.

AGAIN!
LARRY ADLER (1968)

The exclamatory title of *Again!* was appropriate: it had been nine years since the Baltimore-born harmonica virtuoso's last Audio Fidelity album. This one included standards, such as "Night and Day" and "Someone to Watch Over Me."

The jazz label Blue Note is as celebrated for the cover designs of its albums as for the often historic recordings within. Under the imaginative auspices of in-house designer Reid Miles, the Blue Note brand forged a new graphics language between the mid-1950s and mid-1960s that wouldn't have evolved on any format other than twelve-inch vinyl LPs.

Founded in New York City in 1939 by German émigré Alfred Lion, Blue Note initially issued traditional and swing-style jazz. Early releases included boogie-woogie pianists Albert Ammons and Meade Lux Lewis and saxophone star Sydney Bechet. In 1941, Lion was joined by Francis Wolff, a former colleague from Germany, and—after a production hiatus during World War II—the label became particularly identified with modern jazz. Early bebop players on the label included pianist Thelonius Monk, trumpeter Fats Navarro, drummer Art Blakey, and pianist Bud Powell.

In 1951, when Blue Note graduated from producing 78s to the ten-inch long-players, an art department became a necessity. The first designers, all outstanding in their field, were Paul Bacon, Gil Melle, and John Hermansader. Between them the trio produced some of the label's most memorable early sleeve designs.

But it was when *Esquire* magazine illustrator Reid Miles joined the label's art department as primary graphic designer in 1956 that the Blue Note look took shape. Often benefiting from Wolff's stunning photography, Miles's designs made imaginative use of sans-serif typefaces, bold rectangles of a single color, and tinted monochrome photographs.

Reid had graduated from Los Angeles's prestigious Chouinard Art Institute. His stint at *Esquire* in the early 1950s put him under John Hermansender, through whom Wolff hired

OLD STACK O'LEE BLUES
(SIDNEY BECHET)
BECHET-NICHOLAS BLUE FIVE
(BN 277-1)   54-B

NOT LICENSED FOR BROADCASTING

BLUE NOTE

SIDNEY BECHET .... clarinet
ALBERT NICHOLAS .... clarinet
ART HODES .... piano
GEORGE "POPS" FOSTER .... bass
DANNY ALVIN .... drums
BLUE NOTE RECORDS, 767 Lexingt. Ave. NYC

Miles on a permanent basis when the label began releasing twelve-inch LPs. Miles designed several hundred covers for the label yet wasn't a jazz enthusiast himself; he gave his complimentary copies of LPs he'd designed to friends or sold them to second-hand record dealers. But he conjured up his iconic images around Wolff's photographs of the musicians working, or—dispensing with pictures—derived inspiration from the label executive's descriptions of the recording sessions.

The label stood at the forefront of the hard bop movement in the latter half of the 1950s, and seminal records by exponents, such as Lou Donaldson, Stanley Turrentine, Cannonball Adderley, Freddie Hubbard, and Lee Morgan, became indelibly associated with the cover art accompanying them. "The sociological impact of Blue Note was as great for me as Bob Dylan's, or The Beatles', or the Stones'," recalled producer Don Was, who became president of the label in 2012. "I wanted to be one of those guys. I had my mom go out and get me a top hat and a trench coat so I could look like Ornette Coleman on the cover of *Live at The Golden Circle*. I didn't achieve the look, but it wasn't for lack of trying."

Liberty Records bought the label in 1965. Reid Miles left in 1967, around the time that Alfred Lion retired. Francis Wolff died in 1971, but his company continued as a force to be reckoned with, thanks to a new generation of stars, such as Herbie Hancock and Donald Byrd.

Dormant by the first half of the 1980s, Blue Note found subsequent life as an EMI imprint. It found success via Cassandra Wilson and Dianne Reeves and enjoyed its most spectacular commercial impact (now as part of the Universal empire) in the twenty-first century courtesy of Norah Jones, whose *Come Away with Me* (2002) sold ten million in the United States alone.

With the advent of CDs, most of the classic back catalog was gradually rereleased. In recent years, much of that has found its place back on vinyl—in its classic format, where a new generation of fans can enjoy the full glories of the sleeve art of Blue Note.

∧ Pianist Thelonius Monk initially struggled to find work due to his unusual playing technique, but his talent was recognized by Alfred Lion and he made several recordings for Blue Note between 1947 and 1958.

⌐ Trumpeter Fats Navarro recorded with Blue Note between 1947 and 1949, before heroin addiction and tuberculosis tragically led to his death in 1950, at the age of twenty-six.

〉 Drummer Art Blakey appeared on more than sixty records released by Blue Note between 1947 and 1964, including several LPs from his highly influential band the Jazz Messengers.

THE RUMPROLLER
LEE MORGAN (1965)

This April 1965 session may not be the most remarkable in which trumpeter Morgan, saxophonist Joe Henderson, pianist Ronnie Mathews, bassist Victor Sproles, and drummer Billy Higgins participated, but Reid Miles's imaginative graphics are in keeping with the design era of Saul Bass.

GRAVY TRAIN
LOU DONALDSON (1961)

Lengthy workouts open each side of this soulful gem: the eight-minute title track and a nine-minute interpretation of the 1940s standard "Candy." The album also includes "Polka Dots and Moonbeams," popularized by the likes of Sinatra and Sarah Vaughan, and Al Jolson's "Avalon." Cut in New Jersey in 1961, it finds alto saxophonist Donaldson accompanied by bassist Ben Tucker, conga player Alec Dorsey, pianist Herman Foster, and drummer Dave Bailey. As usual, the eye-catching cover is by Reid Miles, but with photography by Ronnie Brathwaite instead of Francis Wolff.

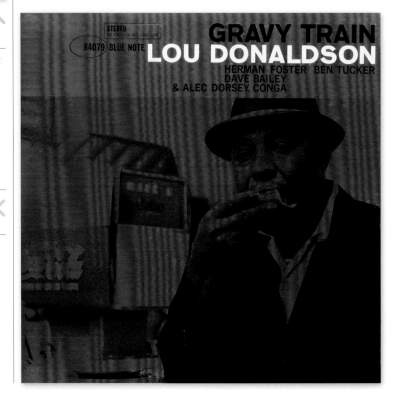

MIDNIGHT BLUE
KENNY BURRELL (1963)

"Kenny Burrell—that's the sound I'm looking for," remarked Jimi Hendrix of the man whose guitar graced classics by the likes of Billie Holiday and Jimmy Smith. Having recorded for Blue Note in the 1950s before dallying with Verve and Columbia, Burrell returned for *Midnight Blue*, cut on January 7, 1963. Accompanied by bassist Major Holley Jr., drummer Bill English, saxophonist Stanley Turrentine, it opened with his soulful signature cut "Chitlins Con Carne." The album's Reid Miles-designed cover was lovingly pastiched by Elvis Costello's *Almost Blue* (1981).

UNIT STRUCTURES
CECIL TAYLOR (1966)

Reid Miles's Warholian artwork, based on a photo by Francis Wolff, befits a cutting-edge free jazz classic. Produced by Alfred Lion, it boasts titles that would make Radiohead proud: "Steps," "Enter Evening (Soft Line Structure)," "Unit Structure / As Of A Now / Section," and "Tales (8 Whisps)."

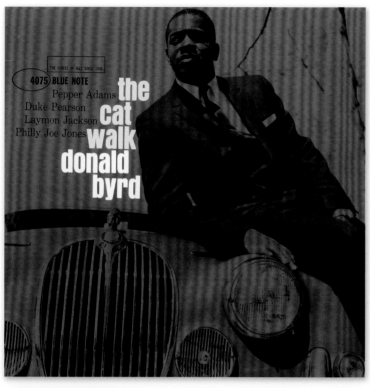

SHOUTIN'
DON WILKERSON (1963)

Tenor saxophonist Don Wilkerson's final album as a bandleader ended his "solo" discography on a high. Recorded in July 1963 with Grant Green, Ben Dixon, and John Patton, it features four of his own compositions and two covers, the latter including the movie theme and jazz standard "Easy Living."

VOL. 2
SONNY ROLLINS (1957)

One of Blue Note's quintessential, and much imitated, sleeve designs was by Harold Feinstein rather than Reid Miles, albeit with photography by Francis Wolff. Its contents are no letdown, with tenor saxophonist Rollins being accompanied by pianists Horace Silver and Thelonious Monk, drummer Art Blakey, trombonist Jay Jay Johnson, and bassist Paul Chambers. A nine-minute take on Monk's "Misterioso" includes both its composer and Silver, but it's hard to pick a highlight from the blissful forty minutes taped in April 1957 under the watchful eye of producer Alfred Lion.

THE CAT WALK
DONALD BYRD (1962)

The Cat Walk is the apex of a formidable gathering of talents: trumpeter Donald Byrd, saxophonist Pepper Adams, and pianist Duke Pearson. The latter wrote four of the album's six cuts, while the title track was by Byrd himself and "Cute" was the work of trumpeter and Batman theme tune composer Neil Hefti. Recorded in New Jersey in May 1961 with bassist Laymon Jackson and drummer Philly Joe Jones, and produced by Alfred Lion, it's described by *Allmusic* as "an essential Byrd purchase" thanks to the star's "sleek and lyrical playing, and Adams's sturdy, husky baritone."

TRUE BLUE
TINA BROOKS (1960)

Hard bop heaven is attained on Harold Floyd "Tina" Brooks's sole album in his own right in his lifetime—his career being curtailed by heroin. Cut in June 1960 and featuring Freddie Hubbard, Duke Jordan, Sam Jones, and Art Taylor, it's blessed with another bold cover by Reid Miles and Francis Wolff.

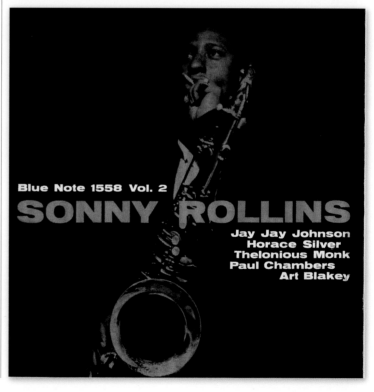

The Spoken Word

Since the advent of sound recording, spoken word has had its place in record label catalogs, be it poets reading their work, political speeches, readings from classic novels, or live performances of the works of Shakespeare.

The first machine to reproduce the human voice was Thomas Edison's cylinder-playing phonograph. When Edison introduced his invention in 1877, one of the uses that he proposed for the phonograph was as an aid to the blind via talking books.

Cylinders were used for spoken-word recordings in the early twentieth century, but their four-minute duration made extended works like books and plays impractical. The 78 rpm disc improved matters; while each side was similarly restricted timewise, the records could be sold as "albums," as were longer works of classical music.

One of the first spoken word artists to find success was actor Ronald Coleman reading Charles Dickens's *A Christmas Carol* on the Decca label (1941). Other significant releases included Columbia's Masterworks series, with an acclaimed album of excerpts from Shakespeare's *Richard III*, and a mammoth eighteen-disc set of a complete Broadway production of *Othello* featuring the black singer Paul Robeson in the title role.

However, multi-disc versions of extended works were cumbersome, and only the introduction of the LP really made spoken word a viable proposition for many companies and customers. Initially, many of the 78 rpm albums were transferred to LP, but the new format saw a boom in freshly produced spoken word.

Founded in 1952, Caedmon Records helped pioneer the genre. Its first release captured Dylan Thomas reading his own poems, while other landmark releases included the complete

works of Shakespeare and newer plays, such as Tennessee Williams's *The Glass Menagerie* and Arthur Miller's *Death of a Salesman*.

At the end of the 1950s, jazz-oriented labels issued recordings of Beat Generation writers, including Jack Kerouac on Verve and Allen Ginsberg on Fantasy. Meanwhile, Columbia, which introduced LPs in 1948, continued their Masterworks with original Broadway cast recordings of plays, including *Who's Afraid of Virginia Woolf?* (1962) and Richard Burton's

production of *Hamlet* (1964). Columbia's rival RCA likewise immortalized theater productions, including a four-album set of Laurence Olivier as Othello, and the UK National Theatre's production of *Much Ado about Nothing*, starring Albert Finney and Maggie Smith. With younger listeners in mind, Disneyland Records launched in 1956. Its first spoken word album, Robert Louis Stevenson's *A Child's Garden of Verses*, was followed by narrated versions of their classic movies.

Comedy on vinyl included musical talents, such as Tom Lehrer, and stand-ups, such as Lenny Bruce and Bob Newhart. The latter's 1960 debut *The Button-Down Mind of Bob Newhart* ("The Most Celebrated New Comedian Since Attila the Hun") topped *Billboard*'s Top 200, and won Album of the Year at the Grammys. In the UK, comedy radio shows were transcribed to LP, including Tony Hancock's *Hancock's Half Hour* and the seminal *Goon Show*. Many shows appeared on vinyl on BBC Records, founded in 1967 to exploit the corporation's vast archive.

Spoken word recordings have served history well. Documentaries have covered major events, and recordings preserved speeches by leaders including Harry S. Truman, Winston Churchill, John F. Kennedy, and Martin Luther King Jr.

Spoken word thrived with the move to cassettes in the late 1970s, which brought a boom in audio books—complete novels read by well-known actors—then CDs, with their longer playing time. But the true innovators were those same pioneers of vinyl: the producers and labels who recognized the potential of the LP in preserving works unsuited to earlier formats.

GOON SHOW CLASSICS
THE GOONS (1974)

Spike Milligan, Harry Secombe, and Peter Sellers perform Milligan's "The Dreaded Batter Pudding Hurler of Bexhill-on-Sea" (broadcast on BBC radio in October 1954) and "The Histories of Pliny the Elder" (broadcast in March 1957). The Ray Ellington Quartet play "Old Man River," "You Made Me Love You," and "This Can't Be Love," and Max Geldray contributes "Get Happy" and "They Were Doing the Mambo." The Goons' absurd flights of fancy and sonic invention strongly influenced on Monty Python and The Beatles, John Lennon citing them as "proof that the world was insane."

BASIL RATHBONE READS EDGAR ALLAN POE
BASIL RATHBONE (1954)

The star of fourteen Sherlock Holmes movies in the 1930s and 40s reads classics by the master of horror—including "The Raven" and "The Masque of the Red Death"—for the Caedmon label ("A third dimension for the printed page").

THE VOICE OF PRESIDENT JOHN F. KENNEDY (circa 1961)

The Golden Records label put out a variety of novelty records. This seven-incher, which makes the most of the young president's good looks, features highlights of his nomination acceptance speech in 1960, and his oath of office and inaugural address in 1961.

READING FROM . . .
TENNESSEE WILLIAMS (1960)

The Glass Menagerie and *A Streetcar Named Desire* elevated Tennessee Williams to the realm of playwright greats in the 1940s. Both became movies in the early 1950s, sealing his reputation worldwide. By the end of that decade, another seven of his plays had hit Broadway, including *Cat on a Hot Tin Roof*. So this Caedmon LP captured the Mississipian genius at the close of his peak period. As an added bonus, the eye-catching cover art is by Andy Warhol, at whose Factory studio Williams subsequently guested. The playwright, said photographer David McCabe, "was belle of the ball."

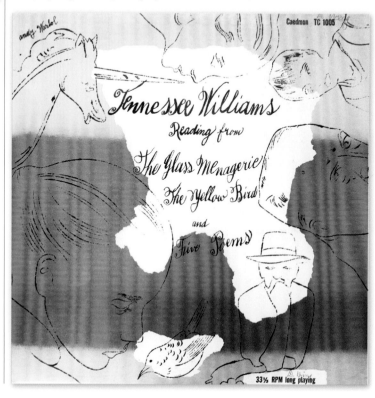

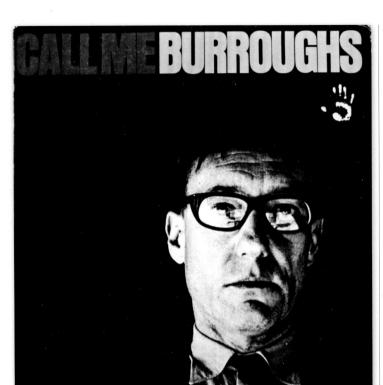

CALL ME BURROUGHS
WILLIAM BURROUGHS (1965)

Author William Burroughs reads excerpts from *Naked Lunch* and *Nova Express* on this LP from Parisian label The English Bookshop (reissued in the United States the following year by New York's avante-garde ESP Disk label, as illustrated above). "His voice," observe sleevenotes by poet, painter, and performer Emmett Williams, "is terrifyingly convincing." Burroughs, an influence on David Bowie among others, created a highly varied spoken word catalog before his death in 1997, including a 1981 LP with Laurie Anderson entitled *You're the Guy I Want to Share My Money With.*

OTHELLO
PAUL ROBESON (1944)

Columbia's eighteen-disc set of 78s (later reissued on LP) was a groundbreaking full-length recording of a Shakespeare play. The sleevenotes make no mention of the casting of an African-American in the title role, emphasizing instead Paul Robeson's "vocal splendor."

LAFF YOUR HEAD OFF
REDD FOXX (1965)

A key influence on Richard Pryor and Chris Rock, comedian Redd Foxx was a vinyl veteran by 1965. This was his first LP on his own MF Records label; later album titles included *Is Sex Here to Stay*, *Three or Four Times a Day*, *Mr. Hot Pants*, *Restricted*, and *Strictly for Adults*.

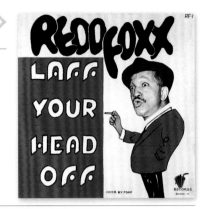

DYLAN THOMAS NARRATING UNDER MILK WOOD (1953)

Serendipity smiled on The Poetry Center in New York on May 14, 1953. An enterprising soul thought to record the first reading of Dylan Thomas's *Under Milk Wood* with a single microphone, laid on the stage floor. Thus was captured the only recorded performance with the author as part of the cast. (Thomas's death six months later put paid to plans for a studio version.) Caedmon issued the recording as two single LPs in 1953 then a double album in 1956. The same label also issued *An Evening with Dylan Thomas Reading His Own and Other Poems* in 1963.

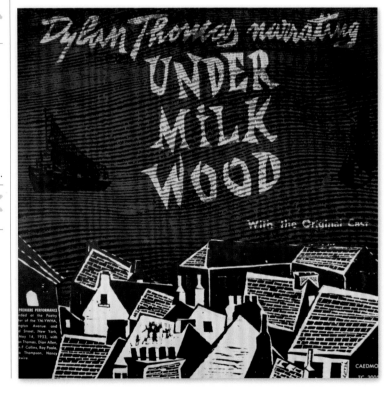

THE GREAT MARCH TO FREEDOM
MARTIN LUTHER KING (1963)

Issued on the Motown imprint Gordy (after the label's founder Berry Gordy), this commemorates the Reverend Martin Luther King's speech to a 25,000-strong congregation at Detroit's Cobo Hall, two months before his celebrated Great March on Washington.

WHO'S AFRAID OF VIRGINIA WOOLF?
ORIGINAL BROADWAY CAST (1963)

Running to four albums and over three hours, this original cast recording would have been highly unwieldy in any pre-LP format. It was issued in mono and stereo variants, but all with a lavish booklet that boasted both photographs from the Broadway production (which premiered in 1962) and essays by drama critics Harold Clurman and Walter Kerr. A droll introduction by the author, Edward Albee, marveled, "I cannot conceive of anyone wanting to buy [this] massive album; but . . . every playwright wants as much permanence for his work as he can get."

THE MONTY PYTHON INSTANT RECORD COLLECTION (1977)

With just one, extremely brief sketch that hadn't already appeared on a Python album ("Summarized Proust Competition"), this set contained little to excite completists, hence its self-deprecating subtitle "The pick of the best of some recently repeated Python hits again, Vol. II" (there was, naturally, no Vol. I). Nonetheless, it repaid investment thanks to an elaborate foldout design by Terry Gilliam that gave the impression of a stack of 65 LPs, with titles such as *The Beatles Chauffers Live!*, *Pet Smells, Young, Gifted, Black, and Furry*, and *Get Bach—The Best of The Welsh Beatles*.

READINGS BY JACK KEROUAC ON THE BEAT GENERATION
JACK KEROUAC (1960)

Kerouac's third and last spoken word album followed 1959's *Poetry for the Beat Generation* and *Blues and Haikus*. Its closing "Visions of Neal (Neal and the Three Stooges)" draws from drafts for his best-known work, *On the Road*.

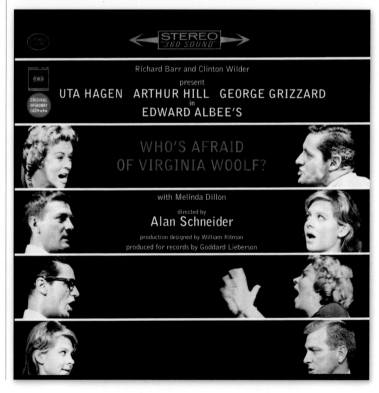

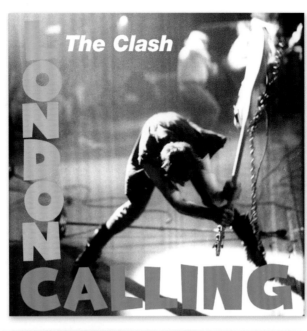

▽ A vintage copy of the classic *Elvis Presley* cover, with bass player Bill Black in the background. As with all of their LPs of the period, RCA Victor marketed it as "A 'New Orthophonic' High Fidelity Recording."

≫ A similar shot from the same Elvis Presley performance that generated the famous album cover.

▷ The celebrated pastiche by the Clash on their third album, *London Calling* (1979), with cover artwork by Ray Lowry featuring a photograph by Pennie Smith of Paul Simonon smashing his guitar.

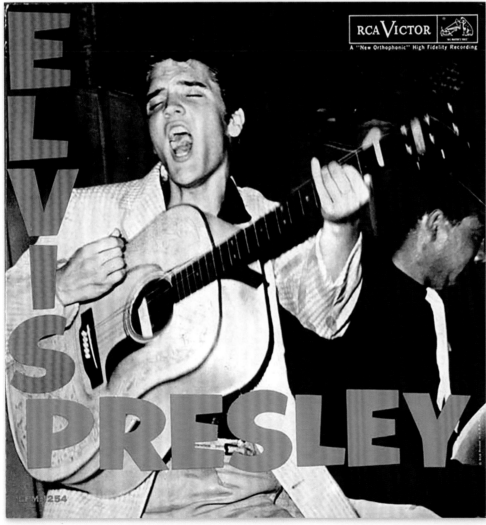

The first rock 'n' roll album to top the charts and sell more than a million copies, *Elvis Presley* was released by RCA Victor on March 23, 1956, following the singer's chart-topping single "Heartbreak Hotel," issued two months earlier.

Having acquired Presley's contract from Sun Records in 1955 for an unprecedented $35,000, RCA determined to cash in on the single's success. Sessions in January yielded eleven tracks, but as was common practice, the label wanted to save any hit potentials for singles. Consequently, the LP consisted seven new numbers and five, dating back to July 1954, that RCA had inherited from Sun. These earlier tracks—including Rodgers and Hart's ballad "Blue Moon," and the R&B number "Tryin' to Get to You"—were produced by Sun boss Sam Phillips and featured guitarist Scotty Moore, bassist Bill Black, and drummer D. J. Fontana.

The newer songs varied from rock 'n' roll (Little Richard's "Tutti Frutti") to R&B (Ray Charles's "I Got a Woman" and Clyde McPhatter's "Money Honey"). The opening track was a classic already: "Blue Suede Shoes" by Elvis's ex-Sun labelmate Carl Perkins. RCA promised Sun that if Elvis

Elvis Presley

recorded the song, they would delay its release as a single to give Perkins's version a chance. Perkins duly hit number two in March 1956, while Elvis made number twenty in September.

Confirming Elvis as *the* rock 'n' roll star, the album topped the US chart for ten weeks. (RCA also issued it as six singles.) In the UK, the LP—on the His Master's Voice label—hit the top of the chart with a modified track list that emphasized rock instead of ballads, including Elvis's Sun debut "That's All Right," the rockabilly tour-de-force "Mystery Train," Lloyd Price's R&B hit "Lawdy Miss Clawdy," and Joe Turner's "Shake, Rattle, and Roll."

The cover (the UK version of which added the subtitle "Rock 'n' Roll" on the back) was for many fans outside the United States the first enduring image they had seen of their idol. Captured in full flight at one of his sensational appearances as a regional star yet to crack the big time, Elvis was photographed at the Fort Homer Hesterly Armory in Tampa, Florida, in July 1955 by William V. "Red" Robertson. The uncredited graphic design, with its striking pink-and-green typography, remains one of the most pastiched icons of vinyl artwork.

Verve

Verve is one of the iconic record companies to emerge from the vinyl revolution of the 1950s. Founded in 1956, when the twelve-inch long-playing record was taking over as the vinyl standard from its ten-inch predecessor, it was the creation of legendary producer and concert promoter Norman Granz.

Founder of the Clef label in 1946 and Norgran in 1953, with his "Jazz at the Philharmonic" concerts and jam session albums, Granz stood on the cutting edge of the jazz scene when he decided to form Verve in 1956, partly to absorb its predecessors' catalogs into one company. His other immediate aim for the label was to act as a vehicle for vocalist Ella Fitzgerald, whom he managed at the time. He engineered her exit from Decca and swiftly established Verve. "I started on a Monday," recalled operations director Buddy Bregman. "We did not have a name on Tuesday, and by Wednesday, Norman had come up with Verve."

The label debuted with *Ella Fitzgerald Sings the Cole Porter Songbook* (1956), the first of seven albums celebrating the great American songwriters. Granz had petitioned Decca to undertake the project but, as he said, "They had one thing in mind and that was finding hit singles. I was interested in how I could enhance Ella's position, to make her a singer with more than just a cult following among jazz fans . . . So I proposed to Ella that the first Verve album would not be a jazz project, but rather a songbook of the works of Cole Porter. I envisaged her doing a lot of composers. The trick was to change the backing enough so that, here and there, there would be signs of jazz."

Granz's recording and promoting heritage bequeathed to Verve one of the strongest catalogs in jazz. Notable signings, including Bill Evans, Ben Webster, Billie Holiday, Stan Getz, Lester Young, and Oscar Peterson, further bolstered the list. Granz also managed Peterson ("I never had a contract with Ella or Oscar," he noted. "I told Ella, If you want the luxury of saying, 'Norman, I quit,' you're off. Go for yourself, but I want the luxury of quitting you, too. So we had a nice relationship. Ella lasted for maybe forty or forty-five years, Oscar well over fifty."). Like Granz's Jazz at the Philharmonic projects, Verve's output in the 1950s strongly tied to the visual style of graphic artist David Stone Martin, whose distinctive work dominated the releases.

When Granz sold Verve to MGM in 1961, Creed Taylor took over as producer, and the label spearheaded the Brazilian-influenced bossa nova craze with the seminal *Jazz Samba* (1962) by saxophonist Stan Getz and guitarist Charlie Bird and the best-selling *Getz/Gilberto* (1964) with Getz, Brazilian guitarist Joao Gilberto, and Gilberto's vocalist wife, Astrid Gilberto. Unusually for an album-oriented jazz label, Verve enjoyed hits: "Desfinado," from *Jazz Samba*, hit number fifteen in the United States; "The Girl from Ipanema" from *Getz/Gilberto* peaked at number five and won a Grammy in 1965.

The label branched out into roots music with Verve Folkways (later Verve Forecast), founded in association with Folkways Records founder, Moses Asch, in 1964. It nurtured such artists as Richie Havens, Tim Hardin, and Laura Nyro, while issuing established blues names, including Odetta, John Lee Hooker, Lightnin' Hopkins, and Lead Belly (the last of whom Asch recorded in the years leading to his death in 1949).

In the mid-1960s, Verve signed its first major rock act, Frank Zappa's Mothers. Rechristened the less suggestive Mothers of Invention at the label's insistence, they produced *Freak Out!* (1966), the second double album in rock history (the first being Bob Dylan's *Blonde on Blonde*). The other historic Verve release on the rock front, though not a hit at the time, was *The Velvet Underground & Nico* (1967), produced by Andy Warhol and featuring the iconic banana cover.

Verve won huge sales with Diana Krall and today is part of the Universal conglomerate.

Oscar Peterson was already a star in his homeland of Canada before Norman Granz brought him to the United States in 1949 for a surprise debut at a *Jazz at the Philharmonic* show at Carnegie Hall in New York.

In addition to the seven songbooks recorded by Ella Fitzgerald, Verve also released several landmark concert albums by the singer.

Tim Hardin II, released in 1967, was the second album by folk artist Tim Hardin.

Tenor saxophonist Stan Getz, live at the Ridgecrest Inn, Rochester, New York, 1957.

. . . AT NEWPORT
COUNT BASIE (1958)

Originally issued on Clef in 1957, this Norman Granz-produced set captured pianist Basie's set at the Newport Jazz Festival that year. He was accompanied by, among others, tenor saxophonists Frank Foster, Illinois Jacquet, Lester Young, and Frank Wess, and, in fine form, vocalist Jimmy Rushing.

TRIO '65
BILL EVANS TRIO (1965)

The most remarkable thing about *Trio '65* isn't the music, even though its eight pieces—produced by Creed Taylor and played by pianist Evans with bassist Chuck Israels and drummer Larry Bunker—are highly enjoyable. The miracle is that it exists at all, given Evans's crippling drug habits. It was suggested that he joined Verve because it offered better distribution and, therefore, higher profits to be spent on pharmaceutical pursuits than his previous label, Riverside. Often self-critical, Evans provided erratic work for Verve, but when he did it right, few could touch him.

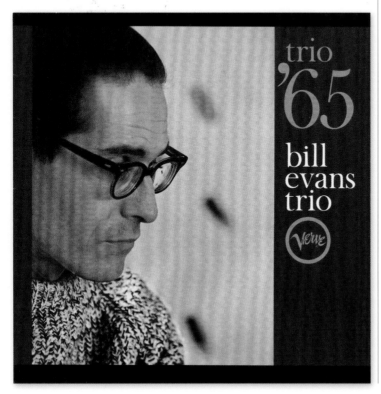

ELLA FITZGERALD SINGS THE RODGERS AND HART SONG BOOK (1956)

After a successful start with *Ella Fitzgerald Sings the Cole Porter Songbook*, Verve quickly followed it with an ambitious double set focusing on the work of Richard Rodgers and Lorenz Hart (the first of whom contributed sleevenotes, as did Oscar Hammerstein II and producer Norman Granz). Thereafter, the great singer tackled similar themed sets focusing on songwriters Duke Ellington (1957), Harold Arlen (1961), Jerome Kern (1963), Johnny Mercer (1964), and—to Grammy-winning effect—Irving Berlin (1958) and George and Ira Gershwin (1959).

JAZZ SAMBA
STAN GETZ AND
CHARLIE BYRD (1962)

Recorded in Washington, D.C., in February 1962, this Creed Taylor-produced set found guitarist Byrd and sax player Getz accompanied by Charlie's brother Gene on bass and guitar, Keter Betts on bass, and Bill Reichenbach and Buddy Deppenschmiddt on drums.

JAZZ BAND BALL
AL HIRT'S BAND (1958)

Wrapped in a charming cover by David Stone Martin, this featured trumpet player and bandleader Hirt with clarinetist and tenor saxophonist Pete Fountain. The sleevenotes promised that this "Swinging Dixie from Dan's Pier 600—New Orleans" would be a tonic for listeners "weary of the dreary."

ABSOLUTELY FREE
THE MOTHERS OF INVENTION (1967)

Frank Zappa's second album with the Mothers was recorded in November 1966, but its release was delayed until May 1967—due to, he suggested, Verve's misgivings about its lyrics. Chief among these was presumably "Brown Shoes Don't Make It," which graphically imagines a city hall official's fantasies about a thirteen-year-old girl. Nonetheless, "Brown Shoes . . ." became one of his signature songs, and *Absolutely Free* took Zappa tantalizingly close to the US top forty (which he eventually breached with 1968's *Sgt. Pepper*-skewering *We're Only In It for the Money*).

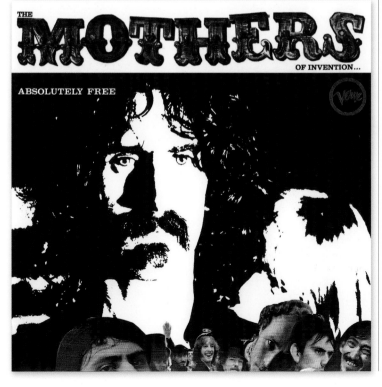

GETZ/GILBERTO
STAN GETZ & JOAO GILBERTO (1964)

Thanks to its opening, "The Girl from Ipanema," this became a jewel in Verve's crown. But its charms begin with painter Olga Albizu's cover. (She also supplied art for *Jazz Samba*.) Recorded in New York in March 1963, tenor saxophonist Stan Getz and guitarist/vocalist Joao Gilberto are joined by pianist Antonio Carlos Jobim and splendidly named drummer Milton Banana. Helmed by Creed Taylor and engineered by Phil Ramone, the record went gold in months and was the first jazz set to win Album of the Year, one of its three victories at the 1965 Grammys.

MOODS FOR GIRL AND BOY
HARRY CARNEY AND HIS ORCHESTRA (1956)

A bandmate of Duke Ellington, Carney was an influential baritone saxophonist whose romantic side is showcased on this Granz-devised set. When Ellington died in 1974, Carney said he had "nothing to live for." He died four months later.

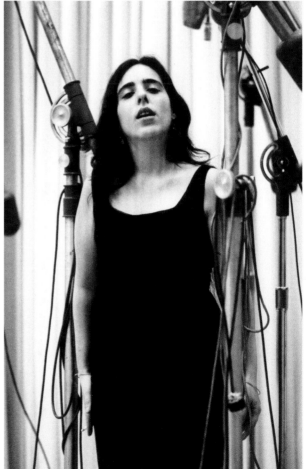

⟨ Legendary jazz trumpeter Dizzy
Gillespie (right) and Verve founder
Norman Granz backstage at a *Jazz
at the Philharmonic* concert, 1955.

∟ Jazz pianist Oscar Peterson
speaking into a microphone,
circa 1955.

∨ Verve Folkways artist Laura Nyro
during a recording session in New
York, 1968.

∧ Billie Holiday's five-year association with Norman Granz and musicians from his *Jazz at the Philharmonic* troupe began in 1952.

⌐ Verve producer Creed Taylor (right) works with a recording engineer to capture Stan Getz and his band performing onstage at Cafe Au Go Go for the live album *Getz Au Go Go* on August 19, 1964, in New York.

❯ Jazz tenor saxophonist Ben Webster, who was also known as "The Brute."

Although coin-operated record machines had been in existence almost as long as record-playing devices themselves, it was with the coming of vinyl that the jukebox really came into its own.

Not long after Thomas Edison introduced his cylinder-playing Phonograph, Louis Glass and William S. Arnold invented a nickel-in-the-slot version in 1890 that had four listening tubes through which to hear the music. This and similar instruments equipped to play only one selection of music were often arranged in "phonograph parlors," in which a group of machines allowed customers a choice of what they might hear.

The jukebox, with its multiple choice of records, first appeared in 1927, manufactured by the Automated Musical Instrument Company, better known later as AMI. It was launched in the era of the ten-inch shellac 78, so early jukeboxes were fairly cumbersome contraptions. Initially, they had eight or ten separate turntables, allowing for listeners to select their choices accordingly, and on most boxes only one side was available to play.

Jukebox Heroes

Through the Great Depression, when many venues across the United States could no longer afford to pay live bands, bars and dance halls relied on the jukebox to provide musical entertainment, which it did in thousands of roadside cafés, diners, and country juke joints. In fact, the jukebox acquired its name from its association with the juke joints of the South, the often ramshackle venues that served as dance hall, bar, and diner to rural blacks. (The word "juke" or "jook" is said to have come from "joog," an African-rooted word meaning rowdy or disreputable, an indication of the bad reputation that these venues often had.)

Into the 1940s, during the Swing era, the Wurlitzer was king. The imposing machines took pride of place wherever they stood, and the designs of engineer Paul Fuller came to epitomize the jukebox of the period with fabulous walnut cabinet styles and animated color lighting effects. They played twenty-four 78s stacked above one another, and the name in general became a byword for jukeboxes. Wurlitzer was overtaken by Seeburg and other competitors during the switch to vinyl 45s in the 1950s, but Fuller's designs were so iconic that they're still used

today as a symbol of the rock 'n' roll era in movies and television shows.

When seven-inch 45s arrived in 1949, jukebox manufacturers saw the potential in the new format. The virtually unbreakable discs, smaller and lighter than the 78, meant jukeboxes needed fewer bulky playing mechanisms, and they could house more discs at any one time. First came Seeburg, who in 1948 already had stolen a march on competitors with their M100A model, the first 78 jukebox to offer both sides of 50 records, giving a choice of 100 tunes. In 1950 Seeburg introduced the M100B, which featured the same "Select-O-Matic" technology to play the records as the M100A, but with the new seven-inch 45s. Again the box carried a total of 100 selections, but later Seeburg models increased the number of discs to 80 (160 sides) and 100 (200 sides) per machine. Seeburg's next model, the M100C, launched in 1952, achieved its own iconic status in the 1970s when it appeared in the opening sequence of the 1950s-set TV series *Happy Days*.

Rock-Ola, along with AMI, Seeburg, and Wurlitzer, was the other major jukebox manufacturer. Despite the name, it didn't originate in the rock era but was named for its founder, David C. Rockola, who famously delivered one of his twelve-selection jukeboxes to the decks of the luxury liner *Queen Mary* on her maiden voyage from New York in 1936. Rock-Ola was best known, however, for its streamlined machines in the 1950s and 1960s, which included the ultramodern looking 434 Concerto, launched in 1967.

< A replica Wurlitzer 1015 Jukebox. Released in 1946, the 1015 sold over 56,000 units during its first eighteen months on the market.

⌐ French singer, actor, and director Serge Gainsbourg peruses a jukebox in October 1959.

> A 1939 Standard Luxury Light-Up, manufactured by Rock-Ola.

In their heyday, jukeboxes were big business, contributing to a significant proportion of record sales. By the mid-1940s, three-quarters of all records produced in the United States went into jukeboxes. Manufacturers, aware of the money-making potential, often set the speed at slightly more than 45 rpm, allowing for more nickels per hour to go in the machines. They were also an important source of income for music publishers, who received a royalty on every song played, as did the record companies. Perhaps not surprisingly, the control of jukeboxes often fell into the hands of organized crime. David Rockola himself had ties to the Chicago mobsters of the 1920s, eventually escaping jail by turning state's evidence.

The demise of the jukebox came about with the spread of portable radios among teenagers in the late 1950s and subsequent mobile players from the Walkman cassette player to the cell phone. However, the jukebox's big sound could never be matched by domestic equipment, let alone portable players, and it remains a symbol of the potent energy of rock 'n' roll records in the mid-twentieth century.

FOLKWAYS

Launched in 1948, just as the vinyl long-playing record appeared, Folkways became one of the world's largest and most influential independent record companies, accumulating a massive catalog of folk music, spoken word, and documentary material.

The label was the brainchild of Moses Asch, who had recorded folk singers, including Burl Ives, Woody Guthrie, Lead Belly, and Pete Seeger, for Asch Records before the business hit financial trouble. All releases on the Asch label appeared on 78s, but when the long-playing record debuted he recognized it as a format more suited to the material he wanted to record. He had his secretary, Marian Distler, set up a new company in her name, circumventing his own bankruptcy, and launched Folkways, dedicated to documenting folk and oral recordings from around the world.

The company recorded material as diverse as Cuban, Native American, and jazz, but its primary focus was folk music, and it played a key role in a folk and blues revival that began in the early 1950s. As well as immortalizing the likes of Guthrie, Lead Belly, and Seeger on album for the first time, it was instrumental in the rediscovery of seminal blues names, such as Lightnin' Hopkins, Sonny Terry and Brownie McGhee, and boogie pianist Speckled Red.

A landmark release came in 1952 with the six-LP *Anthology of American Folk Music*. Compiled by moviemaker and folk collector Harry Smith, the box set consisted of eighty-four folk, country, and blues recordings, originally released as 78s between 1927 and 1932. The compilation caused a sensation. It exposed the work of key performers—many for the first time—and inspired a new generation of musicians, such as Joan Baez, Phil Ochs, and Bob Dylan.

Among the 2,168 releases before Asch's death in 1986, another seminal collection came in 1959: *The Country Blues*. Another set of recordings that had previously appeared as 78s in the 1920s and 1930s, the fourteen tracks included numbers by artists such as Blind Willie McTell, Bukka White, and Robert Johnson. The legendary Johnson was an almost forgotten name at the time, yet to be rediscovered by blues fans. (Among those paying attention were Led Zeppelin, whose cover of "Gallows Pole" took inspiration from Folkways artist Fred Gerlach—who had based his version of the centuries-old folk song on one by Lead Belly.)

Under Asch's hands-on direction, Folkways was ahead of its time in releasing what later became known as world music. Landmark releases included *Music of the World's Peoples*, issued as a series of long-playing records beginning in 1951, and featuring material from as far afield as Iceland, Korea, Madagascar, Russia, and Tibet.

In 1964, the label struck a distribution deal with Verve, creating the Verve Folkways (later Verve Forecast) label, yet the parent company continued to plow a defiantly uncommercial furrow. A hit record, Asch maintained, "would be the end of Folkways."

When Asch died in 1986, the Smithsonian Institution acquired Folkways. It represented an official acknowledgment of the priceless archive the label had built on vinyl for more than forty years, documenting the musical culture of the United States in particular, as well as that of many other parts of the world. As Asch's biographer Tony Olmstead noted, "The Folkways catalog represents what is possible when vision, ingenuity, and creativity come together . . . Folkways has set the standard in terms of the range of sounds that it has preserved, as well as recognizing that sound is meaningless in the absence of context. The whole package—sound and explanation—not only defines Folkways, but has set the standards for any other company that might endeavor to preserve some of the world's sounds."

> Bluesman Lightnin' Hopkins poses for a publicity shot circa 1959 in Houston, Texas.

⌐ Lead Belly received little popular acclaim before his death in 1949, but the songs he recorded for Asch had an enormous influence on the folk music revival that blossomed in the 1950s and 1960s

∨ Woody Guthrie first met Moses Asch in 1944 and recorded hundreds of songs with him.

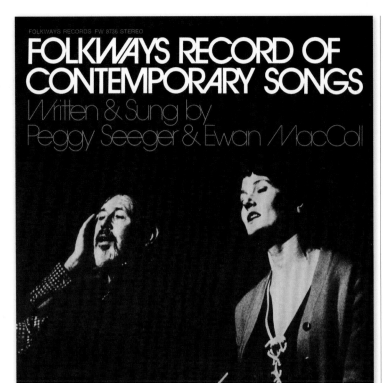

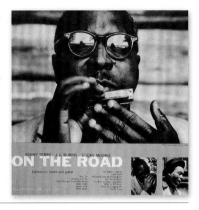

ON THE ROAD
SONNY TERRY, J. C. BURRIS, STICKS MCGHEE (1959)

True blues as nature intended is captured here on wax, with harmonica giant Sonny Terry, J. C. Burris on bones (handheld percussion), and guitarist Brownie "Sticks" McGhee. Cuts include "Jail House Blues" and "Easy Rider."

THE MONTGOMERY MOVEMENT
THE MONTGOMERY EXPRESS (1974)

Recorded in Fort Lauderdale, Florida, in November 1973, this is the sole album by a group described by the Numero Group label (who reissued it in 2014) as "Funk's answer to the Five Blind Boys of Alabama." At their helm was Indiantown, Florida, resident Sandy Montgomery, who—in the words of Folkways' sleevenotes—"is well-known for his work with young people in and around his hometown. He believes that the best way to keep them out of trouble and off the street is to keep them busy doing something useful . . . This album will tell the hard times spent trying to get it to market."

FOLKWAYS RECORD OF CONTEMPORARY SONGS
PEGGY SEEGER & EWAN MACCOLL (1973)

Peggy Seeger is part of an American musical dynasty: her father was a musicologist and her mother a composer. Her siblings included musician Mike and the best-known Seeger, singer and activist Pete. It's the latter with whom she has most in common, being committed to both the preservation of folk music and using it as a vehicle for campaigning. This Folkways LP is one of sixteen that she recorded with her partner and later husband, British folk singer Ewan MacColl.

LIGHTNIN' STRIKES
LIGHTNIN' HOPKINS (1966)

No relation to his 1962 album of the same name on the Vee Jay label, this captures Texas-born Sam John "Lightnin'" Hopkins in the company of bassist Jimmy Bond and drummer Earl Palmer. The country bluesman later expanded into psychedelia and influenced the likes of Townes Van Zandt.

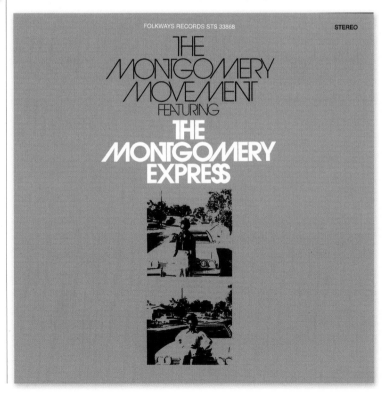

A VISION SHARED—A TRIBUTE TO WOODY GUTHRIE AND LEAD BELLY (1988)

A Folkways album in name only—issued by Columbia—the Grammy-winning *A Vision Shared* nonetheless honored the label by reviving its ethos of bringing songs by pioneering artists to a new generation's attention. Woody Guthrie classics, such as "Pretty Boy Floyd" and "This Land Is Your Land," are performed by Bob Dylan, John Mellencamp, U2, Bruce Springsteen, Willie Guthrie, Emmylou Harris, and Pete Seeger, while Lead Belly gems are tackled by Sweet Honey in the Rock, Little Richard with Fishbone, Taj Mahal, and Brian Wilson.

SONGS AND MUSIC OF TIBET (1962)

Taped in a camp on the outskirts of Kathmandu by Howard Kaufman, this illustrates the astonishing breadth of the label's output—and provides a home for splendid titles, such as "Garpokurkipusa (Song of the Home of a Young Bride)." Other songs praise the land, food, and agriculture of rural Tibet.

BIG BILL BROONZY AND PETE SEEGER IN CONCERT (1956)

The Chicago bluesman and New York folk singer team up for a set taped at Northwestern University by, as the cover declares, the Windy City's fine arts and classical radio station WFMT. Issued on Verve Folkways, it captures the pair in duets and solo performances.

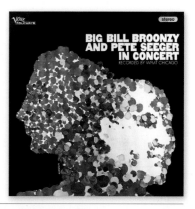

MUSIC OF THE WORLD'S PEOPLES (1951)

This quintessential Folkways set benefited from extensive sleevenotes by compiler Henry Cowell. "The music of some peoples of the world will sound extremely strange on first hearing," he conceded. "Yet all of this music contains richly rewarding values." As the meticulous Smithsonian Folkways site helpfully explains, "Hear a girls' chorus from Madagascar, an Irish reel played on uileann pipes (bagpipes), a Greek Orthodox church choir singing medieval *organum* (an early form of polyphony). Selections also come from Japan, Nigeria, India, France, Tahiti, and Iceland."

1960s

Although singles still dominated, by the end of the 1960s rock music had begun to move toward the long-player market, with the flamboyant graphics of psychedelia matching equally extravagant packaging. Musically, ambitious works like The Beatles' *Sgt. Pepper's Lonely Hearts Club Band* heralded the era of the meticulously crafted concept album.

> Jimi Hendrix in London in 1967. In his hand is an album by the satirical stand-up comedian Lenny Bruce, *Lenny Bruce—Is Out Again* (1966). Leaning against the chair is a copy of Bob Dylan's *Blonde on Blonde* (1966).

MOTOWN

Berry Gordy established his first record label, Tamla Records, in Detroit on January 12, 1959. Its first single was Marv Johnson's "Come to Me." Later the same year he founded the Motown label, which became the parent company of Tamla and a number of other imprints. Gordy's first hit was "Money (That's What I Want)" by Barrett Strong, which hit number two on the *Billboard* R&B chart shortly before the iconic Motown Record Corporation was incorporated in 1960.

Although the Motown label was established in 1959, most of Gordy's early singles were leased to other labels (Anna, End, Chess, Fury, etc.)— a cautious start to one of the biggest success stories in record history. The debut single on the Motown label was "Bad Girl" (1959) by The Miracles, who also gave the company its first million-copy seller with "Shop Around"(1960).

After his early success, Gordy bought a house on West Grand Boulevard and converted it into offices and a recording studio. He hung a sign over the door reading "Hitsville USA," and over the next decade he acquired adjoining buildings as the business grew. Motown expanded at an astonishing rate as Gordy built up a roster of young artists drawn mainly from the black working-class neighborhoods of Detroit. Martha & The Vandellas, Marvin Gaye, Mary Wells, and others joined Motown's burgeoning list of hit makers, and in 1961 the company had its first pop-chart number one with "Please Mr. Postman" by The Marvelettes. That same year Gordy signed a blind eleven-year-old singer—"Little" Stevie Wonder—who in 1963 delivered Motown's first chart-topping LP: *The 12 Year Old Genius.*

The Miracles' lead singer Smokey Robinson played an important role in Motown's success, producing and writing for new acts, including The Temptations, The Supremes, anvd The Four

℗ 1984 Motown
Record Corporation
Produced by Steve
Barri & Tony Peluso
Arranged by Bobby
Sandstrom & Sam Harris
Re-Mixed by Rusty
Garner. Re-Mix Engineer:
David Leonard
AN ENDLESS MUSIC MIX
Manufactured in the UK

MOTOWN®

A

TMGT 1370
TMGT 1370 A§
Chappell Music Ltd./
Donna Weiss Music
STEREO
45 RPM
SIDE A1
Timing is
approximate

HEARTS ON FIRE (DANCE MIX)
(6.40) (B.Roberts-D.Weiss) Single Version
In Album: "SAM HARRIS" ZL 72237
SAM HARRIS

Tops. The Temptations topped the charts in 1965 with a Robinson composition—"My Girl"— while Brian Holland, Lamont Dozier, and Eddie Holland became the song-writing force behind The Supremes and The Four Tops. By the mid-1960s the Motown sound was, as Gordy put it, "the sound of young America." What had started as an almost exclusively black enterprise was now a solid player in the mainstream music market. Between 1961 and 1971, Motown had 163 entries in the US top twenty, including twenty-eight chart-toppers. However, it didn't

rest on its laurels. New acts in the latter half of the 1960s and into the 1970s included Jr. Walker & The All Stars, Gladys Knight & The Pips, The Jackson 5, and the short-lived partnership of Marvin Gaye and Tammi Terrell.

The early 1970s brought turbulent times, and Motown began to reflect socially conscious themes. Edwin Starr's "War," a strident funk protest against the conflict in Vietnam, was a number-one hit in 1970. The following year saw the release of one of the strongest musical statements of the era: Marvin Gaye's *What's Going On.*

Throughout the 1970s, Motown artists, including Gaye and Diana Ross (now a solo star), continued to make records of the highest quality alongside new acts, such as the Commodores, who had five albums in the top ten between 1977 and 1980. However, the decade belonged to Stevie Wonder, who broke barriers with each new release, including three Grammy Award winners—*Innervisions* (1973), *Fulfillingness' First Finale* (1974), and *Songs in the Key of Life* (1976).

The Motown brand was still at the cutting edge of soul and soul-related music in the 1980s. Rick James hit a high with *Street Songs* in 1981 on Motown's Gordy label, and Lionel Richie struck out on his own with three best sellers: *Lionel Richie* (1982), *Can't Slow Down* (1983), and *Dancing on the Ceiling* (1986). In 1988, Gordy sold Motown Records to MCA, ending the label's history as an independent record company. Its run had spanned some of the greatest years in rock, pop, and soul music, confirming Motown as one of the preeminent names in the recording industry.

> Label founder Berry Gordy in the Motown control room.

⌐ Marvin Gaye plays piano as he records in a studio, circa 1974.

∨ Stevie Wonder's first number one hit for Motown was "Fingertips, Part 2" (1963).

HEY HARMONICA MAN
STEVIE WONDER (1964)

For all its greatness, Motown was far from infallible. One of its most notorious errors was trying to fit Stevie Wonder into a pop straitjacket: 1964's *Stevie at the Beach*, a bid to board the Beach Boys bandwagon with a surf 'n' sea concept album, from which "Hey Harmonica Man" was a minor hit.

TOGETHER
THE SUPREMES & THE TEMPTATIONS (1969)

Less than a year after 1968's triumphant *Diana Ross & The Supremes Join The Temptations*, Motown tried to repeat the trick. In a nifty foldout sleeve, *Together* contained a mishmash of covers, including The Band's "The Weight" and Sly & the Family Stone's "Sing a Simple Song" alongside more obvious fare by Smokey Robinson and Marvin Gaye. Ultimately, it represented neither The Temptations, then pursuing a psychedelic path on the simultaneous *Puzzle People*, nor Diana Ross & The Supremes, then on the verge of splitting into two factions.

WHAT'S GOING ON
MARVIN GAYE (1971)

"*What's Going On* forever changed the sound and subject matter of popular music, influencing and inspiring every generation since," reflected Smokey Robinson. "Speaking boldly and passionately about social and political issues . . . *What's Going On* provided a soundtrack to life in America—and still does." Gaye had to threaten to strike to convince Motown to release it but ultimately took full advantage of the LP format; the songs segue from one to another, and a gatefold sleeve accommodates his beautiful lyrics and a personal sleeve note.

STREET SONGS
RICK JAMES (1981)

Rick James became the flagship act of the Gordy imprint in the late 1970s, but funk sleaze masterpiece *Street Songs* pushed him into the major league. Thanks to its side-opening smashes "Give It to Me Baby" and "Super Freak," it sold by the million and crashed the top three of the pop chart.

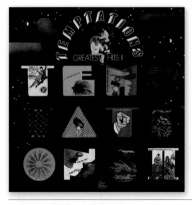

GREATEST HITS II
THE TEMPTATIONS (1970)

A gorgeously packaged collection on the Gordy subsidiary, this captures The Temptations as they ascended to the title "Emperors of Soul" with gems such as "Cloud Nine," "I Wish It Would Rain," "Ball of Confusion (That's What the World is Today)," "I Can't Get Next to You," and "Psychedelic Shack."

GREATEST HITS
COMMODORES (1978)

The chart-topping ballads for which Alabama sextet the Commodores are most widely known open each side of this irresistible package: "Three Times a Lady" and "Easy." However, dig deeper and you'll find stone-cold and much sampled funk classics, such as "Machine Gun" (heard in *Boogie Nights*), "Slippery When Wet," and "Brick House." Despite appearing in the Casablanca company's movie *Thank God It's Friday*, the Commodores were Motown to the core. Discovered while supporting The Jackson 5, they also spawned one of the label's biggest solo stars: Lionel Richie.

PLEASE MR. POSTMAN
THE MARVELETTES (1961)

The Marvelettes—celebrated for this LP's US chart-topping title song—stamped a template for Tamla's girl groups and paved the path to success for the label itself. The album's back cover boasted "A personal letter from The Marvelettes to you": "The last time Mr. Postman walked by our house he delivered to us the happiest letter we've ever received. In it was the news that you have made 'Please Mr. Postman' our first hit record and given us the reason for presenting this album to you . . . Just write us a letter and let us know which song you liked best."

INNERVISIONS
STEVIE WONDER (1973)

Virtually a one-man band, on six of nine tracks Stevie Wonder played piano, drums, harmonica, bass, and synthesizers to create an LP regarded as one of his greatest achievements. At its heart lies a harrowing, seven-minute account of day-to-day existence in the urban ghetto: "Living for the City."

The Commodores performing in 1979.

Formed in the 1950s, Gladys Knight and the Pips only truly took off when they signed with Motown in 1966.

∧ The Temptations perform on *Top of the Pops* in March 1972.

> The Jackson Five in 1970: (left-right) Marlon, Tito, Jackie, Jermaine, and Michael.

Sound quality theoretically declines as a record's grooves run more closely together. It therefore stands to reason that there's an optimum length for long-playing records—hence the convention that a twelve-inch LP lasts between thirty and forty minutes, with a maximum of about twenty minutes per side. For mainstream pop songs, defined in the days of the 78 as being about three minutes long, that meant a maximum of eight songs per side. That holds true for all of The Beatles' albums, with just two exceptions (one side each of "The White Album" and *Abbey Road*).

In the 1950s, budget label Vox crammed an entire sixty-three-minute performance of Beethoven's Ninth Symphony on one disc. Apart from similar budget labels in the pop field, the standard length of vinyl has held steady ever since, with a few notable exceptions.

One example was Todd Rundgren's *Initiation* (1975), which ran to nearly sixty-eight minutes, including the thirty-five-minute, four-part instrumental "A Treatise on a Cosmic Fire." Only in prog rock's heyday did record labels tolerate such indulgence. The inner sleeve even bore a technical note

Really Long LPs

that warned: "Due to the amount of music on this disc (over one hour), two points must be emphasized. Firstly, if your needle is worn or damaged, it will ruin the disc immediately. Secondly, if the sound does seem not loud enough on your system, try rerecording the music onto tape."

Pink Floyd topped fifty-one minutes with *Atom Heart Mother* (1970), while hard rockers UFO hit the one-hour barrier with *UFO 2: Flying* (1971). *Duke* (1980) by Genesis ran to about fifty-five minutes, a couple of minutes longer than the British pressing of The Rolling Stones' *Aftermath* (1966).

Greatest hits packages, especially on budget labels, tended to squeeze more in, at the expense of sound quality. The UK label Pye had a "Golden Hour" series that packed twenty or so tracks on LPs that ran for at least sixty minutes. Artists subjected to such treatment included The Kinks, Donovan, Joan Baez, and Nina Simone.

Most notoriously, when Barry Manilow signed with RCA in 1985, his previous label, Arista, squeezed all his smashes on a single, seventy-five-minute album, *The Manilow Collection: 20 Classic Hits*. Industry insiders at the time claimed it was Arista's revenge for their star attraction leaving the label.

⌃ David Gilmour in Hyde Park in 1970, one of the shows at which Pink Floyd premiered *Atom Heart Mother*'s title cut before its release in October that year.

⌃ In the studio circa 1965, Mick Jagger plays the dulcimer, an instrument that distinguishes the beautiful "Lady Jane" on The Rolling Stones' *Aftermath*.

AFTERMATH
THE ROLLING STONES (1966)

Aftermath ran to fourteen songs (eleven in the United States) and more than fifty-three minutes. For the first time, all the songs were Mick 'n' Keef originals, although Brian Jones proved key to its highlights, playing the dulcimer on "Lady Jane" and marimba on "Under My Thumb." The band also stretched out on the eleven-minute blues jam, "Goin' Home."

ATOM HEART MOTHER
PINK FLOYD (1970)

The most preposterous of Pink Floyd's early LPs was nonetheless their first number one. Its side-long title track—its torturous assembly documented in arranger Ron Geesin's book *The Flaming Cow*—is eclipsed in atrocity only by the closing "Alan's Psychedelic Breakfast," which ended some vinyl editions with a locked groove of endlessly dripping water.

GOLDEN HOUR OF . . .
THE KINKS (1971)

This embarrassment of riches boasts "Waterloo Sunset," "Dedicated Follower of Fashion," "Dead End Street," "Sunny Afternoon," "Victoria," "You Really Got Me," "Days," "All Day and All of the Night," and "Tired of Waiting for You"—a collection that, as the sleevenotes claim, "gives an overall insight into the kind of musical talent that many groups would dearly love to possess."

UFO 2: FLYING
UFO (1971)

Before they replaced guitarist Mick Bolton with Michael Schenker and became a key influence on the likes of Iron Maiden, UFO were a trippier proposition, hence this album's twenty-six minute "Flying." The LP clocks in at just under the billed hour, although that doesn't factor in the time it took for chemically challenged listeners to lift the needle and turn the disc over.

INITIATION
TODD RUNDGREN (1975)

His eyes on psychedelic horizons, Rundgren pushed *A Wizard, a True Star* (1973) to nearly fifty-six minutes. But *Initiation* sailed past that, thanks to "A Treatise on Cosmic Fire," his take on Alice A. Bailey's 1925 philosophical book of the same title. "By the way," say the sleevenotes (somewhat optimistically, as it turned out), "Thanks for buying this album."

DUKE
GENESIS (1980)

The finest of the band's post-Peter Gabriel LPs boasts the hits "Misunderstanding" and "Turn It On Again." But its highlights bookend the set: the opening "Behind the Lines" and "Duchess," and closing "Duke's Travels" and "Duke's End." In 1981, "Behind the Lines" resurfaced on Phil Collins's *Face Value*, which clocked in at forty-eight minutes.

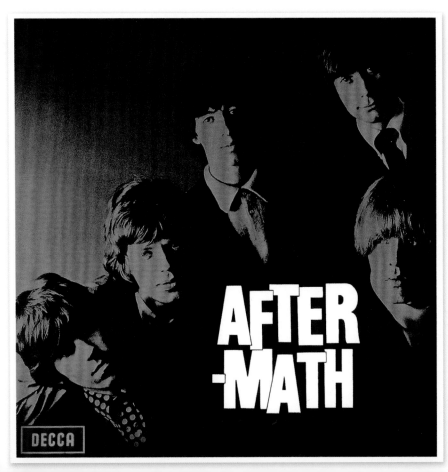

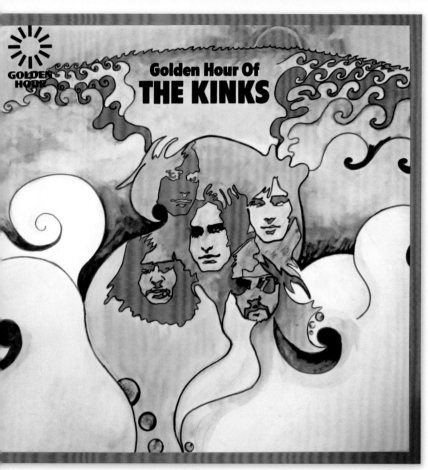

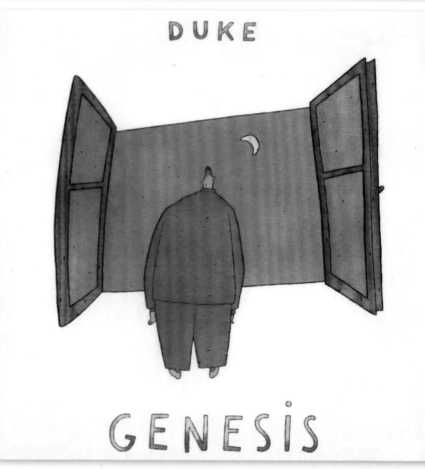

Set the Controls for the Art of the Sun

Rarely was the art of the album cover more potently demonstrated than in the psychedelic era of the late 1960s. Flamboyant designs that evoked hallucinogenic trips wouldn't have worked without twelve-inch canvases.

Classic psychedelic art often appeared on posters by artists such as San Francisco's Rick Griffin, Victor Moscoso, Wes Wilson, and the Mouse & Kelley studios and Britain's Hapshash and the Coloured Coat (Michael English and Nigel Weymouth), Michael McInnerney, and Martin Sharp. These designers also created album designs that became icons of the flower-power period.

A formative example was The Beatles' *Rubber Soul* in 1965. With a deliberately distorted image and cartoony graphics, it anticipated the druggy designs that soon proliferated.

Similarly, *Revolver* (1966) bore an illustration by Klaus Voorman that, although black-and-white, featured the kind of intricate detail beloved of counterculture posters and magazines.

When psychedelia arrived in an explosion of color in 1967, record labels quickly adopted it. In the United States, bands often nominated poster artists whose work they knew. West Coast hippie favorites The Grateful Dead had Mouse & Kelley design their self-titled 1967 debut, while the Steve Miller Band used Victor Moscoso for *Children of the Future* in 1968.

By the close of the decade, Day-Glo colors and swirling typography seethed on hundreds of LP covers. Like the music within, some were memorable, others not so. Among the most celebrated was the second album by British hard rock pioneers Cream, *Disraeli Gears* (1967),

a mind-boggling montage by poster designer and underground magazine illustrator Martin Sharp. Like him, the Dutch designers known as The Fool (Simon Posthuma and Marijke Koger) operated in other disciplines; in the latter case, clothes for The Beatles' Apple shop in London. They made their mark in album design with a quintessential slice of psychedelic fantasy for The Incredible String Band's *The 5000 Spirits or The Layers of the Onion* (1967).

Although the psychedelic period was short-lived, these leaps of imagination on the part of designers influenced the next wave of landmark design. With the onset of progressive rock in the early 1970s, artists such as Roger Dean and Storm Thorgerson extended the parameters of LP art even farther, taking to their limits the possibilities offered by twelve-inch showcases.

The Beatles in June 1967: the start of the psychedelic Summer of Love they had helped to create

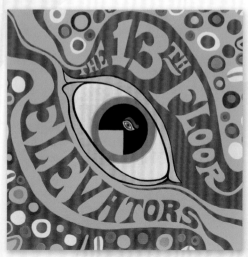

THE PSYCHEDELIC SOUNDS OF THE 13TH FLOOR ELEVATORS
THE 13TH FLOOR ELEVATORS (1966)

This psychedelic rock essential is blessed with a cover by Texan designer John Cleveland, to which Matt "The The" Johnson paid tribute with the artwork of his *Burning Blue Soul* (1981).

INCENSE AND PEPPERMINTS
THE STRAWBERRY ALARM CLOCK (1967)

So 1967 that it should have come with free acid, The Strawberry Alarm Clock's debut album was named after their US number one hit. Guitarist and cowriter Ed King went on to Lynyrd Skynyrd.

DISRAELI GEARS
CREAM (1967)

Disraeli Gears' cover, said Australian designer Martin Sharp, "is a collage colored with fluorescent paints. I was aiming to reproduce visually the warm electric sound of Cream."

THE 5000 SPIRITS OR THE LAYERS OF THE ONION
THE INCREDIBLE STRING BAND (1967)

"Sound of a pixie voice tiptoeing over the strings of a golden guitar and the dawn comes creeping up when it thinks I'm not looking," wrote *Rolling Stone*, enthusiastically albeit incomprehensibly.

FEATURING THE HUMAN HOST ...
HAPSHASH AND THE COLOURED COAT (1967)

Michael English and Nigel Waymouth made clothes worn by The Beatles and The Rolling Stones, designed posters for Pink Floyd, and cut their own influential psychedelic classic.

CHILDREN OF THE FUTURE
STEVE MILLER BAND (1968)

Victor Moscoso—who graduated from poster designs to Robert Crumb's *Zap Comix*—has several LP covers to his credit, of which the best known is Herbie Hancock's *Head Hunters* (1973).

∧ The US edition, which topped the *Billboard* chart for fifteen weeks

≫ The Beatles pose with *Pepper* at manager Brian Epstein's home

› Frank Zappa's 1968 pastiche *We're Only In It for the Money.*

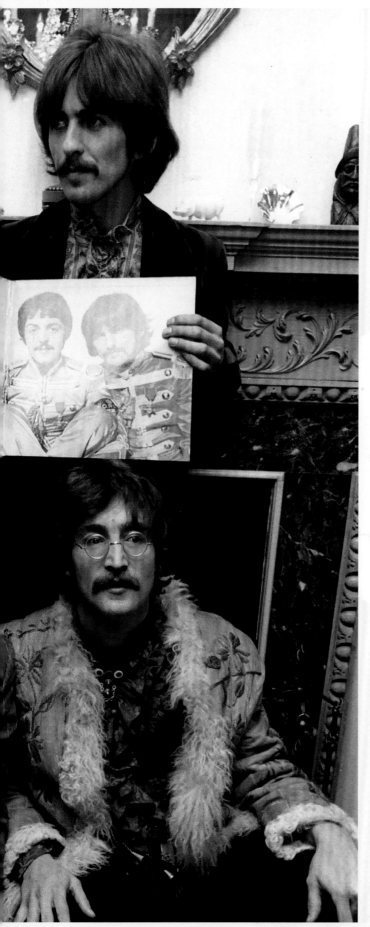

With its conceptual basis and lavish packaging, *Sgt. Pepper's Lonely Hearts Club Band*, released on June 1, 1967, broke new ground in treating the vinyl LP as a stand-alone work of art.

Concept albums already existed, going back to Frank Sinatra's *In the Wee Small Hours* in 1955, but the title alone suggested *Pepper* was going to be different. After seven best-selling LPs, The Beatles came up with the audacious idea of creating a work by a fictitious band "played" by the Fab Four in the military-esque outfits displayed on the cover. The songs were unconnected thematically, but sound effects of an audience and a reprise of the welcoming title track conjured the illusion of a concert by the titular band.

The songs couldn't have been more diverse. The jaunty "With a Little Help from My Friends" eases into the trippy "Lucy in the Sky with Diamonds" and achingly sad "She's Leaving Home." *Pepper* presented a kaleideoscope of words and music, climaxing with "A Day in the Life," its last crashing chord sounding as if it would last forever. And last forever the LP could: at the end was a tape of chat and

Sgt. Pepper's Lonely Hearts Club Band

laughter on a locked groove that played ad infinitum for anyone without an auto-return on his or her record player.

Pepper's packaging was as innovative as the music. With pop artist Peter Blake and his sculptor wife, Jann Haworth, The Beatles conceived a life-size tableau of pictures and mannequins of their heroes and heroines, in front of which they posed as the Pepper band. The stunning result, shot in a Chelsea studio by photographer Michael Cooper, became one of the most iconic sleeves in the history of vinyl—promptly parodied by Frank Zappa and the Mothers of Invention on their 1968 LP *We're Only in It for the Money*. Zappa even had a sheet of cutout images inserted in the sleeve, just as The Beatles did in *Pepper*. Blake recalled that his first idea was to have a small package with badges and gifts inside, an idea the EMI label nixed on grounds of cost.

The gatefold sleeve opened into a panoramic picture of the band and—to complete the immersive experience—the back cover was one of the first to carry the album's entire lyrics.

Pepper took 129 days to make and blazed a trail for LPs to become more than simply vinyl vehicles for pop.

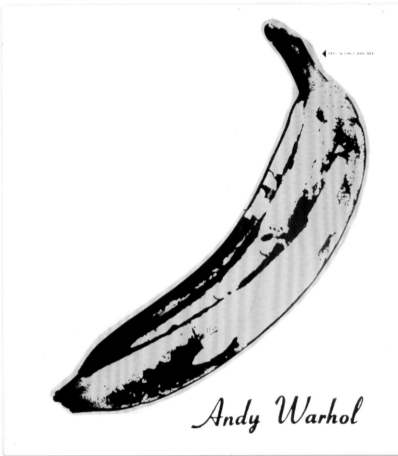

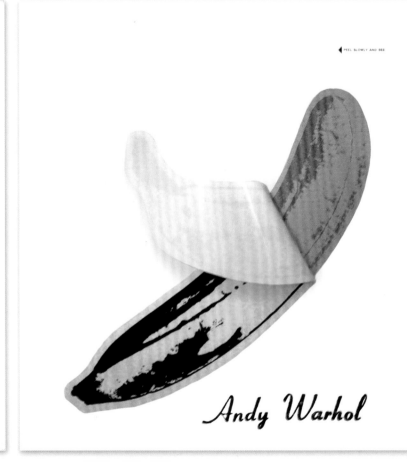

All Wrapped Up

The expanse of the twelve-inch album cover gave designers ideas beyond the limits of a thin laminated cardboard sleeve and even beyond the double possibilities of the open-up gatefold.

The Beatles paved the way with *Sgt. Pepper's Lonely Hearts Club Band*, but even that gatefold, cutout, and lyric-embellished effort (see pages 112–113) paled beside the Small Faces' *Ogdens'*

Nut Gone Flake (1968). An oversize pastiche of a tobacco tin, it was one in a growing field of what might now be deemed interactive LP covers, of which these are three fine further examples.

THEIR SATANIC MAJESTIES REQUEST
THE ROLLING STONES (1967)

In a seemingly blatant attempt to go one better than the Beatles' *Sgt. Pepper* cover, the Rolling Stones hired Michael Cooper (who had taken the *Pepper* sleeve shot) to create a 3-D lenticular image of the band. The original idea was for the picture to take up the entire front cover, but it was too expensive. Dressed in what can be described only as pantomime costumes, the Stones struck a slightly ludicrous image against a bright landscape of hippie-inspired fantasy.

THE VELVET UNDERGROUND & NICO
THE VELVET UNDERGROUND (1967)

Andy Warhol adopted The Velvets, so it was inevitable that the pop artist would create their debut LP cover. The front duly displayed his illustration of a banana on a plain background. Early copies, however, invited purchasers to "peel slowly and see." Doing so revealed a flesh-colored banana. A special machine was needed to create the covers, but MGM (which then owned the Verve label) calculated that Warhol's association would reap big sales. It didn't.

STAND UP
JETHRO TULL (1969)

When Jethro Tull toured the United States in 1969, their manager hired professional woodcarver James Grashow to capture them in his medium—an idea credited in part to graphic designer John Williams, later responsible for many Frank Zappa covers. From that came a novelty gatefold sleeve that, when opened, presented a pop-up image of the band based on the woodcut. *Stand Up* went on to win that year's *NME* award for best album artwork.

Turntable Treasures

While portability was still a key factor in mass market players—the ubiquitous Dansette was still the most popular UK brand after being launched in the late 1950s—the 1960s saw a move toward more ambitious luxury models at the high end of the range, where sound quality took precedence over convenience.

> The Hydraulic Reference was designed by Transcriptors in 1964, and later produced under licence by Michell. It appeared in several scenes in the 1971 movie *A Clockwork Orange*.

> A Laboratory series 4-speed single record player SP25, manufactured by Garrard. Launched in 1965, the SP25 was a popular model that continued to be produced until the Mark IV version.

> Designed by architects Pier Giacomo and Achille Castiglioni in 1965, the Brionvega RR126 had a modular structure that allowed it to be formed into either a cube or a long rectangle.

> The Sonni portable record player was made by Kurt Ehrlich KG in Pirna, East Germany, in 1960. The leather case both protected the turntable and enabled it to be carried easily.

Got Live If You Want It

The advent of rock added a fresh element to the live album genre, from cheap and cheerful cash-ins, such as the Stones' *Got Live If You Want It!*, to weighty classics, such as Cream's *Wheels of Fire*. Meanwhile, in R&B, live sets proved career makers for Stevie Wonder (1963's US number one *The 12 Year Old Genius*) and James Brown (the same year's iconic *Live at the Apollo*). However, the last word in live albums of the 1960s went to Detroit's proto-punks the MC5, who provided one of *the* quotes of the decade: "Kick out the jams, motherfuckers!"

LIVE AT THE APOLLO
JAMES BROWN (1963)

Funded by "Mr. Dynamite" himself when his record label declared it had no faith in the concept, *Live at the Apollo* proved a chartbusting sales sensation and an oft acclaimed classic.

TEMPTATIONS LIVE!
THE TEMPTATIONS (1967)

No Motown act of the 1960s was finer in concert than The Temptations. They prove that here with a set that flows flawlessly from their hits, such as "My Girl," to standards, such as "Ol' Man River."

AT FOLSOM PRISON
JOHNNY CASH (1968)

"I shot a man in Reno, just to watch him die" is one of *the* great rock 'n' roll lines, and here "Folsom Prison Blues" finds its rightful home on a career-revitalizing set taped at the jail itself.

GOT LIVE IF YOU WANT IT!
THE ROLLING STONES (1966)

Artificially expanded from a British EP of the same title, and disowned by the Stones, this US LP remains a thrilling record of the band plying hits and covers to shrieking teenyboppers.

WHEELS OF FIRE
CREAM (1968)

The studio half of this double LP boasts gems, such as "White Room," but it is for the four extraordinary songs on the live disc, taped in San Francisco, that *Wheels of Fire* is celebrated.

KICK OUT THE JAMS
MC5 (1969)

"A lot of pressure," guitarist Wayne Kramer told *Classic Rock* of the taping of this classic. "I hear me making clumsy mistakes." However, tracks such as "Motor City Is Burning" make it essential.

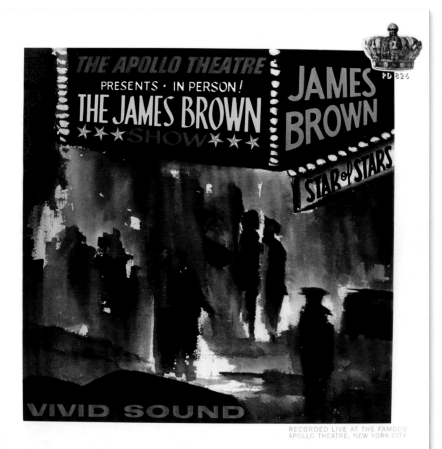

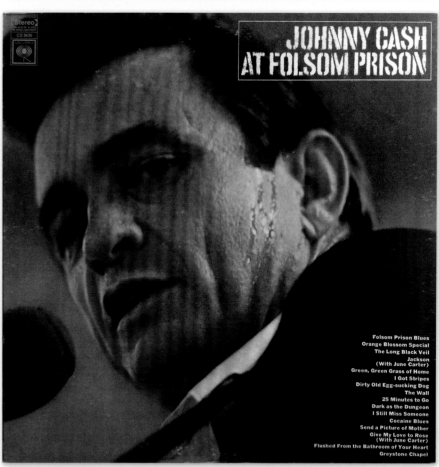

Folsom Prison Blues
Orange Blossom Special
The Long Black Veil
Jackson
(With June Carter)
Green, Green Grass of Home
I Got Stripes
Dirty Old Egg-sucking Dog
The Wall
25 Minutes to Go
Dark as the Dungeon
I Still Miss Someone
Cocaine Blues
Send a Picture of Mother
Give My Love to Rose
(With June Carter)
Flushed From the Bathroom of Your Heart
Greystone Chapel

ISLAND

Chris Blackwell, Graeme Goodall, and Leslie Kong founded Island Records, one of Great Britain's most important independent labels, in Jamaica in 1959. Blackwell, raised on the island, was fascinated by the many bands on the local music scene and set up the company to record the ska—a forerunner of rocksteady and reggae—that proliferated there. The first two artists on his fledgling label were Laurel Aitken and Ernest Ranglin.

In 1962, Blackwell relocated the company to England to push the music to the newly established West Indian community and a burgeoning white market beginning to take an interest in black music. Other key Jamaican musicians and singers with Island at the time included Owen Gray, Jimmy Cliff, Derrick Morgan, and the Blues Busters.

"I never expected Island Records to grow into the intentional phenomenon it became," Blackwell admitted in *Keep on Running: The Story of Island Records*. "When I was starting out making my first record with Lance Hayward in 1959, all I wanted to do was get that one album released. Even in Britain, when at first I was only releasing Jamaican singles, I felt I was in a different business entirely from the world of EMI and Decca. They controlled ninety-five percent of the UK pop business but that wasn't my world."

Bolstered by the smashes "My Boy Lollipop" (1964) by Millie Small and "Keep On Running" (1965) by The Spencer Davis Group—both issued via Fontana—Blackwell began signing British rock acts direct to Island. "I was looking for a label for popular material because Island

was identifiable as a label just doing Jamaican music," he recalled. "Then I realized I couldn't get rid of the name Island, because it was the overall name of the company. So that's when

Limited Edition

BABY I LOVE YOU SO
(H. Swaby) (2.30)

Published by Blue Mountain Music Ltd

45 RPM

IPR 2009-B

℗ & © 1977 Island Records Ltd

AUGUSTUS PABLO

PRODUCED BY AUGUSTUS PABLO
A ROCKERS PRODUCTION

I came up with the idea of the pink Island label, because I thought it was so far away from Jamaican music that people wouldn't make the connection." That pink label became synonymous with LPs on which many a joint was rolled, exemplified by 1967's *London Conversation* by John Martyn, *The Story of Simon Simopath* by the original Nirvana, *Mr. Fantasy* by Traffic, and *Hard Road to Travel* by Jimmy Cliff.

The label continued to wave its rock and soul banners into the 1970s with Jethro Tull,

Emerson, Lake & Palmer, King Crimson, Roxy Music, and Robert Palmer. However, it retained its high-profile Jamaican links with reggae giants, including Sly and Robbie, Toots and the Maytals, and Bob Marley and the Wailers.

"At that time, reggae wasn't considered serious music, whereas rock music had been considered serious for some time," Blackwell reminded *Interview*. "Jimi Hendrix was a model, in a sense, because I felt like Bob could be that big. And so I worked on *Catch a Fire* (1973). I moved things around. I had rock guitar, synthesizers, and expanded into solos, because reggae never had solos—although ska did—so I put that element back into the music." (For his part, Marley grumbled to *Melody Maker*: "Chris Blackwell didn't help me. I had to work hard while Blackwell flew out and enjoyed himself. But he had the contacts at the time that we felt we needed.")

In the late 1970s, Island continued to defy convention giving a home to Georgia madcaps The B-52's, British punks The Slits, 1960s survivor Marianne Faithfull, and Jamaican model-cum-diva Grace Jones. It continued to flourish in the 1980s—despite Marley's death in 1981—with colorful acts such as Kid Creole and the Coconuts and Tom Tom Club.

In 1989, Blackwell sold Island to Polygram, and today—after another untimely death in the form of Amy Winehouse—its idiosyncratic roster ranges from Bon Jovi and The Gaslight Anthem to PJ Harvey and Florence and the Machine. However, it was back in the 1970s heyday of the vinyl album that it was a fearless force to be reckoned with.

Amy Winehouse performs for the fiftieth Grammy Awards ceremony in 2008, at which she won five of her six nominations.

Jamaican-born Grace Jones signed with Island in 1977, after becoming a hit in the New York nightclub scene.

Bob Marley at a signing at Tower Records in Hollywood, 1979.

Kid Creole performs on stage to celebrate fifty years of Island Records at Shepherds Bush Empire, London, 2009.

FIRE AND WATER
FREE (1970)

Free's finest LP, unfortunately, wound up overshadowed by its hit, "All Right Now." "The minute Chris Blackwell came into the studio and heard it, he said, 'That's a hit,'" said drummer Simon Kirke. "Then he said, 'But it's too fucking long.' You can still hear the place he cut it. But we had to admit it worked."

ROXY MUSIC
ROXY MUSIC (1972)

Even minus the hit "Virginia Plain" (released two months later and added to reissues of the album), Roxy's debut was rich with future classics, such as "Re-make/Re-model," "Ladytron," and "If There Is Something" (the last covered by Bowie's Tin Machine). Cover star Kari-Ann Muller—"One of the rare Roxy models who didn't date Bryan Ferry," notes Discogs.com—later appeared in the Bond movie *On Her Majesty's Secret Service* and married Mick Jagger's brother. "The colors remind me of a marshmallow, like something really delicious," she told *Q*. "Fleshy, in a word."

IN THE COURT OF THE CRIMSON KING
KING CRIMSON (1969)

King Crimson "were very much a departure for me," Island founder Chris Blackwell told writer Tim Noakes. "Their music was so very different from a lot of stuff that had been happening before. It was great musicianship, very intelligent music. It was not really pop—it was just great music. So that's why I signed them: I really liked them." Befitting a debut that opens with the crunching "21st Century Schizoid Man," *In the Court of the Crimson King* is wrapped in prog rock's very own *The Scream*—the only LP cover created by British artist and computer programmer Barry Godber.

BUMPERS
VARIOUS ARTISTS (1970)

Twenty-nine shillings and eleven pence ($2.27 or £1.50) bought you this two-LP sampler, including Spooky Tooth's take on "I Am the Walrus," plus cuts by Traffic, Mott the Hoople, Jethro Tull, Blodwyn Pig, Jimmy Cliff, John Martyn, King Crimson, Nick Drake, Cat Stevens, Fairport Convention, and Free.

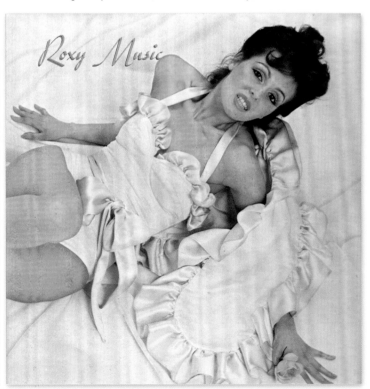

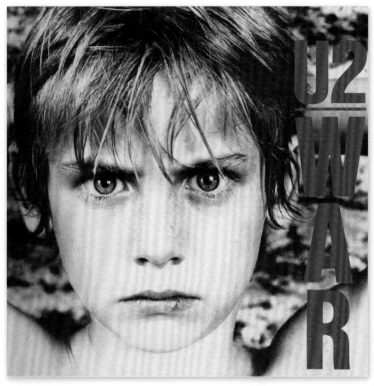

WAR
U2 (1983)

U2's first British chart topper was also their international breakthrough, shooting them into the US top twenty and Australian top ten. In the aftermath of Bob Marley's death, Chris Blackwell told the *Telegraph*, "U2 became the group that carried the flag for Island. . . . When I first saw them, they were nothing like as accomplished as they are now, but they absolutely had something where you just knew that they were going to be great. All the labels turned them down. . . . The most spectacular was CBS, who said, 'Well, if you fire the drummer, we'd probably sign them.'"

THREE LITTLE BIRDS
BOB MARLEY (1980)

Originally issued on 1977's *Exodus*, the irresistible "Three Little Birds" was issued belatedly as a single in 1980 (backed with the instrumental "Every Need Got an Ego to Feed," based on "Pimpers Paradise" from 1980's *Uprising*). The A side's cheery "Don't worry 'bout a thing" chorus secured its immortality.

EMERSON, LAKE & PALMER
EMERSON, LAKE & PALMER (1970)

The supergroup's smash debut featured the only record cover by painter Nic Dartnell. "They didn't pay me anything like enough money," he told RockPop Gallery, "and I had expected to get the painting back, but I never did."

SNEAKIN' SALLY THROUGH THE ALLEY
ROBERT PALMER (1974)

Steve Winwood, The Meters (including Art Neville), Little Feat's Lowell George, drummers extraordinaire Simon Phillips and Bernard Purdie, and R&B guitarist Cornell Dupree were among the cast of the former Vinegar Joe singer's solo debut. "Here was this white English kid coming to New Orleans and New York to work with bands I had only heard on vinyl," he marveled. But like its follow-up *Pressure Drop* (1975), the LP charted only in the United States, where it fell outside the top 100. It wasn't until 1979's *Secrets* that Palmer finally found success commensurate with his talent.

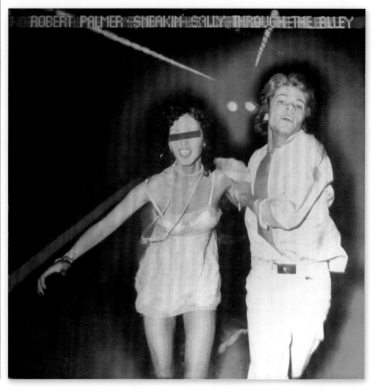

1970s

Vinyl technology allowed for much more invention in the recording studio, resulting in ambitious projects by artists as diverse as Pink Floyd and Stevie Wonder. At the same time, the singles-driven dub and reggae scene emerged, in which the turntable culture of DJs began to create its own unique sounds.

> Debbie Harry in 1978, around the time that Blondie began their ascent to superstardom. Their 1960s-influenced pop made them torchbearers for vinyl on 45 and 33.

Dream Double Albums

As pop evolved into rock courtesy of the increasingly ambitious and regularly stoned likes of The Beatles and Bob Dylan, not even the generous running time of vinyl LPs could accommodate their every whim. The solution? Double albums. The conceit occasionally reaped artistic dividends, and, as the marketing of rock became a bigger investment on the part of record labels, their designers, photographers, and graphic artists had a field day coming up with cover designs as groundbreaking as the music within.

BLONDE ON BLONDE
BOB DYLAN (1966)

Following his transition from folk hero, Dylan made rock's first double, which opened with the stoned "Rainy Day Women #12 & 35" and boasted emotional classics, such as "Visions of Johanna." Fans may have felt shortchanged with the eleven-minute "Sad Eyed Lady of the Lowlands" taking up the whole of side four, but few complained—especially those whose gatefold sleeve included a later withdrawn photograph of Italian actress Claudia Cardinale.

FREAK OUT!
MOTHERS OF INVENTION (1966)

Released by Verve, the first disc of *Freak Out!* included future favorites, such as "Who Are the Brain Police?" and "Any Way the Wind Blows." The second featured more idiosyncratic flights of fancy, including the nine-minute "Help, I'm a Rock (Suite in Three Movements)" and twelve-minute "The Return of the Son of Monster Magnet (Unfinished Ballet in Two Tableaus)." The similarly elaborate artwork included a pastiche of a newspaper.

THE BEATLES
THE BEATLES (1968)

In contrast to the eye-popping *Sgt. Pepper*, the follow-up had a simple sleeve that birthed its nickname "The White Album," with the band's name embossed upon it. The music, however, was anything but monochrome, ranging from the delicate "Blackbird" via the ominous "Happiness Is a Warm Gun" to the raging "Helter Skelter." George Harrison contributed a highlight in the form of "While My Guitar Gently Weeps," and the set went gold in the United States within days.

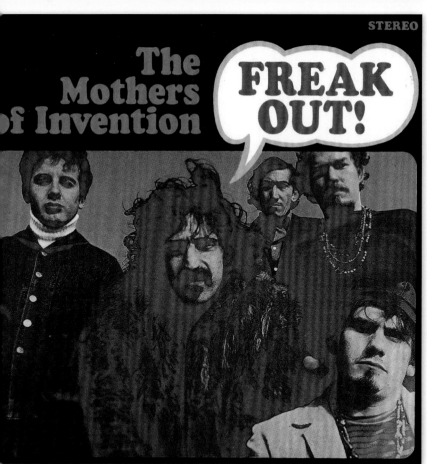

DIRECTIONS IN MUSIC BY MILES DAVIS

MILES DAVIS BITCHES BREW

BITCHES BREW
MILES DAVIS (1970)

Miles Davis first began to explore the electronic-rock world on *In a Silent Way* (1969). His second foray featured just six tracks: "Pharaoh's Dance" on side one, "Bitches Brew" on side two, "Spanish Key" and "John McLaughlin" on side three, and "Miles Runs the Voodoo Dawn" and "Sanctuary" on side four. With a stellar lineup (including saxophonist Wayne Shorter, keyboards man Chick Corea, and guitarist John McLaughlin), the expanse of a double LP gave him the freedom to experiment fully. The resulting hypnotic grooves, rooted in rock and African music, heralded a watershed in jazz and had a significant impact on rock. The album sold more than half a million copies and earned Davis his first gold record. The striking cover art, which captured the zeitgeist of free love and flower power, was created by Abdul Mati Klarwein on Davis's personal invitiation.

EXILE ON MAIN ST.
THE ROLLING STONES (1972)

"The Rolling Stones at their most dense and impenetrable," grumbled *Rolling Stone* reviewer (and Patti Smith Group guitarist) Lenny Kaye. "In the tradition of Phil Spector, they've constructed a wash of sound in which to frame their songs, yet where Spector always aimed to create an impression of space and airiness, the Stones group everything together . . . a tangled jungle through which you have to move toward the meat of the material." This high-profile verdict fostered the myth that *Exile* was poorly received, yet other critics loved it, and it topped the US chart for four weeks. Now acclaimed as *the* Stones album, it showcases the band at their hardest ("Rip This Joint"), spookiest ("I Just Want to See His Face"), most soulful ("Let It Loose"), and most joyful ("Happy"). "It's a double album so there's more range on it," observed Keith Richards, "but it also is the pointer."

PHYSICAL GRAFFITI
LED ZEPPELIN (1975)

"A group whose specialty is excess should be proud to emerge from a double LP in one piece," conceded *Village Voice* reviewer Robert Christgau. This underwhelmed response wasn't echoed by the millions who whisked it to number one on both sides of the Atlantic. The two LPs provided a home for freshly minted classics—notably the pounding epics "Kashmir" and "In My Time of Dying"—and outtakes, such as "Night Flight" and "Houses of the Holy." Intended as the debut of Zeppelin's (Atlantic-distributed) Swan Song label, *Physical Graffiti* was delayed for months by its expensively elaborate packaging: a die-cut affair (by Peter Corriston, who also created Rod Stewart's die-cut *Sing It Again Rod*) that revealed scenes on the inner sleeves through the cover's windows. In the meantime, Bad Company's self-titled debut (1974) became Swan Song's first number one.

ALIVE II
KISS (1977)

Double live albums are as 1970s as platform boots and space hoppers. But before 1976's era-defining *Frampton Comes Alive!*, hard rockers were making the most of the expanded format. Humble Pie's *Performance: Rockin' the Fillmore* (1971) was an acknowledged influence on Kiss, whose last-ditch stab at record sales commensurate with their in-concert popularity yielded 1975's blockbusting *Alive!* With that having become a bible for aspiring rockers, a sequel was inevitable. After an abortive attempt at a live-in-Tokyo set, they put together the atrociously produced but thrilling *Alive II*. The band's eighth release in just four years, it came packaged with a color booklet and temporary tattoos, but most impressive was the inner gatefold: a posed shot for which the band simultaneously detonated all the pyrotechnics in their eardrum-annihilating stage show.

THE WALL
PINK FLOYD (1979)

Pink Floyd's first double LP since *Ummagumma* (1968) might have been a triple had the group and producer Bob Ezrin not whittled it to more manageable proportions. Among the casualties were "What Shall We Do Now?" and "When the Tigers Broke Free," but a freak hit, "Another Brick in the Wall part two," put *The Wall* second only to *Dark Side of the Moon* as the band's best seller. Number one in the United States for fifteen weeks in 1980, it sold millions around the world and has never stopped doing so. The sonic sheen of CDs may be in keeping with Pink Floyd's highfalutin hi-fi, but *The Wall* is best experienced on vinyl, thanks in part to Gerald Scarfe's artwork, which rages across the inner gatefold and onto individual designs for each of the four sides' labels. For anyone willing to risk wrecking his or her stylus, there's a bit of backward masking on "Empty Spaces."

SIGN "O" THE TIMES
PRINCE (1987)

Even before the release of 1986's *Parade*, Prince began conjuring a new album. Known as *Dream Factory*, its various configurations included the likes of "Last Heart." However, after the dissolution of his band The Revolution, Prince abandoned it and channeled his energy into an LP by his alter ego, Camille, then a triple album entitled *Crystal Ball*. When Warner Bros balked at this commercial folly, he cherry-picked cuts from all three sets to create *Sign "o" the Times*. Packaged in a single instead of gatefold sleeve —albeit with Princely inner sleeves and labels— it was a delight from start to finish. Double vinyl suited an album that paid homage to 1970s icons, such as George Clinton and Joni Mitchell, and allowed for splendid indulgences, such as drummer Sheila E rapping an Edward Lear poem down a telephone line on the nine-minute live jam "It's Gonna Be a Beautiful Night."

Dub, a vinyl phenomenon in the 1970s, features reggae mixes reshaped by producers for whom the mixing desk was as much an instrument as a tool. Techniques include removing the vocals, boosting the drums and bass, and applying echo, reverb, delay, and, sometimes, excerpts from other works.

Its roots can be traced to a unique West Indian vinyl scene in the 1950s. After World War II, US troops based in Jamaica and other Caribbean islands created an influx of jazz and R&B records, with which DJs developed sound systems. They fitted trucks with generators, turntables, and speakers to play at street parties, making money by charging admission.

When the record supply ran dry, producers Coxsone Dodd and Prince Buster cut their own versions with local players, in the process birthing ska. While ska morphed into reggae, the sound systems held sway as live events.

A seed of dub was sown in 1968 when Kingston sound system operator Rudolph "Ruddy" Redwood cut a "dub" plate (as the demo-type acetates were called) of the Paragons' "On the Beach." The vocal was accidentally omitted, but he took it to a show at which his DJ "toasted" over the

Dub Culture

instrumental. The response inspired engineer Osbourne "King Tubby" Ruddock to create instrumentals from vocal records, starting with "Ain't Too Proud to Beg" by Slim Smith. Tubby took mixing a step further, isolating the vocals, then the music, then combining the two. Rivalry among sound system operators, each wanting unique versions, led to dub as we know it. It evolved to LP-length with 1970's *Undertaker* by Derrick Harriott and The Crystalites, engineered by Errol Thompson, another pioneer. He and the iconic Lee "Scratch" Perry realized there was a market for records of this live phenomenon. In 1973, Perry released the now-classic *14 Dub Blackboard Jungle* by his house band The Upsetters.

In the wake of late 1970s punk, dub made its presence felt in the work of important artists, including UB40, The Police, and The Clash. Since then, bands as diverse as Culture Club, Massive Attack, and the Beastie Boys have reflected its influence. The preservation of the "pure" dub tradition, as demonstrated by New York's Victor Axelrod, Rootah in Germany, and the Moonlight Dub Experiment from Costa Rica, among many others, is testament to this essentially "vinyl" movement showing no signs of disappearing.

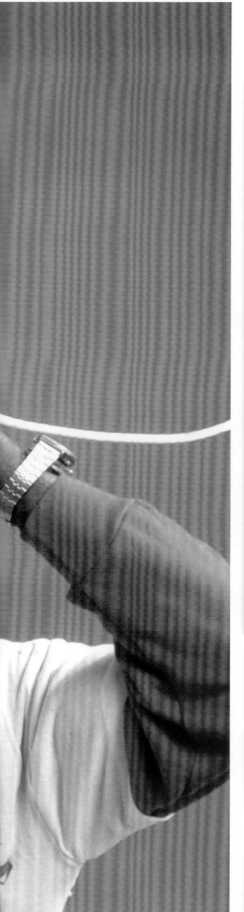

∧ The international version of Lee "Scratch" Perry and The Upsetters' 1973 classic *14 Dub Blackboard Jungle*.

《 Dub pioneer Lee "Scratch" Perry, whose use of technology, such as drum machines and phase shifters, gave his mixes a cutting-edge sound.

< Jamaican record producer Clement "Sir Coxsone" Dodd in 1980. His Studio One recording facility had an enormous influence on the development of reggae.

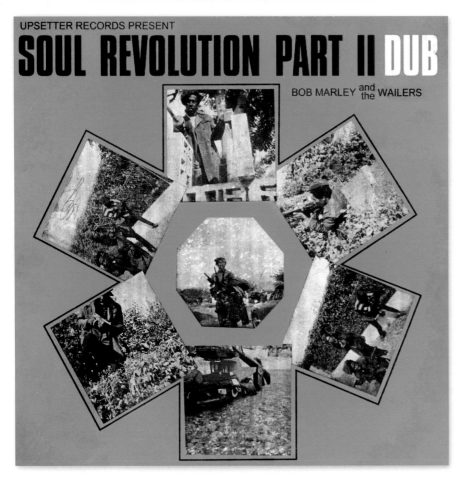

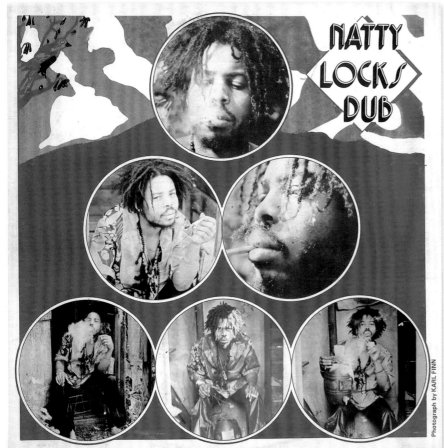

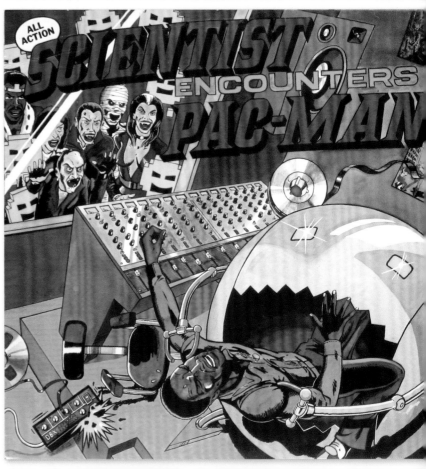

SOUL REVOLUTION PART II DUB
BOB MARLEY & THE WAILERS (1971)

Bob Marley and Lee "Scratch" Perry's working association lasted under a year but yielded no shortage of gems. This is the dub counterpart to *Soul Revolution Part II*—for which Perry produced Marley's band The Wailers—with the vocals stripped from early classics, such as "Don't Rock My Boat" and "Sun Is Shining."

KUNG FU MEETS THE DRAGON
THE MIGHTY UPSETTER (1975)

Long before Wu-Tang mastermind RZA began lacing sparse and spooky rhythms with martial arts themes, Lee "Scratch" Perry was doing it in style. On this pioneering, mostly instrumental gem—inspired by Bruce Lee's 1973 movie *Enter the Dragon*—Perry is joined by The Upsetters and multi-instrumentalist Augustus Pablo.

RETURN OF THE SUPER APE
THE UPSETTERS (1992)

With 1976's *Scratch the Super Ape*, Lee "Scratch" Perry's Upsetters had created one of *the* dub LPs. Fittingly, its sequel was the last to be cut at Black Ark before he covered every inch of the studio in hieroglyphic Magic Marker, then burned it to the ground. (This reissue trades the original's green background for blue.)

NATTY LOCKS DUB
WINSTON EDWARDS (1974)

Winston Edwards was the cousin of influential producer Joe Gibbs, one of the first to recognize Lee "Scratch" Perry's potential. Edwards ran a record store in Jamaica before relocating to the UK to launch the short-lived Fay Music label, for which this LP—hailed by Reggay.se as "one of the holy grails of dub"—formed the flagship.

SCIENTIST ENCOUNTERS PAC-MAN
SCIENTIST (1982)

Producer Linval Thompson—another graduate of Lee "Scratch" Perry's Black Ark studio—helmed this LP by Overton "Scientist" Brown, himself a protégé of King Tubby. It was one of a series on the Greensleeves label (issued, Scientist claimed, without his consent) that also pitted him against space invaders and vampires.

NO PROTECTION
MASSIVE ATTACK V MAD PROFESSOR (1995)

Rooted in dub from their start as the Wild Bunch sound system, trip hop giants Massive Attack went all out with a remix of their second LP by Guyanese producer Mad Professor, who had worked with Lee "Scratch" Perry. The makeover extended to new titles, so "Protection" became the Perryesque "Radiation Ruling the Nation."

>> Drummer Nick Mason and bassist/
lyricist Roger Waters, live in 1975.

> Did Pink Floyd's designers
Hipgnosis own this 1942 Alex
Steinweiss design?

∨ The British version, issued on EMI's
progressive rock imprint, Harvest.

It appeared at the height of progressive rock, but *Dark Side of the Moon* represented a move away from the instrumental indulgences that marked Pink Floyd's earlier work. Full of songs about inner conflict, avarice, and mental illness, it was lifted it into a league of its own by sheer technical audacity. From an age before digital recording and reproduction, it remains a testament to the sonic potential of analog vinyl.

At the end of 1971, the band began discussing a new album and agreed to lyricist Roger Waters's suggestion that they shed the abstract lyrics of previous works in favor of addressing issues that concerned them. For the music, they mixed Waters's new songs, such as "Money," with unfinished material plundered from previous projects. An outtake from keyboard player Richard Wright's music for the movie *Zabriskie Point* spawned "Us and Them," while "Breathe" was a rewrite of a piece Waters created with *Atom Heart Mother* cowriter Ron Geesin for the 1970 documentary *The Body*.

The new material debuted as *Dark Side of the Moon: A Piece for Assorted Lunatics* in Brighton, England, in January

The Dark Side of the Moon

1972. Following a well-received press preview in London, Pink Floyd refined the embryonic album on the road before returning to London to record at Abbey Road. Ensuing sessions were interrupted by another tour, but work was completed by January 1973, prior to the release of the album in March. The recording utilized tape loops and synthesizers, while effects ranged from muted speech and a simulated heartbeat to chiming clocks and cash registers.

Dark Side of the Moon—later covered in full by the Easy Star All-Stars, The Flaming Lips, and Phish—catapulted Pink Floyd from an arena-filling cult band to a stadium-packing supergroup. Aside from its musical lushness and thematic universality, factors in its success included pristine sound and iconic packaging (the latter of which initially included a gatefold sleeve, stickers, and two posters), both marking iconic highs for vinyl. Watch out for a 1978 picture disc version issued by Pink Floyd's US label Capitol in a die-cut sleeve, a 1979 sonically superduper "Original Master Recording" that sealed the reputation of its makers the Mobile Fidelity Sound Lab label, and a 2011 vinyl remaster.

Gorgeous Gatefolds

A packaging innovation strongly associated with the twelve-inch vinyl album format, the gatefold sleeve literally doubled the creative opportunities available to artists, photographers, and designers. Embracing this potential, they responded with some of the most striking, era-defining cover designs ever crafted, making the packaging as much of an incentive to buy a record as the music.

ELECTRIC LADYLAND
JIMI HENDRIX (1968)

Jimi Hendrix envisaged that his double album masterpiece would bear photographs (by David Sygall and Linda Eastman) of his band the Experience—completed by bassist Noel Redding and drummer Mitch Mitchell—posing on an Alice In Wonderland sculpture in Central Park. To his dismay, his UK-based Track label instead used a shot by photographer David Montgomery. "Folks in Britain are kicking against the cover," he observed. "Man, I don't blame them . . . but it wasn't my decision."

FREE YOUR MIND
FUNKADELIC (1970)

"Let's see if we can cut a whole album while we're tripping on acid," suggested bandleader George Clinton to his Funkadelic colleagues. The resulting *Free Your Mind... And Your Ass Will Follow*, dominated by a guitar-crazed, ten-minute title track, suggested that mission had been accomplished. Funkadelic were linked to the trippy art of Pedro Bell, but this lasciviously literal gatefold was by design team The Graffiteria, who created a similarly outrageous cover for Isaac Hayes's 1971 classic *Black Moses*.

BLACK SABBATH
BLACK SABBATH (1970)

Fans of Blue Cheer, Iron Butterfly, and Steppenwolf may howl in protest, but heavy metal as we know it was spawned on Friday February 13, 1970, with the unleashing of Black Sabbath's self-titled debut. At the Vertigo label's behest, designer Keith Macmillan put an inverted cross on the inner gatefold with a poem whose last lines linked the artwork to the opening track. The spooky wraparound shot featured an unidentified, black cat-clutching model in front of Oxfordshire's Mapledurham Watermill.

THE JIMI HENDRIX EXPERIENCE ELECTRIC LADYL

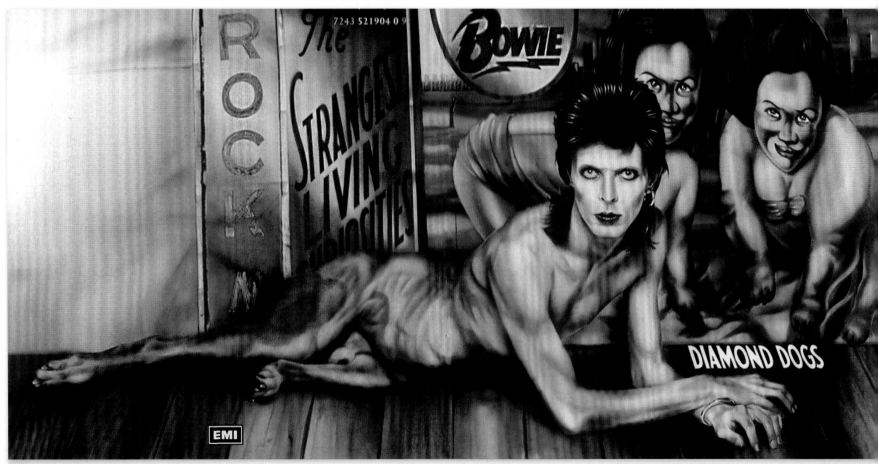

LED ZEPPELIN IV
LED ZEPPELIN (1971)

Fans call Led Zeppelin's untitled fourth album—home of "Stairway to Heaven"—*Zoso* or *Symbols*, referring to the characters chosen by each of the four members to represent them. The Recording Industry Association of America calls it *Led Zeppelin IV* and notes that its twenty-three million sales in the United States alone place it behind only *Thriller* and the Eagles' *Their Greatest Hits* in the ranks of all-time best sellers.

The inner gatefold bore a picture of a hermit, based, as Jimmy Page told *Guitar World*, on "a painting of Christ called *The Light of the World* by the pre-Raphaelite artist William Holman Hunt." The more familiar outer artwork—whose urban and rural elements reflected the electric and acoustic sides of the music—deliberately omitted any mention of the band or contents. "We stripped everything away," Page declared, "and let the music do the talking."

DIAMOND DOGS
DAVID BOWIE (1974)

Mick Jagger rued the day he told David Bowie about hiring Belgian Guy Peellaert to create a sleeve for The Rolling Stones' *It's Only Rock 'n Roll*. Bowie promptly engaged the artist for his own *Diamond Dogs*, issued five months before his rival's set. The artwork was based on a photograph of Bowie, itself modeled on a 1926 shot of performer Josephine Baker.

Peellaert—who shot into the spotlight with his 1973 book *Rock Dreams*—originally blessed the canine Bowie hybrid with genitalia. The design was signed off by RCA, but partway through the pressing of the record the label changed its mind due to concerns that the album would be banned in US record stores. The offending area was airbrushed out and the sleeve reprinted, but only after a few—now extremely valuable—versions of the untouched artwork escaped into the market.

BORN TO RUN
BRUCE SPRINGSTEEN (1975)

"We only shot in the studio for a couple of hours," recalled photographer Eric Meola of *Born to Run*, "but came up with an iconic image."

Iconic indeed: The tousled troubadour and his E Street Band's "Big Man" Clarence Clemons became indelibly linked with Springsteen's breakthrough LP. The gatefold sleeve—on the front of which The Boss wears an Elvis Presley fan club badge—reflected a remarkable show of faith on the part of the Columbia label, which had considered dropping the singer after indifferent sales of his first two albums. On the reverse were lyrics that were poetic without the florid excesses of their predecessors.

"It all came together on that album," Meola told BermanGraphics.com of the stellar success that redefined Springsteen's sound *and* image. "From that point on he was equally interested in photography and being photographed."

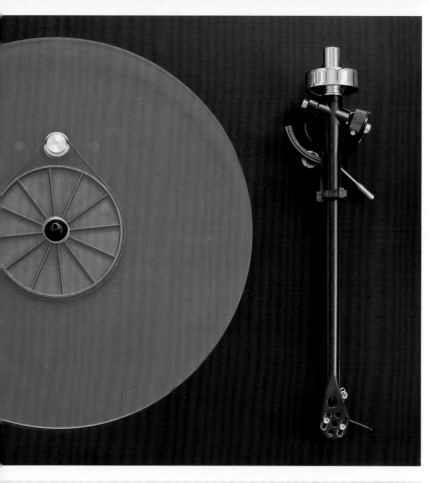

Turntable Treasures

Turntable design in the 1970s focused mainly on the practical function of hi-fi equipment. Models like the Technics 1200 and Robotron emphasized the technical over the ornamental, creating their own aesthetic style in the process. DJ activity also emphasized the tactile nature of physically playing records, making the Technics 1200 a favorite.

《 The Sony Wega Concept 51k, designed by Hartmut Esslinger in 1976, has a turntable, tape player, and tuner. Today, it features in the collection of the Museum of Modern Art in New York.

〈 Released in 1977, the belt-driven Rega Planar 3 was unusual at the time for featuring a solid plinth instead of a compliantly-suspended chassis or sub-chassis.

L A Robotron 4000 stereo set, made in 1976 by VEB Robotron-Elektronik. Based in Dresden, the company was the largest electronics manufacturer in East Germany.

V First manufactured in 1972, the Technics SL-1200 became popular among DJs due to the direct-drive high-torque motor that enabled the push-button cueing and starting of tracks.

All Wrapped Up

Sgt. Pepper and peelable bananas seemed nifty in the 1960s, but the next decade yielded an over-the-top crop of album cover craziness. You could construct a cardboard replica of ELO's *Out of the Blue* spaceship, fondle the faux snakeskin sleeve of Alice Cooper's *Billion Dollar Babies*, wield Kiss' plastic *Love Gun* shooter, pore through the cuttings file in Fairport Convention's *"Babbacombe" Lee*, collect all six variants of Led Zeppelin's *In Through the Out Door*, savor the bootleg stylings of The Who's *Live at Leeds*, and find a special place on your shelves for these.

STICKY FINGERS
THE ROLLING STONES (1971)

Pop artist Andy Warhol conceived the close-up of a male crotch in tight jeans with a working zipper (which opened to reveal white briefs, on which a gold rubber stamp bore a copyright notice with Warhol's name on it). The task of packaging it all fell to Craig Braun, and it was he who Atlantic threatened to sue when the zipper was found to be damaging the vinyl when the records were in transit. Braun's solution was to draw the zippers down before shipping, so they pressed on the label instead of the record.

BE GOOD TO YOURSELF ...
MAN (1972)

On *Be Good to Yourself at Least Once a Day*, said Manband-archive.com, "all the elements combined perfectly to produce a genuine classic." The Welsh prog rockers—known for psychedelic jams and tongue-in-cheek titles—rewarded fans with a map of Wales packaged with their seventh LP. Created by David Anstee of Flying Colours, it expanded to four times the size of the cover and was full of little details, including cartoons of the group. The inner sleeve boasted an endearingly tangled family tree.

THICK AS A BRICK
JETHRO TULL (1972)

When Tull front man Ian Anderson came up with the idea of a spoof twelve-page newspaper accompanying the band's next album, the Chrysalis label said it would be too expensive. He duly insisted that if a real newspaper could be produced at low cost, so could a mock one.

The result—a pastiche of a small-town English paper, complete with news reports, children's competitions, ads, and an account of the album written by Anderson under a pseudonym—took longer to produce than the album itself.

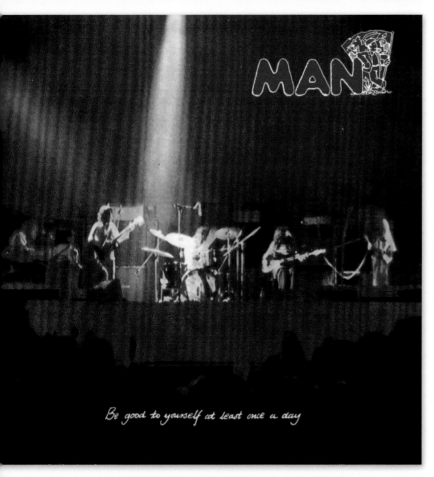

MANS MAP OF WALES

★ FAMILY FUN PAGES ★

CHILDRENS' CORNER

Hello, who's Fluffy the Duck talking to this week?
(Join the dots and find out!)

St. Cleve Crossword

ACROSS
1 See 1 down.
5 A damp version of 29 Down, with 9 Down. (3)
8 More than 20 in anal c.w.t. in reverse. (4)
11 Long John Silver definitely had one of these. (6)
12 Maybe the reason behind a scar included from us. (4)
15 Long John Silver's pet. (6)
16 Similar to the latter part of 15 Down. (4)
17 Covering for the end of a golfing enthusiast's iron. (4)
20 Could it be at the bottom of an overt umbrella? (4)
21 What Captain Beefheart's Wilke is doing. (7)
26 Why Little — Peep couldn't go to sleep twice. (4)
28 Always comes behind 28 Down. (4)
30 Heaps of grapes. (7)
31 23 Down in reverse. (4)
32 Latter part of 32 Down. (4)
34 A sort button-up fly. (3)
35 The start of a sauna, but at the rear. (4)
37 Shapely bearded seafood. (5)
39 Upstanding Donald Swan and Michael Flanders animal. (5, 3)

DOWN
1 Canine leftovers (see 1 Across). (3, 4)
2 Initially intransigent tympanum. (2)
3 Initially tintinabulation cupidor. (2)
4 The end. (3)
6 What Mac gives it. (5)
7 The cat did this when it entered the crypt. (5)
9 The latter part of 5 Across. (3)
11 Continually left behind by 11 Across. (9)
14 To puncture. (4)
15 The Flanders-Swan animal has reared its ugly 'head' again. (3, 4)
17 An odorous breeze. (4)
18 A courageous smart. (5)
22 Enormous dinner-dances of the past? (3, 5)
23 Very descriptive of what a cow may do with it's tongue. (3, 4)
24 The reverse of 31 Across. (4)
25 Female clerics surplus (see 29 Down) (1)
33 There's no business like show business. (3)
36 'Underground' animal. (4)
28 Latter part of 25 Down. (4)
32 Small rodents affectionately carressings (see 32 Across) (3)
33 The beginning of a curtailed non-rabbit. (3)
36 A capital sort of Derek Small's underwear. (2)
39 Small single curtains that sheep may leave behind them. (2)

THICK AS A BRICK
By Gerald "Little Milton" Bostock

We print here, for all to read, Gerald Bostock's controversial poem "Thick as a Brick" which caused so much controversy —Ed

Really don't mind if you sit this one out.

My words but a whisper—your deafness a SHOUT. I may make you feel but I can't make you think. Your sperm's in the gutter—your love's in the sink. So you ride yourselves over the fields and/you make all your animal deals and/your wise men don't know how it feels to be thick as a brick. And the sand-castle virtues are all swept away in the tidal destruction/the moral melee. The elastic retreat rings the close of play as the last wave uncovers the newfangled way. But your new shoes are worn at the heels and/your suntan does rapidly peel and/your wise men don't know how it feels to be thick as a brick.

And the love that I feel is so far away: I'm a bad dream that I just had today—and you/shake your head and/say it's a shame.

Spin me back down the years and the days of my youth. Draw the lace and black curtains and shut out the whole truth. Spin me down the long ages: let them sing the song.

See there! A son is born—and we pronounce him fit to fight. There are black-heads on his shoulders, and he pees himself in the night. We'll/make a man of him/put him to a trade/teach him/to play Monopoly and/how to sing in the rain.

the house is far away. The horses stamping—their warm breath clouding in the sharp and frosty morning of the day. And the poet lifts his pen while the soldier sheaths his sword.

And the youngest of the family is moving with authority. Building castles by the sea, he dares the tardy tide to wash them all aside.

The cattle quietly grazing at the grass down by the river where the swelling mountain water moves onward to the sea; the builder of the castles renews the age-old purpose and contemplates the milking girl whose offer is his need. The young men of the household have/all gone into service and/are not to be expected for a year. The innocent young master—thoughts moving ever faster—has formed the plan to change the man he seems. And the poet sheaths his pen while the soldier lifts his sword.

And the oldest of the family is moving with authority. Coming from across the sea, he challenges the son who puts him to the run.

What do you do when/the old man's gone—do you want to be him? and/your real self rises the day. Do you want to free him? No one to help you get up steam—and the whirlpool turns you 'way off-beam.

LATER.

damn sure that no-one judges me.

You curl your toes in fun as you smile at everyone—you meet the stares. You're unaware that your doings aren't done. And you laugh most ruthlessly as you tell us what not to be. But how are we supposed to see where we should run? I see you shuffle in the courtroom with/your rings upon your fingers/your downy little sidies and/your silver-buckle shoes. Playing at the hard-case, you follow the example of the comic-paper idol who lets you bend the rules.

QUOTE
We will be geared toward the average rather than the exceptional/ God is an overwhelming responsibility/ we walked through the maternity ward and saw 218 babies wearing nylons/ cats are on the upgrade/ upgrade?

So!
Come on ye childhood heroes! Won't you rise up from the pages of your comic-books/ your super-crook/and show us all the way. Well! Make your will and testament. Won't you? Join your local government. We'll have superman for president/let Robin save the day.

So! Where the hell was Biggles when you needed him last Saturday? And where are all the Sportsmen who always pulled you through? They're all resting down in Cornwall —writing up their memoirs for a paper-back edition of the Boy Scout Manual.

LATER.

See there! A man is born—and we pronounce him fit for peace. There's a load lifted from his shoulders with the discovery of his disease.

We'll take the child from him/ put it to the test/teach it/to be a wise man/how to fool the rest.

LATER
We will be geared toward the average rather than the exceptional/ God is an overwhelming responsibility/ we walked through the maternity ward and saw 218 babies wearing nylons/ cats are on the upgrade/ upgrade?

In the clear white circles of morning wonder, I take my place with the lord of the hills. And the blue-eyed soldiers stand slightly discoloured (in neat little rows) sporting canvas frills. With their jock-straps pinching, they slouch to attention, while queueing for sarnies at the office canteen. Saying—how's your grannie and/ good old Ernie: he coughed up a tenner on a premium bond win.

The legends (worded in the ancient tribal hymns) lie cradled in the seagull's call. And all the promises they made are ground beneath the sadist's fall. The poet and the wise man stand behind the gun, and opted for the attack of down. Light the sun.

Do you believe in the day? Do you? Believe in the day! The Dawn Creation of the Kings has begun. Soft Venus (lonely maiden) brings the ageless one.

Do you believe in the day? The fading hero has returned to the night—and fully pregnant with the day, wise men endorse the poet's sight.

Do you believe in the day? Do you? Believe in the day!

Let me tell you the tales of your life of the cut and the thrust of the knife: the timeless oppression; the wisdom instilled: the desire to kill or be

killed. Let me sing of the lovers who lie in the street as the last bus goes by. The pavements are empty: the gutters run red—while the fool toasts his god to the sky. So come all ye young men who are building castles! Kindly state the time of the year and join your voices in a hellish chorus. Mark the precise nature of your fear. Let me help you to pick up your dead as the sins of the fathers are fed with/ the blood of the fools and/ the thoughts of the wise and/ from the past under your bed. Let me make you a present of song as the wise man breaks wind and is gone while the fool with the hour-glass is cooking his goose and/ the nursery rhyme winds along.

So! Come all ye young men who are building castles! Kindly state the time of the year and join your voices in a hellish chorus. Mark the precise nature of your fear. See! The summer lightning casts its bolts upon you and the hour of judgement draweth near. Would you be: the fool stood in his suit of armour or/ the wise man who rushes clear. So! Come on ye childhood heroes! Won't your rise up from the pages of your comic-books/ your super-crooks/and show us all the way. Well! Make your will and testament. Won't you? Join your local government. We'll have superman for president/ let Robin save the day. So! Where the hell was Biggles when you needed Him last Sunday? And where are all the Sportsmen who always pulled you through? They're all resting up there in Cornwall —writing up their memoirs for a paper-back edition of the Boy Scout Manual.

OF COURSE.
So you ride yourselves over the fields and/ you make all your animal deals and/ your wise men don't know how it feels to be thick as a brick.

Distribution Photogravure S.S.A. - Printed and made in Italy.

HEAD INJURY

DIRECTOR ACCUSED

U.F.O. SIGHTING SENSATION

LITTLE MILTON IN SCHOOL— GIRL PREGNANCY ROW

Mongrel dog soils actor's foot

QUAD'S STORE
HIGH STREET, ST. CLEVE
GOOD SERVICE PLUS STAMPS AT

Local Feud Over Kitchen Window

DOG HANDLER AT WORK ON FILM

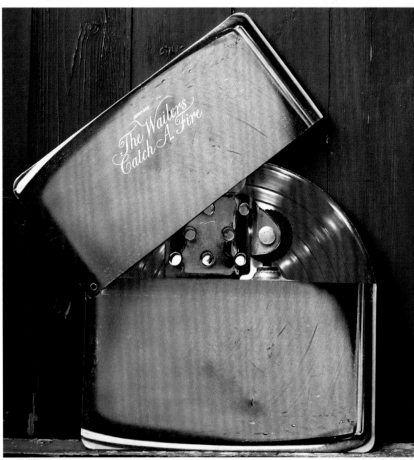

SCHOOL'S OUT
ALICE COOPER (1972)

The flip-top cover was a no-brainer, but the record-wrapping panties were genius. "I'd read a newspaper article about flammable panties from Europe being confiscated and thought, 'I've got to use that,'" manager Shep Gordon told *Shortlist*. "I never told Warner Bros, but I bought legal, nonflammable panties, which were made in Canada. I also bought 3,000 pairs of flammable panties from Europe, flown through Washington, as there was a journalist I knew there. Customs got a tip from someone—I can't imagine who—that these panties were coming in. The front page of the *Washington Post* read: 'Largest pantie raid in history.'" Having broken a law that decreed clothes be resistant to fire, Warner claimed they were just packing material. The Federal Trade Commission didn't buy it. "I know we're hot right now," Alice cracked, "but I never thought our panties would catch on fire."

CATCH A FIRE
THE WAILERS (1973)

Before Bob Marley was billed ahead of his band, The Wailers' *Catch a Fire* was their first release on Island. An international success upon its release, the songs on the album covered everything from the state of urban poverty ("Concrete Jungle") to love ("Stir It Up"). The original vinyl came in a cover, designed by graphic artists Bob Weiner and Rod Dyer, that resembled a giant Zippo lighter—and, like the iconic lighter case, opened on a central side hinge to access the record. As with many extravagant covers, it appeared with only the first pressing—in this case, 20,000 discs—before the packaging reverted to a more conventional format that didn't have to be hand-assembled. The cover of subsequent pressings featured an Esther Anderson portrait of Marley smoking a joint and credited the album to Bob Marley and the Wailers.

WALLS AND BRIDGES
JOHN LENNON (1974)

After 1972's woeful *Some Time in New York City* and 1973's patchy *Mind Games*, John Lennon's output required some restoration. Remarkably, despite being made during his "lost weekend" (a prolonged estrangement from Yoko Ono), *Walls and Bridges* did just that, topping the US chart and giving him his first number one single, "Whatever Gets You Thru the Night." Its sleeve, credited to the Capitol label's art director Bob Kohara, featured foldout flaps with which different versions of the cover could be created. The back boasted a portrait of Lennon by photographer Bob Gruen, while the front bore paintings that the former Beatle had made at the age of eleven. "That was very important to John," Ono explained to Billboard author Craig Rosen, "because that had a lot to do with the music on the album. He was really delving into his youth and bringing out emotions from it."

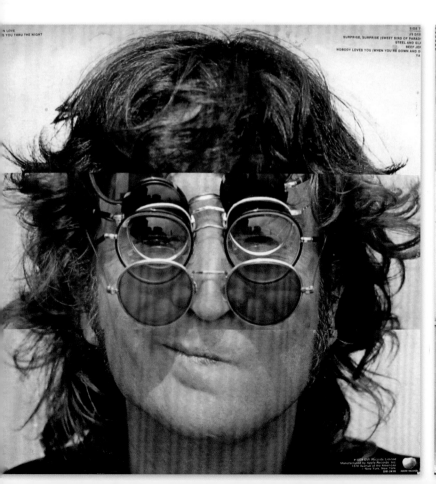

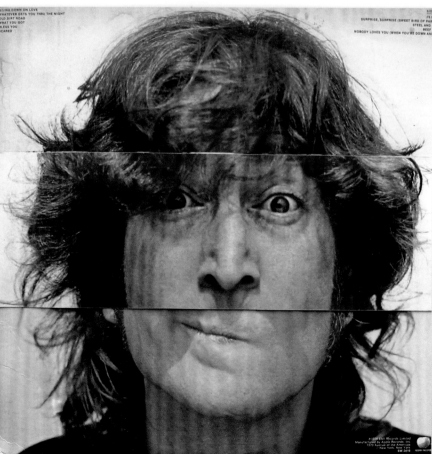

SHININ' ON
GRAND FUNK (1974)

"Nobody knows the band Grand Funk?" asked an incredulous Homer Simpson in 1995. "The wild, shirtless lyrics of Mark Farner? The bong-rattling bass of Mel Schacher? The competent drum work of Don Brewer? Oh man." Two decades earlier, you'd have had to work hard *not* to know Grand Funk, who enjoyed nine hit albums in just four years. *Shinin' On* maintained their momentum with a chart-topping cover of "The Loco-Motion," but it failed to garner the critical and popular acclaim of the band's previous album. "We just didn't prepare long enough,"admitted Brewer to Vintagerock.com. "I think it's a good album, but I don't think it has the cohesiveness of *We're an American Band*. The songs didn't stick together quite as well." *Shinin' On*'s packaging, however, was stunning: an awesome 3-D sleeve and poster, complete with 3-D glasses.

WISH YOU WERE HERE
PINK FLOYD (1975)

In the aftermath of *Dark Side of the Moon*, Pink Floyd conceived an album that, as designer Aubrey "Po" Powell noted, "is primarily about absence and about their disenchantment with the music business." Powell and his Hipgnosis partner Storm Thorgerson evoked that absence by hiding their work in black shrink-wrap. The band's US label, Thorgerson recalled, "thought we were completely nuts"—a view echoed by stores who, to prevent theft, had to slice the artwork to remove the vinyl before the sleeves were displayed. The cover sticker of mechanical hands reflected the music biz machinations of "Welcome to the Machine," while the flame-engulfed Bond movie stuntman Ronnie Rondell conveyed the sense of "getting burned" to which "Have a Cigar" alluded. Befitting the album title, the eerie package also included a postcard of a swimmer posed mid-dive in perfectly still water.

METAL BOX
PUBLIC IMAGE LTD. (1979)

After quitting the Sex Pistols, John Lydon formed Public Image Ltd, whose second album was issued as three 45 rpm twelve-inchers, the better to showcase its dub-influenced emphasis on drums and bass. These were packaged in a metal film canister (after which the LP was named), with the band's name embossed on the front. The box proved influential, but expensive and problematic, with the discs being tricky to remove without scratching. (After the first pressing of 60,000, the set was reissued in a conventional sleeve as 1980's *Second Edition*). Still, it could have been worse. Guitarist Keith Levene told Superseventies.com that they had considered both sardine-can-style packaging that could be opened only with a key —"except we wouldn't give the key"—and a "sandpaper-type record, which would fuck up all your other records when you put it in your collection."

GUN
THE GUN (1968)

Dean's first high-profile piece graces this cult classic that features Paul and Adrian Gurvitz (the latter later a solo star with songs such as "Classic"). Coincidentally, an earlier lineup of The Gun featured future Yes man Jon Anderson.

OSIBISA
OSIBISA (1971)

Dean's heyday was heralded by this sleeve for the British funk act, establishing his style and familiar typeface. "The first of a new era," he told GilmourDesign. The winged elephants returned on that year's follow-up, *Woyaya*.

FRAGILE
YES (1971)

"Before I started painting *Fragile*," Dean told GilmourDesign, "I had already written a story about it. So *Fragile* was the world within which this story took place, and the story continued through *Yessongs* and other Yes albums."

THE MAGICIAN'S BIRTHDAY
URIAH HEEP (1972)

This was Dean's second cover for the British rockers, following his "sea of light" for the same year's *Demons and Wizards*. Appropriately, given his Yes links, the music marked Heep's evolution from hard rock to a more progressive sound.

RELAYER
YES (1974)

Aiming to depict "the ultimate castle, the ultimate wall of a fortified city" for Yes' sole album with Patrick Moraz, Dean conjured up what he hailed as "my masterpiece of drawing . . . a highpoint of my draftsmanship."

GRAVITAS
ASIA (2014)

When former Yes members Geoff Downes and Steve Howe launched Asia in 1982, Dean's art provided a link to their past. Over three decades on, the association endures, despite the absence of Howe, once again a full time Yes-man.

Roger Dean

One name that leaps to mind when contemplating album art of the progressive rock era of the early 1970s is Roger Dean. Along with Storm Thorgerson and Aubrey Powell at Hipgnosis, his work epitomized the flights of fancy in which designers indulged at the time. But whereas the Hipgnosis covers were cleverly staged visual events, often involving everyday images amid surreal situations, Dean created amazing fantasy landscapes invented in his imagination.

Born in 1944, Dean attended Canterbury College of Art before graduating to a furniture design course at London's Royal College of Art. It was via furniture design that he earned a first commission for rock album illustration. He had designed seating for Ronnie Scott's London jazz club, and that musical connection led to his first album cover. The Gun, he explained to Progarchives.com, "were managed by Ronnie Scott and they saw my work . . . and asked to use one of my sketch book paintings as a cover." The result housed the band's 1968 debut.

In 1971, he created the cover for the self-titled debut by the Afro-rock band Osibisa. Its spectacular image of a hybrid between a flying insect and an elephant was a taste of the style for which Dean became famous.

The artist met his best-known muse in the form of the archetypal prog rock band Yes, beginning with the cover for *Fragile* (1971). On the band's next LP, *Close to the Edge* (1972), he introduced the familiar "bubble" logo for the band's name, and on the live *Yessongs* (1973) came a hint of the fantastical landscapes that became iconic for act and artist. (*Yessongs* was in fact painted for *Dark Side of the Moon*, before Pink Floyd opted to stick with Hipgnosis.) *Tales from Topographic Oceans* (1973) and *Relayer* (1974) cemented Dean's otherworldly approach with mysterious creatures, floating islands, and spectacular stones. These landscapes became a signature style that he applied to LP by bands including Gentle Giant, Uriah Heep, Budgie, and Asia. In 1989, when discord in the Yes ranks led Jon Anderson, Bill Bruford, Rick Wakeman, and Steve Howe to create an album under their own name, they retained Dean to reassure fans who may have assumed "Anderson Bruford Wakeman Howe" was a team of lawyers.

Dean's fantasy worlds have been echoed in sci-fi book covers, posters, graphic novels, other record sleeves, and—according to the artist, albeit not the judge who dismissed a copyright infringement lawsuit—James Cameron's *Avatar*.

Dean holds his 1975 book *Views* amid his *House Complex* sculpture at London's Institute of Contemporary Arts.

Three is the Magic Number

2 2 2
3
1 4 4 4

While for most mortals the extra running time of a double album was sufficient for the most extravagant of whims, the triple album surfaced to represent An Event instead of a mere collection of songs. Appropriately, the first triumph of this quintessentially 1970s conceit commemorated an actual event: the Woodstock festival, whose soundtrack went gold in days.

The triple album called for more complicated packaging than its smaller relatives, so record labels had to be convinced the investment was worth it. The Grateful Dead's *Europe '72* (1972), Yes's *Yessongs* (1973), Paul McCartney's *Wings over America* (1976), and The Band's *The Last Waltz* (1978) were live albums by acts with loyal audiences, so gambles were worth taking. In other instances, acts went the extra mile to satisfy the appetites of fans—or themselves. Both boxes were checked by Emerson, Lake &

Palmer's *Welcome Back My Friends, to the Show That Never Ends—Ladies and Gentlemen . . .* (1), a characteristically grandiose package from the prog rock trio. Even their equipment trucks had the members' initials stenciled on the roofs, so the die-cut flaps of this three-leaf package were in keeping with the ELP ethos of excess in all areas. Vindication came in the form of a gold award, just one month after its release in 1974.

In 1995, The Smashing Pumpkins' *Mellon Collie and the Infinite Sadness* (2) harked back to progressive follies, bandleader Billy Corgan having been raised on the likes of Pink Floyd. Admirably, however, thought was invested to distinguish the vinyl format from its double CD incarnation: the track list was revised, "Tonite Reprise" and "Infinite Sadness" were added, and the lovely packaging included labels that traced the album's arc from "dawn" to "starlight."

The Clash's *Sandanista!* (3) was a curious mix of altruism and indulgence. "We wanted to give value for money," explained drummer Topper Headon, "and release as much material as we could." That meant the band taking a cut in royalties so the set could be sold at affordable rates. But it also meant indulging their fondness for dub—which fans could have done without. "It was," grumbled Kurt Cobain, "so bad."

George Harrison's *All Things Must Pass* (4) also arose from an outpouring of creativity, albeit with more acclaimed results. "I was only allowed to do my one or two on Beatle albums, so I had a backlog of songs," he recalled. Nonetheless, he explained to Billboard's Craig Rosen, the 1970 set "was really only a double album. The third album, which was called *Apple Jam*, was supposed to be a free record. . . . (It) was just a jam session, not a proper album."

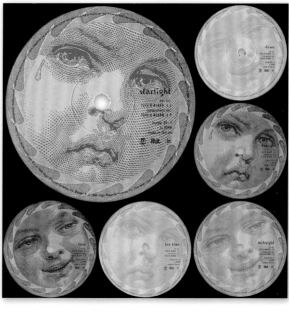

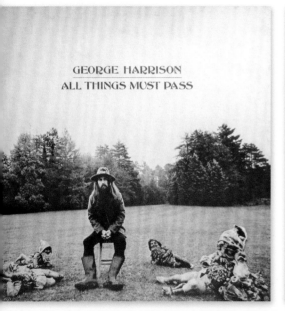

Bootleg!

Popular use of the word "bootleg" dates from the 1920s, when liquor—banned in the United States during the Prohibition era—was smuggled in the legs of tall boots. For nearly half a century since the late 1960s, however, it has been associated with the illicit recording of music.

Although it flouts copyright laws, bootlegging should not be confused with the illegal copying and counterfeiting of already-released material. That is piracy, often a product of organized crime. In contrast, bootlegging of otherwise unreleased performances, usually from live shows, is overwhelmingly by fans and for fans.

The most celebrated of early bootlegs was *Great White Wonder* by Bob Dylan, issued by the Trademark of Quality label in 1969. Testament to its impact is that many of its cuts have since been officially released, as has since been the case

with many classic bootlegs. Frank Zappa even bootlegged the bootlegs with his *Beat the Boots* series, the first eight volumes of which were collected as a ten-LP box in 1991. That same year, Columbia began to issue unreleased Dylan material as *The Bootleg Series*—an inspired idea that, as of 2014, had spawned eleven volumes.

The LPs could be poorly packaged with lamentable sound, but sophisticated labels, such as Trademark of Quality, prided themselves on high quality and imaginative covers. In the mid-1970s, it was reported that tens of thousands of fans had purchased Pink Floyd's *British Winter Tour 74*—boasting three then-unreleased tracks—under the misapprehension it was an official follow-up to *Dark Side of the Moon*.

The most bootlegged acts—including Dylan, Pink Floyd, Led Zeppelin, The Beatles, and

The Rolling Stones—tended to take a benign view of such releases, although this tolerance never extended to their paymasters. Zeppelin manager Peter Grant, for example, was known to smash any that he found in record stores. The much-bootlegged Bruce Springsteen quipped "Roll your tapes" during a radio broadcast of a live show in 1978, but was less amused when demos for the album that became *The River* hit the streets before their official release.

Later, however, a policy pioneered by The Grateful Dead—to allow anyone who wanted to do so to record shows—signaled a sea change, embraced by trendsetters such as Nine Inch Nails' Trent Reznor. In its vinyl heyday, the bootleg was a required complement to any serious fan's record library. Today, those illicitly produced records are prized collectors' items.

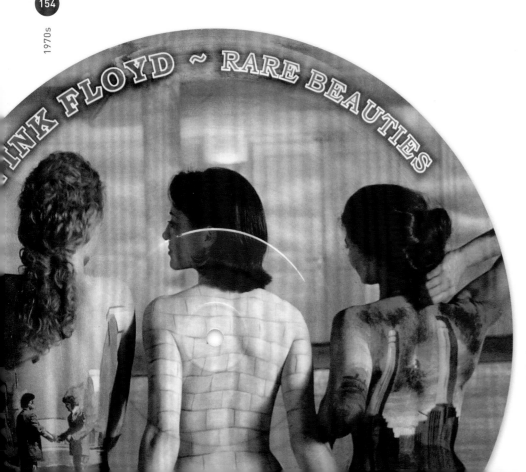

Outtakes from *Dark Side of the Moon* are among the attractions of this latter-day picture disc bootleg.

SEEMS LIKE A FREEZE OUT
BOB DYLAN (1971)

A collection of mid-1960s outtakes, named after a phrase with which Dylan would introduce one of its songs, "Visions of Johanna," in concert. "GWW" is a tip of the hat to the Trademark of Quality's pioneering *Great White Wonder* bootleg.

GOING TO CALIFORNIA
LED ZEPPELIN (1973)

This incomplete but still extraordinary double album finds Page, Plant, Bonham, and Jones in barnstorming form at the Berkeley Community Center in September 1971. The then-unreleased "Stairway to Heaven" earns an ovation.

GUITAR BANDIT
ROBIN TROWER (1973)

An FM radio broadcast from California's Record Plant—taped after the Procol Harum guitarist's solo debut *Twice Removed from Yesterday* (1973) but before the classic *Bridge of Sighs* (1974)—is immortalized by the Amazing Kornyphone label.

TALES FROM THE WHO
THE WHO (1974)

Sheathed in a tribute to the comic *Tales from the Crypt*—one of designer William Stout's extraordinary covers for the Trademark of Quality label—this double album is drawn from a *Quadrophenia* show in Pennsylvania in 1973.

"TIKI GODS"
ADAM AND THE ANTS (1983)

With killer cuts, such as "Physical (You're So)" and "Kings of the Wild Frontier," this captures the British influence in the United States in 1981. The untitled double LP set is known as "Tiki Gods" due to its artwork.

JAPAN 1986
THE CURE (1988)

Bootlegs don't always hit the nail on the head. In this instance, the performance is from 1984, and the venue is in the Netherlands, not Japan. But a vintage Cure selection, including "Primary" and "One Hundred Years," is some compensation.

"Like some big Hollywood studio blockbuster," marveled *Rolling Stone* reviewer Vince Aletti in late 1976, Stevie Wonder's *Songs in the Key of Life* "comes to us already weighed down with words, stabbed with exclamation points and wrapped—or is it shrouded?—in great expectations. Two years in the making, the album's imminent release was announced several times, and each time it was withdrawn to be haggled over, reworked, expanded, and gossiped about until its release at the end of September."

Talking Book (1972), *Innervisions* (1973), and *Fulfillingness' First Finale* (1974) had set the commerical bar high, with the last being Wonder's first number one on *Billboard*'s pop chart since 1963. More importantly, they had vindicated the star, who wrested control of his output from Motown to create immortals, such as "Superstition," "Living for the City," and "You Haven't Done Nothin'"—characterized by increasingly pointed lyrics and electronic sophistication. But Wonder, at the peak of his creativity, was not about to resort to formula. "I knew that I wanted the album to be different," he told *Billboard* author Craig Rosen. Crucially, "I knew that I had a

Songs in the Key of Life

lot of material"—so much, in fact, that only a double LP could accommodate it. "You're crazy," was Motown head Berry Gordy's reaction, "but go ahead and do it." (In the midst of recording, Wonder signed a new multimillion-dollar deal with Motown that made him pop's highest-paid performer.)

Wonder duly spent so long on the album that engineer Gary Olazabal created a T-shirt that read, "We're almost finished." However, the result was spectacular, with so much music that four of its songs were cut on a seven-inch single included with the gatefold, double LP package. From the gorgeous "Knocks Me Off My Feet" to the furious "Black Man," the music, as *Rolling Stone* observed, "varies so widely that even after weeks of listening it's difficult to get a critical fix on." Its best-known song (at least until Coolio revamped "Pastime Paradise" as "Gangsta's Paradise") was the last composed for the album: the irresistible "I Wish," a US chart topper in January 1977.

Before then, however, *Songs in the Key of Life* had become only the third album (after Elton John's *Captain Fantastic and the Brown Dirt Cowboy* and *Rock of the Westies* in 1975) to enter at the top of the *Billboard* pop chart—a feat not repeated until Bruce Springsteen's *Live/1975–85* in 1986.

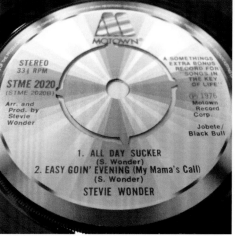

《 The twenty-seven-year-old genius promoting *Songs in the Key of Life* in September 1976.

∧ The lavishly packaged original LP's sticker mentions "A Something's Extra" . . .

‹ . . . which was this four-track bonus single, tucked into the gatefold sleeve.

One of the most celebrated labels of the 1970s, Casablanca Records was founded in 1973 by record executive Neil Bogart, and from the start it was conspicuous by virtue of its big-budget, energetic approach to the promotion of its artists and their records. At the cutting edge of commercial pop, its signings included over-the-top rock group Kiss, disco queen Donna Summer, funk pioneer George Clinton, and club favorites Village People.

Bogart was employed as chief executive of Buddah Records in the early 1970s, but when the opportunity came to break away and form his own label, with financing from Warner Brothers, he seized it. Named after Bogart's favorite movie, *Casablanca* (1942), the groundbreaking label was home to an eclectic roster of artists. The first signing was "hot" rock band Kiss. According to Kiss cofounder Gene Simmons, Bogart wasn't enamored by the band's face paint but "let Kiss be Kiss." The group wasn't an immediate success: its first three albums—*Kiss* (1974), *Hotter Than Hell* (1974), and *Dressed to Kill* (1975)—made only a modest impact and confirmed Warner's doubts about the band. However, Kiss had a growing cult following, based largely on their spectacular stage shows, and Bogart persuaded them to release a live album. The double album *Alive!* (1975) saved Casablanca, for a while, by providing the first top ten entry for both the label and the band.

Already involved with Bogart via Buddah Records, outlandish George Clinton was a natural choice for Casablanca, and he signed with his funk outfit, Parliament, in 1973. The first Parliament hit on the label was the title single from *Up for the Down Stroke* (1974), but it was their third LP for Casablanca, *Mothership Connection* (1975), that became the group's first million seller. It also led to Clinton's crazy creation, the P-Funk Mothership: a huge flying saucer stage prop for the P-Funk Earth Tour.

In the era of the burgeoning disco scene, Bogart struck gold when he signed vocalist Donna Summer to Casablanca. Her sexually charged debut "Love to Love You Baby" (1975) was such a hit that an extended, seventeen-minute version was released as a twelve-inch single: a landmark in the history of vinyl. Despite being banned by many US radio stations, the song made it to number two on the *Billboard* Hot 100 and catapulted Summer to superstardom. By the end of the decade, her success had cemented Casablanca's reputation as the go-to disco label. Indeed, she was its best-selling artist, with several gold and platinum albums to her name, and four number ones in the singles chart. As the uncrowned queen of disco, she also had no fewer than eleven chart toppers on the *Billboard* Hot Dance Club listing, and her biggest album success, *Bad Girls* (1979), sold more than eight million copies worldwide.

In 1977, disco group Village People joined the "rogues and rebels" at Casablanca and became another instant success for the label. Originally aimed at the gay disco audience, their singles "YMCA" (1978) and "In the Navy" (1979) crossed over into big hits in the mainstream pop market, and the first five of their Casablanca albums went gold or platinum with their US sales alone. However, the disco craze couldn't last forever, and Bogart's debts were huge and mounting.

The label's great success throughout the 1970s was not to be repeated in the next decade. When the giant PolyGram acquired a 50 percent interest in Casablanca, Bogart's days with the label he had founded were numbered. However, with his severance money from PolyGram, he set up a new label, Boardwalk Records, and signed the ex-Runaways singer Joan Jett. Unfortunately, it was his last hurrah, and Joan Jett & The Blackhearts' *I Love Rock 'n Roll* (1981) was his last hit. Tragically, Neil Bogart died from cancer in 1982 at the age of thirty-nine, and a year after his demise, the new label folded.

> Donna Summer's "Love to Love You Baby" came to Bogart's attention after he made a deal with Giorgio Moroder and Pete Bellote to distribute records from their Oasis label in the United States.

⌐ Casablanca cofounder Larry Harris poses with Kiss and their gold discs, backstage at the Nassau Coliseum in Uniondale, New York, December 1975.

∨ Neil Bogart—according to Harris, "no person or company in that era of narcissism and druggy gluttony was more emblematic of the times than Casablanca Records and its magnetic founder."

TAKE ME HOME
CHER (1979)

Cher's Casablanca debut went gold in months, and its title track became her fifth US top ten hit of the 1970s. Its conception was far from easy; according to one biographer, she "hated all six" songs cut with producer Ron Dante. Teamed instead with Bob Esty, who helmed Donna Summer's "Last Dance" and Barbra Streisand's "The Main Event," she was obliged to work on disco material that, Esty recalled, "bugged the shit out of her." Cher had no qualms, however, about a gold bikini—also immortalized on a picture disc—that was inspired by her boyfriend, Gene Simmons of Kiss.

LOVE TO LOVE YOU BABY
DONNA SUMMER (1975)

Initially issued on producer Giorgio Moroder's German label Oasis, the erotically charged *Love to Love You Baby* was picked up and developed into an international sensation by the wily Neil Bogart. Oasis became a Casablanca subsidiary while the singer became *the* disco superstar.

ALIVE!
KISS (1975)

"There are those who regard this concert double as a de facto best-of that rescues such unacknowledged hard rock classics as 'Deuce' and 'Strutter' from the sludge," wrote *The Village Voice*'s Robert Christgau. "There are also those who regard it as the sludge." Forty years on, the former view has tended to prevail.

MOTHERSHIP CONNECTION
PARLIAMENT (1975)

Two months after issuing one of hard rock's definitive albums—Kiss' *Alive!*—Casablanca unleashed the decade's funkiest LP. Parliament's third in sixteen months, it boasted subsequently much-sampled cuts, including "P. Funk (Wants to Get Funked Up)" and "Give Up the Funk (Tear the Roof Off the Sucker)." Of Casablanca boss Neil Bogart, bandleader George Clinton said: "I had wanted to be with him for years because he was a good promotion man. But he would only do it if I would be the center of attraction. . . . So I reluctantly said yes and that became Dr. Funkenstein."

MACHO MAN
VILLAGE PEOPLE (1978)

Created by French producer Jacques Morali, the Village People proved an instant hit in clubs with their self-titled 1977 debut. Neil Bogart snapped them up and Morali expanded the lineup of Victor Willis, Alexander Briley, and Felipe Rose to a sextet with David Hodo, Randy Jones, and Glenn Hughes, unveiled on *Macho Man*. "Jacques was the hook man," Hodo (the construction worker) told *Popmatters*. "He had a million hooks. Neil knew which hook was the hit. . . . Casablanca was king for a while. That was the label to be on. It was young, it was new, it was vibrant, it was innovative."

FUNKYTOWN
LIPPS, INC. (1980)

Casablanca signed Minneapolis musician Steven Greenberg on the strength of a demo that, he said, had everyone "from secretaries to the vice presidents . . . all packed in this little office dancing around." He repaid them with a worldwide number one that was Casablanca's best-selling single ever.

MUSIC INSPIRED BY STAR WARS AND OTHER GALACTIC FUNK
MECO (1977)

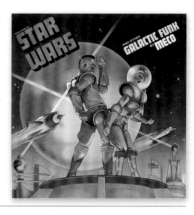

Fans of *Never Mind the Bollocks* may demur, but this set of disco reworkings of John Williams's *Star Wars* music, on the Casablanca-distributed Millennium label, was the LP that best defined 1977.

BAD GIRLS
DONNA SUMMER (1979)

"An incredibly talented lady," said Neil Bogart, even after Summer sued Casablanca for ten million dollars. "She was a concept. We promoted and marketed a concept." That frequently erotic concept peaked with the fantastic *Bad Girls*, her third consecutive double album (the fourth, *On the Radio*, made her the only artist to top the US chart with consecutive double albums). When Bogart first heard the title track, Summer told writer Craig Rosen, "He said, 'This song is not for you.' . . . He thought it was too rock 'n' roll and that I should give the song to Cher, but I refused."

A poster for *The Clones of Dr. Funkenstein* (1976), which became Parliament's second album to be certified gold.

A celebration of the Village People's first three albums being certified gold in 1978.

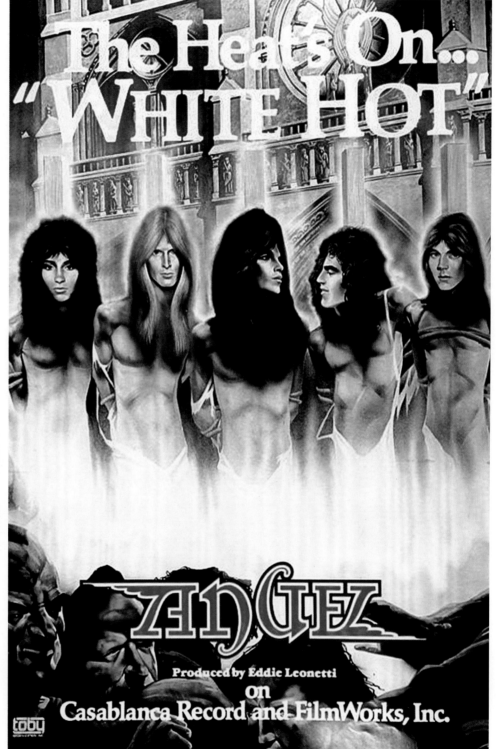

> Discovered by Kiss bassist Gene Simmons, Angel were deliberately marketed by Casablanca as the antithesis to Kiss.

> Casablanca tried to repeat Kiss' success with hard rockers The Godz, to little commercial avail.

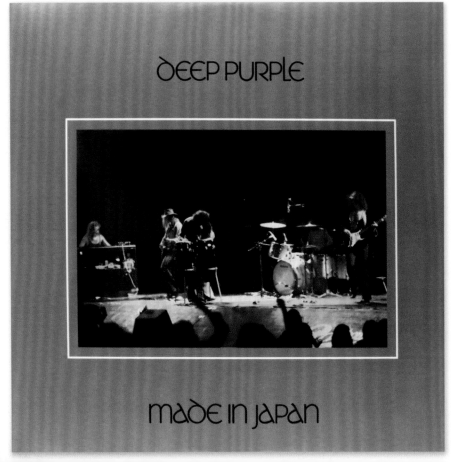

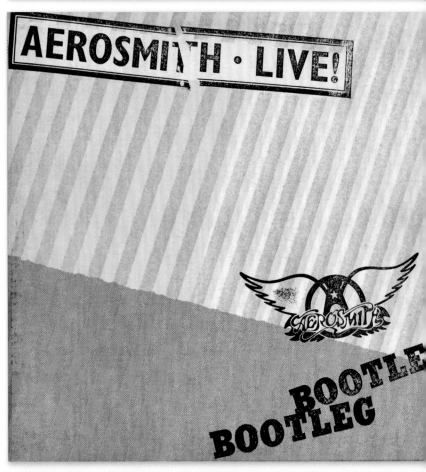

Got Live If You Want It

Live LPs in the 1970s were excuses for excess, as in Yes's triple *Yessongs* and Led Zeppelin's *The Song Remains the Same*. Yet they yielded gems such as Donna Summer's *Live and More*, Peter Frampton's *Frampton Comes Alive*, and Cheap Trick's *At Budokan*. In the lo-fi arena were The Beatles' *Live at the Hollywood Bowl* ("The sound rings clearly and powerfully through the shrieking," wrote Robert Christgau, "and the songs capture our heroes at their highest") and Iggy & the Stooges' *Metallic KO*, on which you can hear the firecrackers and breaking glass.

LIVE AT LEEDS
THE WHO (1970)

The original vinyl version of this much reissued classic is the one to get: it trims the *Tommy* fat from The Who's set, and its mock-bootleg sleeve houses all kinds of delightful ephemera.

MADE IN JAPAN
DEEP PURPLE (1972)

Drummer Ian Paice's assessment of this as "the best live rock 'n' roll album ever" is immodest but not too far from the truth. Metallica founder Lars Ulrich cites it as his favorite album.

ALOHA FROM HAWAII . . .
ELVIS PRESLEY (1973)

This souvenir of an entertaining TV broadcast from Hawaii to Japan and the Far East was the king's first US number one album since 1965's *Roustabout* and the ninth and last in his lifetime.

LIVE! BOOTLEG
AEROSMITH (1978)

Seemingly packaged in homage to *Live at Leeds*, this double album captured the quintet at the peak of their 1970s success with glorious R&B covers from a vintage radio session on side four.

TAKE NO PRISONERS
LOU REED (1978)

"There are so *many* favorites to choose from!" Reed deadpans. Taped in New York at a series of shows whose attendees included Springsteen, this is an indulgent but entertaining double LP.

LIVE AND DANGEROUS
THIN LIZZY (1978)

"That was us at our best, before the bad drugs came in," guitarist Scott Gorham told *Classic Rock* of a Tony Visconti-helmed hard rock bible that ranges from raucous to wrenching.

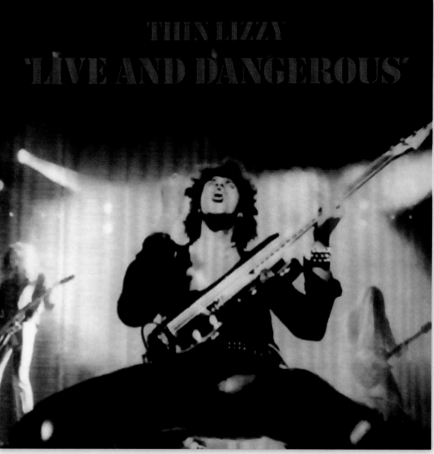

Out of This World Records

This stunning disc launched with 1977's *Voyager 1* and *Voyager 2* space probes. Its contents decided by a committee chaired by Carl Sagan, it bore encoded photographs of Earth and its life-forms, scientific information, spoken greetings from the president of the United States and "the children of the Planet Earth," a "Sounds of Earth" medley (whale sounds, a baby crying, waves breaking on a shore), and music by Mozart, Blind Willie Johnson, Chuck Berry, Valya Balkanska, and other Eastern and Western performers. The disc is mimicked by the cover and vinyl version of *The Great Pretender*, a 2015 LP by Mini Mansions that features Alex Turner of Arctic Monkeys and Brian Wilson.

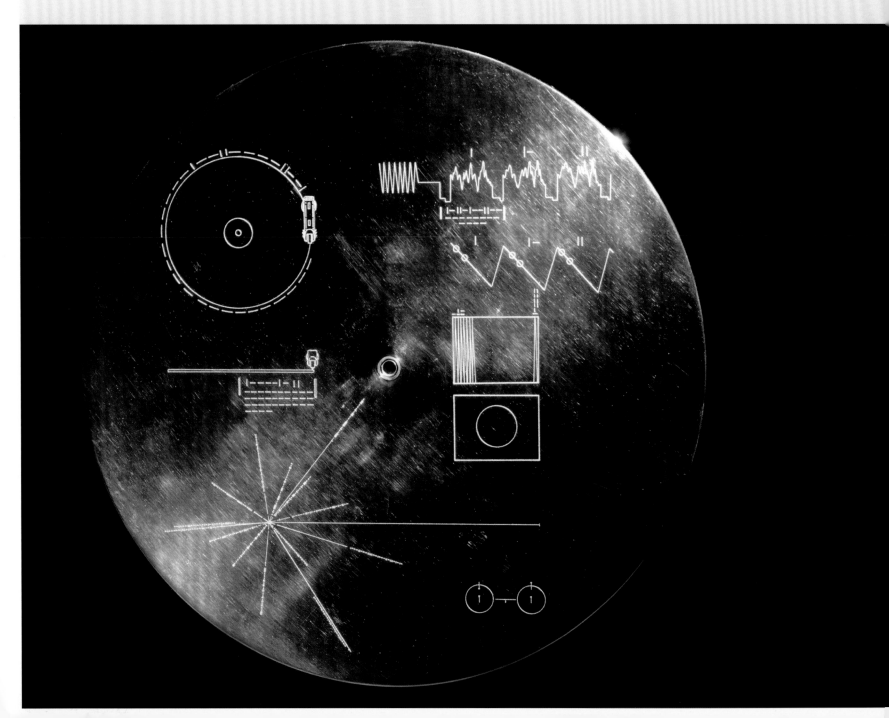

The gold-plated aluminum cover was designed to protect the "Sounds of Earth" records from micrometeorite bombardment but also serves a double purpose in providing an explanatory diagram for how to play the record.

A "Sounds of the Earth" record ready to be attached to one of the identical *Voyager* crafts.

The twelve-inch gold-plated copper disc.

A technician attaches the record to one of the space probes.

The record in its final position, with cover in place.

Sacked by EMI after their 1976 debut single "Anarchy in the UK," due to a much-publicized incident in which they swore during a prime-time TV interview, the Sex Pistols had carved a notorious reputation for themselves. In February 1977, bass guitarist Glen Matlock left the group, and in his place they recruited drummer and Sex Pistols fan Sid Vicious, who could hardly play a note on the bass but looked the part. With Vicious swearing and spitting at fans and foes alike, publicity followed the band wherever they went.

At a bizarre press gathering held outside Buckingham Palace in March 1977, the band signed to the giant A&M label. The publicity tied in with the imminent release of their single "God Save the Queen," but it was put on hold when just a week later A&M canceled the contract, after the group had caused mayhem and abused staff in the company's offices.

The Pistols signed with Virgin in May, and "God Save the Queen" was finally released. It hit number two in the UK, amid suggestions that it had been denied its rightful place atop the chart due to Queen Elizabeth's Silver Jubilee.

Never Mind the Bollocks Here's the Sex Pistols

After signing to A&M, the band had begun recording with *Dark Side of the Moon* producer Chris Thomas, and, on joining Virgin, an album was planned. Comprising their four singles and other tracks recorded between March and June 1977, the LP was eventually released in October that year. Matlock plays bass on "Anarchy in the UK," but Vicious appears only on "Bodies." His playing was so bad that even the Sex Pistols, despite their apparent disregard for technical finesse, couldn't work with him in the studio. As a consequence, guitarist Steve Jones played bass on all the other nine tracks.

On the first release of the album, "Submission" was included as a one-sided seven-inch single, before being included in later twelve-track pressings of the LP.

The striking and ultimately iconic artwork proved as revolutionary as the album itself. "The instant the Sex Pistols brought out *Never Mind the Bollocks* with the cover done by Jamie Reid, which cost about tuppence . . ." admitted Aubrey "Po" Powell, whose company Hipgnosis had clad the likes of Pink Floyd, ". . . we realized that our extravagant and expensive pieces of surreal output were going to die a death."

NEVER MIND THE BOLLOCKS HERE'S THE Sex PiSTOLs

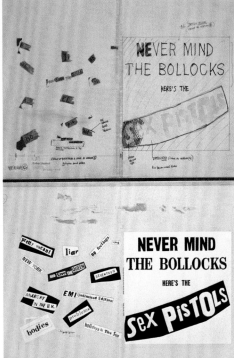

∧ Jamie Reid's much-imitated cover reflected the in-your-face impact of the Pistols' take on punk.

‹ Preliminary artwork for the album, initially titled *God Save Sex Pistols*, but replaced with a phrase Steve Jones overheard from a fan.

« Pre-Vicious Pistols: Glen Matlock, Johnny Rotten, Jones, Paul Cook.

Picture This

Although considered a contemporary phenomenon, colored vinyl was introduced with the very first seven-inch singles, when the format was launched by RCA-Victor in 1949. In the United States, these were color-coded by genre: black for pop, red for classical, blue for Broadway musicals, yellow for children's, green for country, orange for R&B, and teal for international music. This system was ditched, however, when the production process proved too complicated. (Colored—and even transparent—records are created by using chemical compounds to produce the original vinyl pellets. These, like the conventional black pellets, are fed into an extruder that shapes the vinyl from which the record is pressed.)

As a marketing gimmick, colored discs reappeared in force in the early 1970s. With cover artwork providing the major visual identity, the discs themselves offered further artistic opportunities. "Krautrock" band Faust's self-titled 1971 debut, for example, was pressed in transparent vinyl.

In 1978, punk band Penetration issued their *Moving Targets* in luminous vinyl (as did Kiss with 1982's "Creatures of the Night" and Skrillex, with 2011's "Scary Monsters and Nice Sprites"). Indeed, the punk era was big on quirky vinyl, fitting the movement's visual style. In 1978, Devo's debut *Q: Are We Not Men? A: We Are Devo!* featured spattered-color vinyl, while "The Day the World Turned Day-Glo" by X-Ray Spex was bright orange. Meanwhile, the UK success in the same year of The Cars' "My Best Friend's Girl" is credited in part to its then-novel availability as a picture disc.

In the 1980s, picture discs were customarily deployed to persuade the loyal fan bases of huge acts, such as Michael Jackson, Iron Maiden, and Madonna, to shell out for material that they often already owned in conventional formats. A variant of Madonna's "Erotica" (1992) featured her sucking a lucky beneficiary's toe. Due to its echoes of a notorious photograph of British royal Sarah Ferguson, it was withdrawn and was estimated by *Record Collector* magazine in 2010 to be worth more than $3,000 (£2,000).

A characteristically idiosyncratic limited edition from Jack White's Third Man label was the "A Glorious Dawn" seven-inch EP of remixed recordings from Carl Sagan's TV series *Cosmos* and *Stephen Hawking's Universe*, for which glow-in-the-dark vinyl was scatttered into black to evoke a starry sky.

This version of Bon Jovi's breakthrough *Slippery When Wet* (1986) illustrates one of the reasons for its success.

THE WORKER
FISCHER-Z (1979)

Just as a train appears in the lyrics of this British new wave band's song (from their 1979 debut *Word Salad*) as a symbol for a hated daily commute, so it revolves with endless monotony as the disc spins on the turntable.

ROCK AND ROLL OVER
KISS (1982)

Few acts lend themselves to visual trickery so readily as Kiss. Their Dutch label Polygram duly milked the band's back catalog with a series of picture disc reissues, including this LP that used Michael Dorer's cover art from the 1976 original.

LITTLE RED CORVETTE
PRINCE (1983)

Long something of an underachiever on the pop charts, Prince belatedly hit big with his 1982 classic *1999*, whose glorious "Little Red Corvette" and infectious title track are paired on this suitably purple-tinged picture disc.

SHE WAS HOT
THE ROLLING STONES (1984)

The Rolling Stones' trademark tongue makes for an arresting shaped picture disc, but even that couldn't stop this ho-hum rocker from 1983's *Undercover* falling short of the top forty on both sides of the Atlantic.

SWEET CHILD O' MINE
GUNS N' ROSES (1989)

Nearly two years after its initial release on *Appetite for Destruction,* this GN'R classic finally made it into the British top ten, thanks in part to a delightful shaped disc, based on a design for one of Axl Rose's tattoos by Bill White Jr.

KILLERS
IRON MAIDEN (1998)

Exploiting Iron Maiden's iconography—largely based on Derek Riggs's drawings of "Eddie"—and the fanatical loyalty of their fans, the band's US label Columbia reissued their second album, from 1981, as one of their many picture discs.

1980s

Vinyl faced its first rival in the form of the ubiquitous Walkman, but fans soon realized that nothing could match the sheer physicality of owning a vinyl album such as Michael Jackson's *Thriller* or Bruce Springsteen *Live*, both of which were among the biggest hits of the decade.

> Jazz musician Herbie Hancock poses with a record in 1986, the year in which he wrote the Oscar-winning soundtrack to the movie *Round Midnight*.

>> A publicity shot from the title track's video, premiered on December 2, 1983.

> The singer, in his trademark glove, collects one of *Thriller*'s many awards.

∨ The cover of the album, which won a record-breaking eight Grammy Awards in 1984.

It's August 1982, and for Michael Jackson and his producer Quincy Jones things are not going well. "The Girl Is Mine"—a duet with Paul McCartney, recorded in three days at the end of 1981—is battling poor reviews to climb the US chart. But Jackson and Jones have yet to finish its parent album and can no longer rely on goodwill generated by *Off the Wall*, its now three-year-old predecessor. In just four months of work, they've had to complete a new album and a storybook LP for Steven Spielberg's movie *E.T. the Extra Terrestrial*. On the day before the former is due for delivery to the Epic label, the pair pull an all-nighter and, the next day, listen to the final mix.

"It sounded terrible," Jones told *Billboard* writer Craig Rosen. "We had put too much music on each side. Since it was vinyl, you could only have twenty minutes a side. Michael was crying at the time and we all felt terrible." After two days of cooling off, Jones abbreviated the introduction to "Billie Jean" and removed a verse from "The Lady in My Life." "From then on," he observed, "it was like magic."

This wasn't the first time his editing skills had been called upon. For the track list, Jones told *The Guardian*, he whittled

Thriller

800 contenders to nine. "Then I took out the weakest four and replaced them with 'The Lady in My Life,' 'PYT,' 'Beat It,' and 'Human Nature.' Mix that with 'Billie Jean' and 'Wanna Be Startin' Somethin',' and you have a serious album."

Issued in November 1982, *Thriller* failed to displace Men at Work's *Business As Usual* from the US chart peak. But when "Billie Jean" hit in early 1983, the album rose to the top—a position it occupied for thirty-seven nonconsecutive weeks. In January, it earned its first platinum award (a number that rose to twenty in the US alone by November 1984). In March, the star debuted his moonwalk in a Motown TV special, and in July "Human Nature" became *Thriller*'s third hit.

A year after the LP's release, its title track was unleashed as the seventh single, meaning every cut bar "The Lady in My Life" had featured on an A or B side. "People used to do an album where you'd get one good song, and the rest were like B sides," Jackson told *Ebony*. "I would say to myself, 'Why can't every one be like a hit song? Why can't every song be so great that people would want to buy it if you could release it as a single?' So I always tried to strive for that. . . . I wanted to just put any one out that we wanted. I worked hard for it."

Def Jam recordings

Def Jam began as a name rather than a label. "The first record I produced was 'It's Yours' by T La Rock and Jazzy J in '84," recalled Rick Rubin, then a twenty-year-old student at New York University. "I was going to press it up, but then one of the MCs I knew played a tape of it to (producer) Arthur Baker . . . and he put it out." This historic and much-sampled twelve-inch single appeared on Partytime, a subsidiary of Baker's Streetwise, with "Def Jam Recordings" on its label and a latterly iconic drawing of a record player's tone arm on the sleeve. "My aunt worked in the creative services department of Estée Lauder," Rubin explained, "and I went to her offices and used the type there to make the Def Jam logo." A college friend helped him with the drawing: "I asked her to copy an image of the tone arm from my Technics turntable so it would look like a blueprint. I grew up with seven-inch singles. The logos on those, from all of the small indie labels of the 60s and 70s, were the inspiration. I wanted something that fit in that canon."

"It's Yours" caught the ear of rap promoter Russell Simmons, who managed Kurtis Blow and produced his brother's trio Run-DMC. Rubin, he recalled, "convinced me . . . to go into partnership with him. He had a downtown, rock 'n' roll perspective on record. He appreciated the records I'd made because they were loud and abrasive, and we got along because I'd put loud, ridiculous drums on everything."

Also inspired by "It's Yours" was sixteen-year-old James Smith, a.k.a. LL Cool J, who sent a demo to the address on the sleeve—Rubin's university dorm. Adam Horovitz, a friend of the

producer (and one of the Beastie Boys), brought the demo to his attention. Rubin duly called Smith: "He came over to the dorm, and we decided to make records together."

Horovitz, Rubin, and Smith cowrote Def Jam's official debut single, LL's "I Need a Beat," which sold more than 100,000 copies. "We'd have the records pressed up and shipped to the dorm, and send them out to the different distributors," Rubin recalled. "We did everything except promotion, which Russell did from his office."

Def Jam's success led to a distribution deal with Columbia, who reluctantly also took on the Beastie Boys (whose AC/DC-looting "Rock Hard" was the label's second single, in 1985).

LL's *Radio* (1985) became his first of twelve gold albums over two decades and shot Def Jam to fame. Mainstream success was sealed by the Beasties' US chart-topping *Licensed to Ill* (1986), but with fame came fractures. In 1986, Simmons helmed Oran "Juice" Jones's R&B smash "The Rain" while, in stark contrast, Rubin produced Slayer's metal classic *Reign in Blood* (distributed by Geffen after Columbia refused to handle an LP with a song about Nazi Josef Mengele). Def Jam's extremes were illustrated by its soundtrack for the 1987 movie *Less Than Zero*, which veered from Roy Orbison to the label's most significant signing, Public Enemy—who, Simmons observed, "influenced a whole generation of black Americans to be more conscious."

Simmons and Rubin increasingly ran their own teams. "We really didn't know what we were doing," the latter told the *New York Post*, "and then, all of a sudden, we had this big successful company. Instead of finding a way to manage it, I just left!" Rubin duly decamped to Los Angeles to establish Def American (later American Recordings). "We don't have Slayer anymore," Simmons sniffed to *Rolling Stone*. "That's how much it affected us."

As vinyl gave way to CD, so Def Jam became a tamer beast than the one that growled at the industry in the 1980s, but stars such as Jay-Z, Redman, DMX, Method Man, and Rihanna maintained its position. In 2003, Rubin restored Simmons' "loud, ridiculous drums" to Def Jam with his production of Jay-Z's classic "99 Problems." The former partners, Jay noted, "didn't start (Def Jam) with the idea of making a business. They started it as a *need*."

∧ Rubin and Simmons were first introduced to each other at the legendary Manhattan nightclub Danceteria, whose diverse crowd of hardcore rockers and streetwise rappers was symbolic of their own relationship.

⅂ Thanks to the popularity of "I Need a Beat" and *Radio*, LL Cool J (short for Ladies Love Cool James) was one of the first hip-hop acts to achieve mainstream success.

› Chuck D, Flavor Flav, Terminator X, and members of Public Enemy in September 1988.

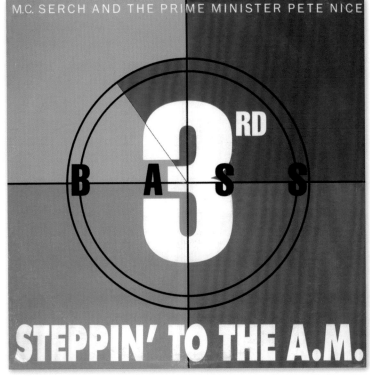

M.C. SERCH AND THE PRIME MINISTER PETE NICE

3RD BASS

STEPPIN' TO THE A.M.

CROSSOVER
EPMD (1992)

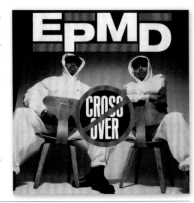

By 1992, Def Jam's funkiest act were on their last legs, yet still adding to their canon of classics with cuts like this new jack swing-flavored single. Before they reunited in 1997, their legacy was kept alive by their protégé Redman, who scored three gold albums on Def Jam from 1992 to 1996.

TEENAGE LOVE
SLICK RICK (1988)

The English-born Ricky Walters is a true hip-hop pop pioneer. He first made waves on Doug E. Fresh's "The Show," but it was that hit's B side, "Lodi Dodi," that proved more influential, not least when it was covered by Snoop Dogg. His first solo singles on Def Jam followed a similar pattern of chart-friendly fare on the A side, and a rap classic on the flip. "Mona Lisa" backed "Hey Young World" while "Teenage Love"—a transparent but fruitful bid to engineer a hit along the lines of LL Cool J's "I Need Love"—boasted the gleefully wrongheaded "Treat Her Like a Prostitute."

STEPPIN' TO THE A.M.
3RD BASS (1989)

Helmed by Public Enemy producers Hank and Keith Shocklee and Eric "Vietnam" Sadler, and featuring chiming clocks from Pink Floyd's "Time," "Steppin' to the A.M." was a cut from MC Serch and Pete Nice's classic *The Cactus Album*. Although 3rd Bass lasted for just two LPs—*Derelicts of Dialect* followed in 1991—they proved the Beasties weren't Def Jam's only funky and witty white boys. Highly rated by Russell Simmons, they also gave early platforms to MF Doom (as Zev Love X on *The Cactus Album*'s "The Gas Face") and Nas (on Serch's solo *Return of the Product*, 1992).

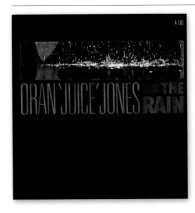

THE RAIN
ORAN 'JUICE' JONES (1986)

Def Jam scored a transatlantic top ten hit with a cut that signposted the label's eventual transition into R&B, but the evocative lament (shown here in its European sleeve) was Jones's sole smash. "Oran 'Juice' Jones . . ." he later reflected to VH1. "He came, he saw, he conquered, he moved on. You dig?"

LICENSED TO ILL
BEASTIE BOYS (1986)

The Beastie Boys and LL Cool J were the formative Def Jam's flagships. Yet such was the reaction to the former's mix of bratty Run-DMC pastiches and hopeless hardcore that, when the Columbia label took Def Jam under its distribution wing, Mike D recalled, "They looked at us as the curse of the whole deal." Even the Beasties didn't have high hopes for their debut, recorded between shows with Madonna and Run-DMC. But in March 1987, three months after its release, *Licensed to Ill*—clad in a witty gatefold by David Gambale—became the first rap album to top *Billboard*'s pop chart.

IT TAKES A NATION OF MILLIONS TO HOLD US BACK
PUBLIC ENEMY (1988)

A sticker on the sleeve of Public Enemy's second LP promised "16 pumpin tracks on black wax," including "cold stompers," such as "Bring the Noise" and "Rebel without a Pause." *Nation* packed nearly an hour on a single album, divided into "Side Silver" and "Side Black," including instrumental interludes and epics, such as "Black Steel in the Hour of Chaos." "Vinyl's function was threefold," front man Chuck D recalled. "The records had the breaks, so you used it as a tool to entertain. With the beats, it was a tool for writing. Then the record was also there to just play."

∧ Ad-Rock of the Beastie Boys sprays the contents of a can of beer over members of the audience from on stage at the Centrum in Worcester, Massachusetts, on April 9, 1987.

≪ LL Cool J in 1990, the year in which his classic album *Mama Said Knock You Out* was released.

‹ To celebrate the label's 30th anniversary in 2014, Def Jam released *DEF JAM 30*, an all-encompassing collection of landmark tracks packaged in a limited edition turntable-style box.

> Jay-Z and Rick Rubin during a Def
> Jam Party at B Bar in New York
> in 2001.

> Russell Simmons (left) and a
> colleague in his Def Jam office in
> 1988. MTV hailed Simmons as "the
> most important businessman in the
> history of rap music."

Turntable Treasures

The first big challenge to vinyl came with the launch of the Sony Walkman audio cassette player in 1979, which for the first time enabled young people to listen to recorded music on the go. Turntable manufacturers reacted by turning their attention to the high end of the market, with the first examples of engineer-driven design.

> Ron Arad's Concrete Stereo (1983) features a turntable deck, amplifier unit, two speaker towers, and two shallow cone speakers, all encased in housing of cement with aluminum mesh.

>> Sony's PS-F5 portable record player was first introduced in 1983. It features a linear tracking tone arm and can play records standing upright, lying down, or hanging on a wall.

Produced from 1981 to 1985, the Technics SL-10 was the first linear-tracking turntable to feature direct drive. Its success spawned numerous imitators throughout the 1980s.

Upon its introduction in 1980, many felt that the Oracle Delphi set a new benchmark for analog playback. Over 10,000 were built and sold throughout the world before production ended in 1994.

Bruce Springsteen's appeal lies as much in the dynamism of his shows as the quality of his albums, and fans had been waiting a long time for a definitive record of the former when *Live/1975–85* was released in November 1986. His concerts were marathons, stretching more than three hours, so what could be more appropriate than a live box set running to the same kind of time, stretching over five vinyl albums?

In a thirty-six-page booklet, Springsteen describes how, on reviewing hours and hours of live tapes, a career-defining "story began to emerge." This opened with "Thunder Road" from the Roxy, Los Angeles, in 1975, with Springsteen's star in the ascendant thanks to his breakthrough, *Born to Run*. Cuts from 1978 fill much of the first two discs, before side four speeds us to Springsteen's arena-filling 1980 tour— beginning with a stirring singalong to his first top ten hit, "Hungry Heart."

The sixth side showcases understated songs, including a trio from the lo-fi *Nebraska*, taped at the Meadowlands Arena in his native New Jersey, and prefaced by Woody Guthrie's unofficial national anthem, "This Land Is Your Land."

Live/1975–85

The final two albums present Springsteen the stadium star, with thunderous takes on Edwin Starr's "War" and his own "Born in the U.S.A.," and a long, evocative introduction to "The River." Finally, after three hours, the set wound down with a gentle, well-received take on Tom Waits's "Jersey Girl."

The forty-track collection had advance orders of more than a million-and-a-half copies, making it the biggest by-the-dollar preorder in record industry history. Across the United States, fans waited in line outside record stores on the morning of its release on November 10, 1986, with one New York retailer selling the album straight off the delivery truck.

Live/1975–85, as Craig Rosen wrote in *The Billboard Book of Number One Albums*, "became Springsteen's first album to debut at the top, as well as the first album to do so since Stevie Wonder's *Songs in the Key of Life* in 1976. It also became the first five-record set ever to hit number one." Within three months, it had achieved triple-platinum status.

By no means the last gasp for live albums—Garth Brooks's 1998 set *Double Live* outsold it by millions—*Live/1975–85* was nonetheless a final stand for the blockbusting vinyl box set— a fitting triumph for an artist steeped in rock 'n' roll heritage.

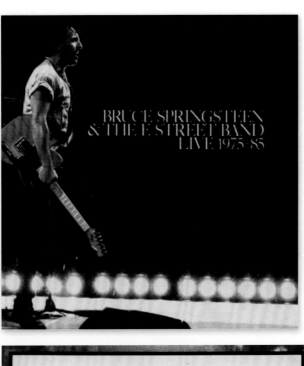

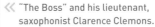

≪ "The Boss" and his lieutenant, saxophonist Clarence Clemons.

‹ A Neal Preston photo adorned the box in which the LPs were packaged.

⌄ Springsteen's handwritten introductory note to the album's sleevenotes.

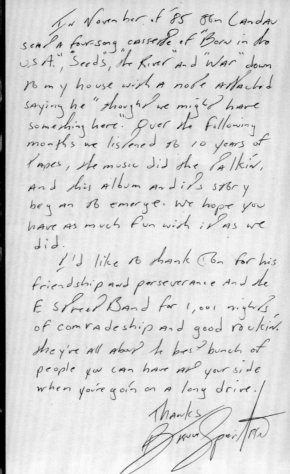

In November of '85 Jon Landau sent a four-song cassette of "Born in the U.S.A.", "Seeds", "The River" and "War" down to my house with a note attached saying he "thought we might have something here." Over the following months we listened to 10 years of tapes, the music did the talkin', and this album and its story began to emerge. We hope you have as much fun with it as we did.

I'd like to thank Jon for his friendship and perseverance and the E Street Band for 1,001 nights of comradeship and good rockin'. they're all about the best bunch of people you can have at your side when you're goin' on a long drive.

Thanks,
Bruce Springsteen

Factory Records

One of the most influential independent British labels, Factory was in the vanguard of a new wave of rock emerging from Manchester in the late 1970s and early 1980s. With vinyl still the dominant medium, the label crafted LPs, EPs, and seven and twelve-inch singles, often prioritizing art over profit.

The Factory name was first applied to a Manchester club, opened by TV presenter Tony Wilson and actor Alan Erasmus in May 1978. Having decided the way forward was records instead of just live promotions, they plotted an EP featuring acts who played the club—Manchester's Joy Division and The Durutti Column, Sheffield's Cabaret Voltaire, and Birmingham's John Dowie.

An important aspect of the punk revolution of the late 1970s was a proliferation of small indie labels, often putting out seven-inch singles and EPs of local acts. Noting the success of one such outfit, Manchester's Rabid Records, with bands such as Slaughter and the Dogs, Wilson and Erasmus set up the Factory label, enlisting Rabid founder Martin Hannett in the process.

The planned EP, *A Factory Sample*, was issued in January 1979 and carried the number FAC-2. It lost first place in the catalog to a poster, Factory having decided that their numbering system would include other artifacts, such as flyers and merchandise. (Celebrated examples of this conceit include FAC-61, a lawsuit launched by Hannett against the label in 1982; FAC-91, an abandoned computer software prototype; and FACT-181, a mooted movie with the Happy Mondays entitled *Mad Fuckers*). The debut EP was designed by Peter Saville,

a partner in the business with Wilson, Erasmus, and Hannett, who would be responsible for much of its distinctive artwork. Two singles followed in May 1979: "All Night Party" by

A Certain Ratio and "Electricity" by Orchestral Manoeuvres in the Dark. A first LP, *Unknown Pleasures* by Joy Division, appeared in June.

Over the next twelve months, Factory stayed at the cutting edge, but tragedy struck in May 1980, when Joy Division's Ian Curtis committed suicide. While "Love Will Tear Us Apart" and *Closer* hit charts, the band recovered and, by the end of the year, had regrouped as New Order.

In May 1982, Factory launched FAC-51: the fateful Haçienda club. Its finances were often

precarious—at one stage it was said to be costing investors New Order £10,000 ($15,000) a month—but, by the mid-1980s, it was a flagship for the nascent techno and acid house scene. Meanwhile, New Order took five Factory albums into the British top ten, including a chart topper with *Technique* in 1989.

Happy Mondays, whom Tony Wilson had discovered at a "battle of the bands" contest at the Haçienda, made their Factory debut with the *Forty Five* EP in September 1985. In late 1986 they recorded their first album *Squirrel and G-Man Twenty Four Hour Party People Plastic Face Carnt Smile (White Out)*, produced by ex-Velvet Underground man John Cale. However, it was *Bummed*, produced by Hannett and released in 1988, that proved to be one of the building blocks of the "Madchester" rave scene that dominated the city at the turn of the decade. The Mondays consolidated their position with 1990's top five *Pills 'n' Thrills and Bellyaches*.

The excess that characterized Madchester eventually caught up with Factory. The Mondays' drug-crazed recording of 1992's *Yes Please!* in Barbados was cited as a factor in the label being forced into bankruptcy, while the £400,000 ($600,000) spent by New Order on *Republic* (eventually released on London in 1993) also contributed to the state of Factory's finances.

The Factory saga would be the subject of the 2002 movie *24 Hour Party People*, and its legacy as a boutique independent label is incalculable, despite the fact that, in the words of New Order's Peter Hook, "It went bankrupt and didn't pay its acts! But then it also transcended the ordinariness of record companies."

187

> The Happy Mondays in 1991, riding
  high on the peak of their popularity
  following the release of 1990's *Pills
  'n' Thrills and Bellyaches*.

∨ Tony Wilson and Peter Saville
  in 1984.

⌐ Bernard Sumner and Ian Curtis
  of Joy Division performing live
  in Rotterdam in 1980.

STILL
JOY DIVISION (1981)

This double LP was issued fifteen months after Ian Curtis's death, initially wrapped in a burlap cover. It collects studio oddities, a cover of The Velvet Underground's "Sister Ray," and an abysmally recorded but thrilling live set from 1980, including a formative version of New Order's "Ceremony."

TECHNIQUE
NEW ORDER (1989)

Factory Records hadn't worked out that "sunny places are not really conducive to working hard," Stephen Morris told the *Telegraph* of the recording of *Technique* on the Spanish island Ibiza. "We started off trying to write an album in the summer," said Bernard Sumner. "But as the season progressed, it moved further and further to the back of our minds. We just went out to clubs." The eventual result, however, proved to be New Order's most successful album, bolstered by its immersion in Balearic beats and the hits "Fine Time," "Round and Round," and "Run."

PILLS 'N' THRILLS AND BELLYACHES
HAPPY MONDAYS (1990)

"I saw the Happy Mondays on TV," Paul McCartney told *NME* in late 1990, "and they reminded me of The Beatles in their 'Strawberry Fields' phase." That phase had begun a year earlier, with the release of the *Madchester Rave On* EP that bequeathed a name to the scene of which the Mondays and fellow Manchester-based The Stone Roses were the leaders. The loose-limbed *Pills 'n' Thrills and Bellyaches* even climbed into the lower reaches of *Billboard*'s top 100, albeit after its original sleeve, illustrated above, had been toned down to remove branded US candy wrappers.

PIGS+BATTLESHIPS
QUANDO QUANGO (1985)

Quando Quango, formed in The Netherlands, are best remembered for early recordings produced by Bernard Sumner, and for being a platform for M People founder Mike Pickering. Their imaginative blend of new wave and Latin music made them an intriguing addition to the Factory roster.

BUMMED
HAPPY MONDAYS (1988)

One of Factory's finest and funkiest releases was clad in a crop of a painting of singer Shaun Ryder. It was a personal favorite of sleeve designers Central Station, whose vibrant work for the Mondays created an entirely different image for Factory than the elegance of Joy Division and New Order.

SEXTET
A CERTAIN RATIO (1982)

A textured and colorful cover painting by Denis Ryan gave a helpful clue that A Certain Ratio's third album had taken them farther than ever from the monochromatic flavor associated with Factory. (The movie *24 Hour Party People* includes a description of them as having "all the energy of Joy Division, but with better clothes.") Purchasers of *Sextet*, *The Quietus* observed, "experienced extraordinary flurries of world beats, samba, flurries of jazz, and even scat singing." In the process, A Certain Ratio influenced a variety of acts, from Heaven 17 to !!! and LCD Soundsystem.

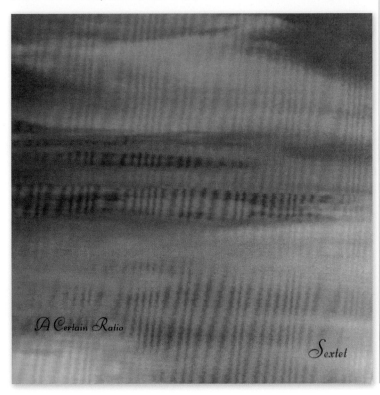

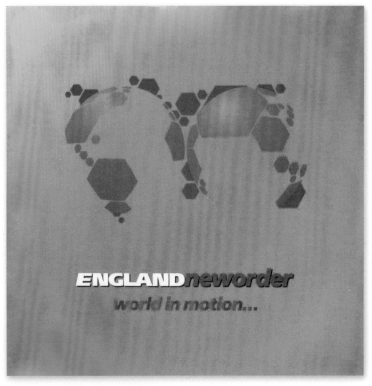

WORLD IN MOTION
ENGLANDNEWORDER (1990)

Factory's only chart-topping single was this anthem for the 1990 soccer World Cup, cowritten by New Order (based on a theme Stephen Morris and Gillian Gilbert had composed for the BBC TV show *Reportage*) and Lily Allen's dad, Keith. It featured English soccer players Chris Waddle, Des Walker, John Barnes, Paul Gascoigne, Peter Beardsley, and Steve McMahon, whose antics in the studio did nothing for the nerves of producer Stephen Hague. In the end, drummer Stephen Morris recalled, Allen corralled them simply by being even drunker and more obnoxious.

A FACTORY SAMPLE
VARIOUS (1979)

This double EP pack, packaged in a plastic bag, was Factory's first record (FAC-1 was a poster). Its four sides—labeled Aside, Beside, Seaside, and Decide—featured two tracks each by Joy Division ("Digital" and "Glass"), The Durutti Column, and Cabaret Voltaire, and three by humorist John Dowie.

<A Certain Ratio performing on
the UK television show *The Tube*
in 1986.

∟ A record in memory of Tony Wilson,
left on the railings outside the
Haçienda club, following his death
of a heart attack in 2007 after a
battle with cancer.

∨ Durutti Column was Tony Wilson's
first signing to Factory Records.

TONY WILSON....

YOU EPITOMISED EVERYTHING
THE MUSIC INDUSTRY SHOULD BE
CREATIVE, EXCITING, FULL OF RISKS,
YOU SINGLE-HANDEDLY MADE MANCHESTER
THE CENTRE OF THE MUSICAL UNIVERSE
A GIANT AMONG MEN IN THE
MUSIC INDUSTRY, THANK-YOU
FOR ALL THE MUSIC YOU HAVE BROUGHT
TO US.
YOU WILL BE SADLY MISSED.
ANOTHER OF MY HEROES
PASSES AWAY.....

^ Revelers at the Haçienda club.

⌐ Formed by the remaining members
of Joy Division following the suicide
of vocalist Ian Curtis, New Order
was one of Factory's flagship bands.

> Depicting the rise and fall of Factory
Records from 1976 to 1992, the 2002
movie *24 Hour Party People* starred
Steve Coogan as Tony Wilson.

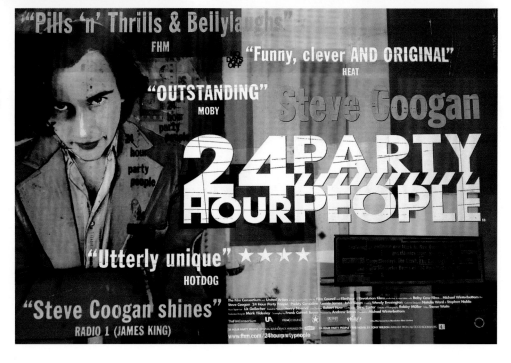

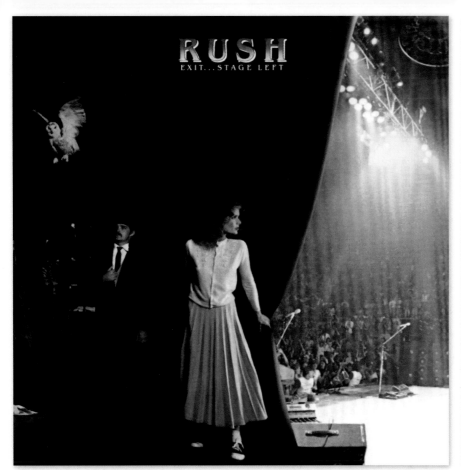

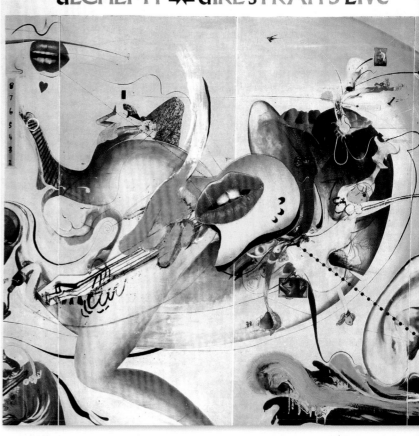

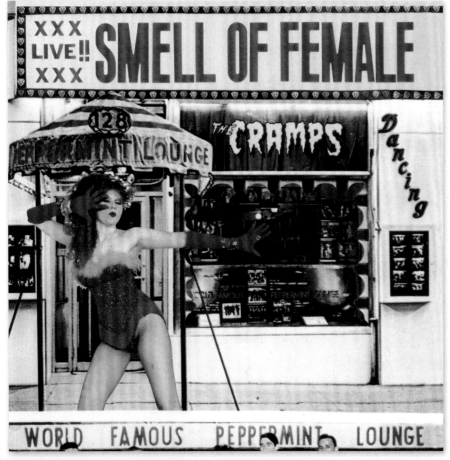

Got Live If You Want It

Touring became truly big business in the 1980s, with the stadium rock era giving us The Rolling Stones' product-sponsored American Tour 1981 (from which 1982's *Still Life* is drawn) and Live Aid. Live albums increasingly seemed like souvenirs rather than events in themselves, and huge sellers, such as Prince, The Police, Madonna, Bon Jovi, and Michael Jackson, didn't bother boarding the bandwagon in the decade that turned them into true superstars. However, a few albums blasted through the corporate stew to etch themselves into immortality.

EXIT . . . STAGE LEFT
RUSH (1981)

Of Rush's ten live sets, this double album is the best. Its title is a catchphrase of the cartoon character Snagglepuss, while its artwork is packed with references to previous Rush sleeves.

SMELL OF FEMALE
THE CRAMPS (1983)

From the *Faster, Pussycat! Kill! Kill!* Russ Meyer movie theme to a cover of The Count Five's "Psychotic Reaction," this twenty-minute mini-LP may provide all the Cramps you'll ever need.

ALCHEMY
DIRE STRAITS (1983)

On their last tour before *Brothers in Arms*, this finds Dire Straits showcasing highlights from 1982's *Love Over Gold*, and revitalizing hits, such as "Romeo and Juliet" and "Sultans of Swing."

UNDER A BLOOD RED SKY
U2 (1983)

After the same year's breakthrough *War*, this sealed U2's reputation as *the* band of the 1980s. Despite appearances, only two tracks are from their iconic show at Colorado's Red Rocks.

LIVE AFTER DEATH
IRON MAIDEN (1985)

"With its gatefold sleeve, complete with highly detailed breakdown of the World Slavery Tour," *Classic Rock* enthused, *Live After Death* "was the last great live album of the vinyl era."

LIVE MAGIC
QUEEN (1986)

Live Killers (1979) caught Queen at their most deliciously decadent. This souvenir of Freddie Mercury's final tour is a more compact set that clung to the UK chart for forty-three weeks.

1990s

Labels such as Warp Records pioneered a move toward club-oriented dance music, where vinyl remained king. Meanwhile, in Seattle, bands including Pearl Jam and Nirvana proved that live music wasn't dead. They were supported, of course, by the obligatory albums, which were still selling in the millions—although a far bigger share was now being taken by CDs.

Jungle Brothers DJ Sammy B scratching in the UK in 1990.

The genesis of Warp Records, one of the UK's leading electronic labels, can be traced back to a Leeds nightclub called the Downbeat in 1989, where DJs George Evelyn and Kevin Harper decided to make their own electro record. Calling themselves Nightmares on Wax, they pressed their own white-label single, "Dextrous." Failing to attract any label interest, they took the demo to a Sheffield record shop called Fon.

Steve Beckett and Rob Mitchell ran Fon, building on their ambitions to start a label. Dedicating themselves to electro-based music, the pair formed Warp Records, with the aid of a government-funded grant of £40 ($60) a week. They distributed five hundred copies of their first single, "Track with No Name" by the local techno group Forgemasters, from the back of a borrowed car. Their next release, the Nightmares on Wax 12-inch single "Dextrous," sold 30,000 copies and made the UK top one hundred.

The label's first big success came with its fifth release, "LFO" by LFO, two teenagers who created the bass-heavy techno classic in their bedrooms. The single sold 130,000 copies and hit number twelve in the charts in July 1990, catapulting Warp into the major leagues.

With the support of indie rock magazines, such as the *NME*, Warp became a high profile label almost overnight. Shortly after the LFO success, another Warp act, Tricky Disco, made number fourteen in the chart with their eponymous single "Tricky Disco." Sweet Exorcist (with Cabaret Voltaire member Richard Kirk) completed a trio of 1990 landmarks for Warp, with the bleep techno single "Testone." Sweet

Exorcist was also responsible for the label's first album, *C.C.E.P.*, which appeared in 1991.

As the rave scene boomed, Warp changed their perspective toward more listenable, experimental music, with a series of compilation releases under the banner of Artificial Intelligence. The first collection was released in 1992 and included key electro artists, such as Aphex Twin, Autechre, and Alex Paterson of the Orb. It ushered in the era of intelligent dance music (IDM). A much-derided term (even Warp had their reservations), IDM nevertheless summed up the more cerebral feeling of much of the music, which nodded to the work of Kraftwerk and Brian Eno while

retaining the functional aesthetic of records designed for the dance floor.

The series was an artistic success and led to individual albums by many of the participants, including *Bytes* by Black Dog, *Incunabula* by Autechre, and *Dimension Intrusion* by Richard Hawtin (as F.U.S.E), all released in 1993. Ambient techno was hugely popular across the UK dance scene, and by the mid-1990s Warp was branching out into other areas, albeit still largely experimental. The Sabres of Paradise hit the charts in 1993 with "Smokebelch II" and *Sabresonic*; drum 'n' bass specialist Squarepusher (Tom Jenkinson) signed to the label in 1995; and the acid jazz trio Red Snapper made their album debut in 1996 with the acclaimed *Prince Blimey*. In 1998, Warp signed Boards of Canada (Scottish duo Michael and Marcus Sandison), whose debut album *Music Has the Right to Children* (1998) received widespread critical praise.

To mark their tenth anniversary in 1999, Warp issued *Warp 10: Influences, Classics, Remixes*, a six-CD set that also came out as three sets of four vinyl LPs. The compilation featured early acid house and techno music that influenced the label, greatest hits from its back catalog, and remixes of familiar Warp material.

The label's cofounder Rob Mitchell died of cancer in 2001, but the company continued in ever-expanding areas, most notably with Warp Films. The record label still prospers with an artist roster including Hudson Mohawke, Brian Eno, and Rustie, plus names long associated with Warp, such as Aphex Twin, Nightmares on Wax, Squarepusher, and Autechre.

> Aphex Twin performs on stage
during day one of the Pitchfork
Music Festival at the Grande Halle
de La Villette on October 28, 2011,
in Paris, France.

∨ Nightmares on Wax Sound System
perform on the Open Air Stage at
The Big Chill Festival in August 2006.

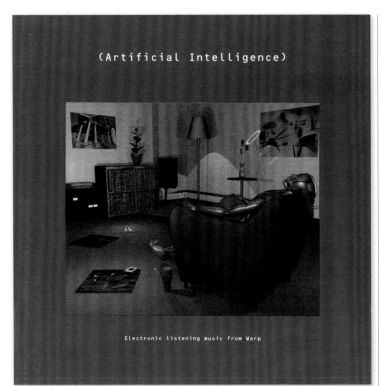

Electronic listening music from Warp

ARTIFICIAL INTELLIGENCE
VARIOUS (1992)

"Electronic music for the mind created by trans-global electronic innovators," promised the first in Warp's celebrated Artificial Intelligence series. Its cover featured a robot with Kraftwerk's *Autobahn*, Pink Floyd's *Dark Side of the Moon*, and Warp's own *Pioneers of the Hypnotic Groove* (issued the preceding year). The equally impressive contents kicked off with Aphex Twin (in his one-off guise The Dice Man), and continued with Autechre, Musicology, I.A.O. (future Black Dog man Ken Downie), techno pioneer Speedy J, UP! (Richie Hawtin), and The Orb's Dr. Alex Paterson.

TRICKY DISCO
TRICKY DISCO (1990)

Alongside LFO's own self-titled single, husband and wife Michael Wells and Lee Newman, as Tricky Disco, led Warp's invasion of the UK top twenty. The duo recorded as Greater Than One and John + Julie, among other pseudonyms, before Newman's untimely death from cancer in 1995.

PRINCE BLIMEY
RED SNAPPER (1996)

Warp indulged the jazz, breakbeat, and dub-influenced instrumental trio with a double LP debut. "Warp was the only label that signed us completely for the music," guitarist David Ayers pointed out at the time. "A lot of other labels were saying, 'Well, they will be very good when they've got a vocalist.'"

MUSIC HAS THE RIGHT TO CHILDREN
BOARDS OF CANADA (1998)

"By the start of the nineties we were making melodic ambient electronic music," Boards of Canada's Marcus Eoin told *De:Bug Musik*, "and it felt to us that almost nobody else out there at the time was interested in melody. I think that is why we gravitated toward the artists on Warp." After releases on Skam and their own Music70, Eoin and Mike Sandison's Warp debut jump-started one of the label's most enduring success stories, culminating in 2013's *Tomorrow's Harvest* crashing transatlantic top twenties. *Music* remains a fan favorite, thanks to cuts such as "Roygbiv."

boards of canada
music has the right to children

RICHARD D. JAMES ALBUM
APHEX TWIN (1996)

Aphex Twin—born Richard David James—commemorated his transition from ambient to a more jungle-inflected sound with a set that lasted barely more than half an hour. "I took longer working on this than on any of my other albums," he protested to *Sonic Press*. "It's about quality, not quantity." To listeners alarmed by its frenetic nature, he suggested simply slowing it down. "Buy it on vinyl," he proposed. "Instead of thirty-three minutes, you actually get forty-five, you understand? And there you have it, an album of standard length."

VENUS NO. 17
SQUAREPUSHER (2004)

Warp mainstay Tom Jenkinson was courted by rival dance labels. "R&S was asking about me," he told *Perfect Sound Forever*, "but I didn't sign with them because they're a pretty shit label. I've never really been that much of a fan of Ninja Tune. I went with Warp because I was more into their music."

TESTONE REMIXES
SWEET EXORCIST (1990)

Sweet Exorcist, notes Discogs.com, were a "seminal 'bleep techno' collaboration between Richard H Kirk and DJ Parrot (Richard Parrott), taking the name from the title of the *Sweet Exorcist* LP by Curtis Mayfield." This remix EP features artwork from a video made by Pulp's Jarvis Cocker.

A WORD OF SCIENCE . . .
NIGHTMARES ON WAX (1991)

Despite its ominous subtitle *The 1st & Final Chapter*, this debut LP began a two-decades-and-counting run of albums by Nightmares on Wax. "Just from my experiences at Warp," cofounder George Evelyn told FACT, "they've allowed the artist to express themselves and allowed them to develop. I don't think there's 100 labels that are like that—there's only a few. . . . The real key to Warp's masterstroke has been, first of all, signing good artists, but then allowing that artist to express themselves. Because at the end of the day, it's not what you are, it's what you are becoming."

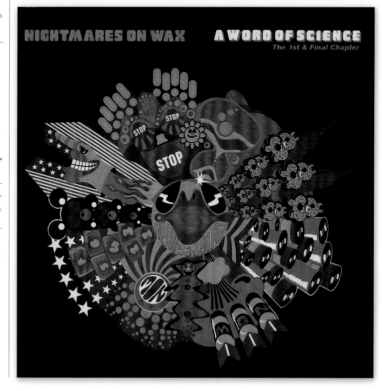

⌃ Mark Bell of LFO, whose albums *Frequencies* (1991), *Advance* (1996), and *Sheath* (2003) were key in pioneering IDM and acid house.

⟨ Rob Mitchell, cofounder of Warp, outside the label's shop and headquarters in Sheffield in 1992.

> Autechre (Rob Brown and Sean Booth) signed with Warp in 1993, following their inclusion on Warp's seminal Artificial Intelligence compilation in 1992.

> Squarepusher performs at HARD Summer music festival at Los Angeles Historical Park on August 4, 2012, in Los Angeles, California.

> Operating between the mid-1960s and 1981, Wigan Casino was a key venue for northern soul music.

⌐ Wigan Casino in 1977. In 1978, *Billboard* magazine voted the nightclub "The Best Disco in the World."

⌐ A poster for one of Wigan Casino's all-nighters.

∨ Open from 1963 to 1971 and a pioneer of Northern Soul, the Twisted Wheel nightclub in Manchester was an important forerunner for 1990s club culture.

THE TWISTED WHEEL CLUB

6 WHITWORTH STREET, MANCHESTER 1

Tel. CENtral 1179

presents

SATURDAY - Forthcoming Attractions

JANUARY

6th THE FERRIS WHEEL
13th LUCAS & THE MIKE COTTON SOUND
20th GENO WASHINGTON & THE
       RAM JAM BAND
27th EDWIN STARR

FEBRUARY

3rd JIMMY JAMES & THE VAGABONDS
10th JAMES & BOBBY PURIFY
17th ROBERT PARKER
24th AMBOY DUKES

ADVANCE TICKETS NOW AVAILABLE
or
PAY AT THE DOOR

POSTAL BOOKINGS ACCEPTABLE (S.A.E.)
No Parking on Whitworth Street, or Minshull
Street South PLEASE
CORPORATION CAR PARK AVAILABLE
Aytoun Street, Every Night (No Charge)

BLUES & SOUL: 151   27

WIGAN CASINO
ALL-NIGHTER

Visit The Heart Of Soul
Every Sat / Sun Morning 2am-8am (Members only)
featuring

RUSS and RICHARD and Lots of Guest D.J.s
playing the top Soul Sounds

Also Every Wednesday (7.30pm — 11pm) & Friday (7.30 — 12 midnight)

"NORTHERN SOUL NIGHTS"
"featuring RUSS plus Guest D.J.s (No Membership Required)
Playing the Top Sounds

The
Brilliant "NEW"
Night Owl
Allnighter Badge
Now Available
Price 60p + SAE

Don't miss out on our other
Two Great Badges . . . .
60p Each + SAE

"Keep The Faith" & "Heart Of Soul"
'Car Stickers' also available
price 30p each + SAE

TO JOIN OUR CLUB
(FREE MEMBERSHIP)
SEND FORM BELOW TO ARRIVE AT LEAST 48 HOURS BEFORE YOU DO

Post to: WIGAN CASINO SOUL CLUB, STATION ROAD, WIGAN WN1 1YQ, LANCASHIRE
              W.C.S.C. APPLICATION FORM FOR MEMBERSHIP

I (name) ....
of (address) ....
do apply for membership to Wigan Casino Soul Club. I am over 18 years of age and agree to abide by the
rules of the club.

(P.S. Don't forget Beachcomber Soul Snack Bar open from 12 midnight to 2 a.m. and 6 a.m. — 10 a.m. for breakfasts (ed). Casino entrance)

We can trace the origins of 1990s club culture back to the British northern soul phenomenon of the 1970s, when DJs began to take precedence over live music. Northern soul grew out of 1960s clubs, such as the Twisted Wheel in Manchester, where the house DJs would play lesser-known American soul records between live bands. The style of music was basically an extension of the Motown sound, and there was an active mission on the part of DJs and fans to discover rare 45s that nobody else was listening to.

By the early 1970s, key venues, such as the Golden Torch in Stoke-on-Trent and the Wigan Casino, had begun to present soul all-nighters for the thousands of fans who had by then evolved their own look and dance routines. Many of the DJs were moving away from a pure post-Motown sound, embracing even harder-to-get labels and artists in the process. The trading of second-hand vinyl was a major feature of the northern soul events, usually in the venue's reception area. (Even when rival formats later seemed to be

Club Culture

taking over from records, northern soul remained a bastion in the preservation of vinyl and its subsequent revival.)

The mid-1980s brought a trend toward larger venues for the types of all-night gatherings that northern soul had pioneered. Again, the Manchester area was at the center of the movement; with the Haçienda club as a permanent flagship, a circuit of informal warehouse spaces began to be used as all-night venues, concentrating on electronic dance music, acid jazz, and early house records. These raves attracted audiences of thousands, as DJ-driven house music caught on across Great Britain. Empty spaces of all kinds were requisitioned for unofficial acid-house parties, with hallucinogenic drugs (particularly ecstasy) adding a psychedelic edge to the proceedings.

The house genre had originated in Chicago in the early 1980s, and records usually featured repetitive beats created by drum machines and synthesized bass parts—not unlike club disco, but with an electronic, minimalist feel. House music quickly caught on commercially, with big hits across

Europe. Typical were "Pump Up the Volume" (1987) by M/A/R/R/S, featuring mixes by DJs Chris C. J. Mackintosh and Dave Dorrell, and "Theme from S'Express" (1988) by S'Express, which both topped the UK charts. By the end of the decade, major labels had offered deals to many Chicago DJs and other house music artists, and the style was adopted by mainstream artists, including Madonna, Björk, and Janet Jackson.

The house club scene, meanwhile, was burgeoning across Europe, with rave venues opening in Germany, Italy, and elsewhere. The fall of the Berlin Wall in 1989 triggered techno house parties in what had been East Berlin, and by the early 1990s a permanent scene was based around a trio of clubs: E-Werk, Der Bunker, and Tresor. Warehouse parties had also taken hold in Australia, in the major cities of Sydney and Melbourne.

⤊ The main dancefloor at the Haçienda on the club's tenth birthday in 1992.

⌃ Two clubbers being searched by members of security as they enter the Haçienda in the early 1990s.

‹ Clubbers at The Fridge nightclub in Brixton, London, in 1997.

« Partygoers on the dancefloor at a Desire rave in 1995.

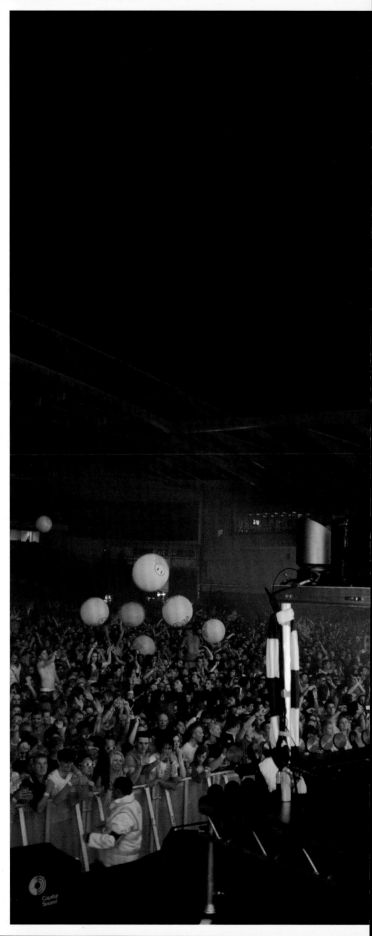

⌃⌃ Trance DJ Tiesto overlooks the crowd at Cream at Amnesia in Ibiza in 2005.

⌃ Paul Oakenfold DJing in London in 1998.

› Fatboy Slim performs in Brighton in June 2012.

≫ A crowd dances at London's Fabric nightclub, voted World Number 1 in *DJ Magazine*'s Top 100 Clubs Poll in 2007 and 2008.

Initiated by British ex-pats and American DJs visiting Europe, rave culture in the United States began to take off in the late 1980s. Major events in the early 1990s included the Impact electronic dance festival in Pennsylvania in 1993 and the New York Storm Raves organized by DJs Frankie Bones and Heather Heart. Other key raves in the country were lavish parties thrown by San Diego's Global Underground Network, whose Opium and Narnia events attracted 60,000 people. Narnia was hailed as the "Woodstock of Generation X" and *LIFE* magazine voted it Event of the Year in 1995.

However, disc-dominated rave culture didn't get any more spectacular than the scene that developed on the Mediterranean island of Ibiza. Huge clubs, such as Manumission, Pacha, and Amnesia, attracted young people and top DJs from all over the world, with acts such as Paul Oakenfold and Fat Boy Slim as the star summer attractions. Amnesia, in particular, became an international mecca for dance music fans; taken over in 1996 by Joseph Mullen, founder of the famed Liverpool dance club Cream, it won Best Global Club in 1996, 1997, 1998, and 1999 at the International Dance Music Awards. The huge success of this turntable-driven dance club scene was instrumental in ensuring the survival of vinyl through the 1990s.

S·U·B P·O·P

Sub Pop Records was inspired by the notion that nearly every major movement in rock music had a regional basis and an independent label to support it, as evidenced by the likes of Motown Records and the Detroit sound, Chess and Chicago R&B, and Sun Records and Memphis rockabilly. Focusing on the local alternative rock scene emerging in late 1980s Seattle, Sub Pop was the pioneer of grunge music.

In 1979, student Bruce Pavitt started a fanzine called *Subterranean Pop*, specializing in news of independent record labels. Soon he was releasing compilation cassette tapes under the Sub Pop banner, with the first—1982's *Sub Pop Number Five*—selling more than two thousand copies. In July 1986, the first Sub Pop album appeared, the compilation *Sub Pop 100*. It featured one track each by thirteen acts, including Sonic Youth, Skinny Puppy, and singer-songwriter Steve Albini.

One of Sub Pop's earliest grunge releases was Green River's EP *Dry As a Bone*, in July 1987. (Green River vocalist Mark Arm is generally credited with introducing the term grunge in 1981, describing his then-band Mr. Epp and the Calculations as "Pure grunge! Pure noise! Pure shit!") Also in July 1987, the label released Soundgarden's debut single "Hunted Down," which was followed in October by the band's first EP, the six-track *Screaming Life*. Suddenly, the fledgling label was in business.

By the end of the year, Pavitt was joined by Jonathan Poneman, who had helped fund the Soundgarden debut. In August 1988 came another major release, Mudhoney's debut single "Touch Me I'm Sick," followed a few months later

by the band's EP *Superfuzz Bigmuff*. Formed by members of the disbanded Green River, Mudhoney was one of the biggest names on the Seattle scene. Though not graced with massive

© 1971 Bizarre Music Inc. & Alive Enterprises (BMI)

℗ 1991 Sub Pop SP121 C

Is It My Body
(A. Cooper, D. Dunway, M.Bruce, N. Smith, G. Buxton)
SONIC YOUTH

Mfg. by ERIKA Records - Cerritos CA. (213) 926 - 8992

commercial success, their ten studio albums exerted a huge influence on grunge and alt-rock.

Sub Pop was always very vinyl oriented in its output, and by the end of the 1980s had amassed a large catalog of singles, EPs, and albums. Producer Jack Endino (responsible for seventy-five releases on the label in its first two years) crafted a cheap but effective trademark sound that ran through all the output. To its growing fan base, the Sub Pop sound was the sound of Seattle.

A major factor in the growth of the label's audience was the introduction of the Sub Pop Singles Club in November 1988. A mail-order subscription service that supplied fans with two singles a month, it had more than two thousand subscribers by 1990. The first release on the service was "Love Buzz," the debut single by a new band called Nirvana. In June 1989, Nirvana released their first album, *Bleach*; popular with college radio stations, it had initial sales of 40,000 copies and went on to sell nearly two million in the United States alone. By the time of their second studio album, *Nevermind* (1991), Nirvana had left Sub Pop for the mainstream world of David Geffen's DGC label.

Sub Pop, meanwhile, attracted the attention of the UK music press. The British rock media and rock public became fascinated by grunge and the Seattle sound, epitomized by the label and its bands. Throughout the 1990s, Sub Pop represented the cutting edge of American indie rock, although some of the label's most successful signings moved to major mainstream labels in the wake of chart-busting sales figures.

Sub Pop gave up its status as an independent when it sold a forty-nine percent share to the giant Warner Bros. company in 1995. Pavitt departed acrimoniously the following year and some poor business choices saw the label's fortunes take a downturn in the late 1990s. After returning to its roots post-millennium, Sub Pop reinstated its reputation as a force to be reckoned with. Current names on the label's roster include Seattle folk band Fleet Foxes, Australian guitar band Deaf Wish, and the New Zealand comedy-rock group Flight of the Conchords.

> Left to right: Chad Channing, Kris Novoselic, and Kurt Cobain, in an early portrait of Nirvana taken in Seattle in May 1988.

⌐ The Afghan Whigs signed to Sub Pop in 1988 after releasing their first album independently.

∨ Mudhoney's early releases on Sub Pop exerted a huge influence on the Seattle music scene, inspiring the dirty, high-distortion sound that was central to grunge.

DICKNAIL
HOLE (1991)

Initially a bigger deal than Nirvana, Courtney Love's band Hole made just one single for Sub Pop: the raging "antimisogynism anthem" "Dicknail." Love was influenced by Mudhoney's *Superfuzz Bigmuff* (1988) and claimed to have bought a single by fellow Sub Pop act Cat Butt in preference to one by Nirvana.

SCREAMING LIFE
SOUNDGARDEN (1987)

"Sub Pop was still in the 'planning' stages," recalled producer Jack Endino of this formative EP, "so Soundgarden was spending their own money at a terrifying fifteen bucks an hour. . . . Matt Cameron, who starved for a year in Skin Yard before leaving amicably and ending up in Soundgarden, is credited cryptically with 'bonus tubs' on the original vinyl. . . . You can hear Chris (Cornell) experimenting with his singing as he starts to realize how much range he has to play with. 'Nothing to Say' was the song that made us all look at each other and go, 'Uh, holy crap, how did we do *this*?'"

THE SEBADOH
SEBADOH (1991)

"Being a scrappy indie, we had to work with bands nobody would touch," Sub Pop founder Bruce Pavitt told *Pitchfork*. "With their crazy lo-fi aesthetic, no major was gonna go near Sebadoh, because so much of what they were all about was their approach to recording. Of course, the first thing majors wanted to do was stick you in a big studio that they owned, and pick back their advance and put it into their own pocket. . . . I think Sebadoh was a perfect example of how we creatively went around the majors. And of course, the Sebadoh records sold really well."

BLEACH
NIRVANA (1989)

"In our press releases, we would announce that the Nirvana album was gonna go double platinum and stuff like that," Bruce Pavitt told *Pitchfork*, "never believing for a minute that would actually happen. . . . I remember *Bleach* in its first year selling forty thousand copies, which was amazing."

NO CITIES TO LOVE
SLEATER-KINNEY (2015)

The first album in a decade by the influential Olympia, Washington, trio found them back on Sub Pop, who issued 2005's *The Woods*. The label had teased the trio's return with the new "Bury Our Friends" on a seven-inch single included with the previous year's retrospective vinyl box set *Start Together*.

SLIVER
NIRVANA (1990)

Sub Pop's best known act issued only one LP and three singles on the label. While the first of the latter—1988's "Love Buzz"—is notable mostly for being the band's debut, "Sliver" showed their true potential. Issued on a bewildering variety of colored vinyl, it showcased the rumbling riffing and singalong songwriting of "Chris Novoselic" and "Kurdt Kobain," as they then credited themselves. In Nirvana's Spinal Tap-esque period before the appointment of Dave Grohl, Mudhoney's Dan Peters drummed on "Sliver," while Chad Channing manned the stool for the B side, "Dive."

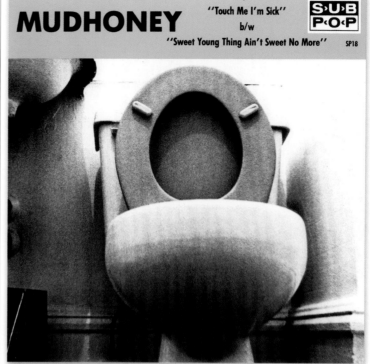

TOUCH ME I'M SICK
MUDHONEY (1988)

"The big stinkin' grunge hit!," crowed Sub Pop, who first issued it on brown vinyl in a plain white sleeve. "The main riff of that song could be traced back to the Yardbirds' 'Happenings Ten Years Time Ago'," front man Mark Arm admitted to Songfacts. "As far as the lyrics go, the line, 'Touch me, I'm sick,' really struck me as being a funny thing to say, and we built verses around that." At the close of 1988, Sub Pop issued a single that thumbed its nose at Christmas: on the A side, Sonic Youth covered "Touch Me I'm Sick," while the B side featured Mudhoney taking on "Halloween."

SUB POP 200
VARIOUS (1988)

Issued as a box set of three twelve-inch singles, Sub Pop 200 featured the yet to be huge Nirvana ("Spank Thru"), Screaming Trees (a cover of Hendrix's "Love or Confusion") and Soundgarden (the scathing "Sub Pop Rock City"). The sleeve was by Charles Burns, later the creator of the graphic novel *Black Hole*.

SUB POP SINGLES CLUB

☆

Hey loser. Wanna find some action? Tired of being left out? Here at SUB POP we've just started a special club for lonely record collectors like yourself: THE SUB POP SINGLES CLUB. Every month we'll send you a limited edition 45. All you have to do is SEND US YOUR MONEY. $35.00 for a full year, $20.00 for 6 months. Your subscription begins the month we receive your $$$.

☆

OUR RELENTLESS SCHEDULE:

NOV 90 **Poison Idea**
DEC 90 **Reverend Horton Heat**
JAN 91 **Nirvana/Fluid**
FEB 91 **Velvet Monkeys**
MAR 91 **Unrest**
APR 91 **Shonen Knife**

Canadian: *$45, **$25   Overseas: *$55, **$30

YES. I am lonely and I want to join your SINGLES CLUB. Here is my money.
☐ $35 Full Year* ☐ $20 6 Months**

NAME _____

ADDRESS _____

_____

SUB POP:
P.O. Box 20645,
Seattle, WA 98102
85

Mark Arm of Mudhoney performs on stage in 1990.

The Sub Pop Singles Club released 62 records over five years, with a similarly eclectic mix of tracks to those Pavitt used on his early Subterranean Pop compilations.

Tad Doyle of grunge band Tad performs on stage at the Islington Powerhaus in London in April 1991.

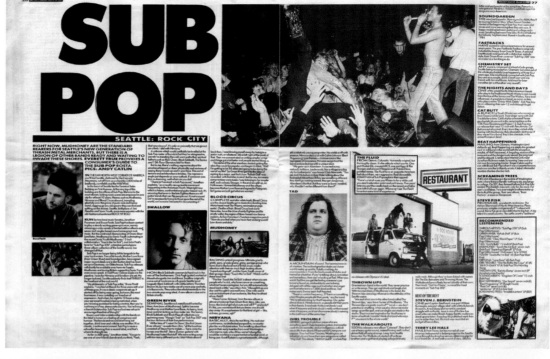

> Everett True's guide to the Sub Pop roster in *Melody Maker*, published on March 18, 1989.

> Fleet Foxes signed to Sub Pop in 2008, the year in which they released their critically acclaimed first full length album, *Fleet Foxes*.

"There's no school to go to for some of the weird shit that happens," Eddie Vedder marveled to *Rolling Stone* in fall of 1993. "The fucking weirdness of it all." Pearl Jam's *Ten* had begun to outsell Nirvana's *Nevermind*, the two having debuted a month apart in 1991. And although Metallica and Guns N' Roses were bigger than both, there was pressure on Vedder and Kurt Cobain to deliver statements befitting their (unwanted) status as spokesmen for the grunge generation.

Both proved defiant. Cobain filled *Nevermind*'s abrasive follow-up *In Utero* with bitter lyrics, such as track title "Radio Friendly Unit Shifter," while Pearl Jam's title for *Ten*'s sequel was *Five Against One*. "That title represented a lot of struggles that you go through trying to make a record," guitarist Stone Gossard explained. "Your own soul versus everybody else's."

Five weeks in the studio between March and May 1993 with producer Brendan O'Brian yielded an intense set that ranged from acoustic laments ("Elderly Woman Behind the Counter in a Small Town," "Daughter") to cranked-up rock reminiscent of The Who and MC5, with evocatively terse titles: "Go," Blood," "Rats," "Leash," "Animal," and "Indifference."

Vs.

Indecision about the title illustrates the pressure on Pearl Jam. *Five Against One* had beaten out guitarist Mike McCready's suggestion of *A Shark in Blood Waters*, bassist Jeff Ament's *Paul Is Dead*, and Vedder's *Al* (after occultist Aleister Crowley). However, in the weeks leading to its release, the album became *Pearl Jam* and, eventually, *Vs.* (i.e. "versus," referencing a recurring theme of conflict). The eleventh-hour final change was the reason that the cover bears no title.

Eager to go against the grain, Vedder insisted the album initially appear on only vinyl, with the CD following several days later. Had this not happened, *Vs.* might have knocked *In Utero* off the US top spot—as it was, Meat Loaf's *Bat Out of Hell II* provided an incongruously old-school buffer. *Vs.* set a new yardstick for the SoundScan era, shifting 950,000 copies in its first week. Vedder duly pushed the envelope even farther with 1994's *Vitalogy*, which was introduced by the ode-to-vinyl "Spin the Black Circle" and released on LP two weeks before the CD. The latter enabled them to make the biggest jump to number one—from number 173—in the history of the US album chart. Vedder, Ament explained, "loves vinyl . . . the way it looks, sounds, and feels."

pearl jam

< Jeff Ament laughs at singer
  Eddie Vedder on stage during
  a 1993 concert.

≪ The vinyl version of the album
  featured different cover art to the
  CD and cassette.

∧ Pearl Jam at the 10th Annual
  MTV Video Music Awards on
  September 2, 1993.

Turntable Treasures

When CDs took over as the most popular audio format in the 1990s, manufacturers turned their focus toward super high-quality turntables that reflected a design trend for "on the outside" engineering, with companies producing Rolls Royce versions of their classics for an increasingly exclusive group of vinyl enthusiasts.

« Michell Engineering launched their flagship Orbe in 1995 in response to the success of the GyroDec model and demands for a higher-end product from its customers.

L Named to mark three decades since SME produced its first tone arm, the SME Series 30 was released in 1990. It took just three-and-a-half months for the design to go from concept to reality.

< The PDX 2000 was released by Vestax in 1999 as part of a flagship range of DJ turntables that was intended to compete with the popular Technics SL1210 and SL1200.

∨ Launched in 1991, the Thorens TD180 was one of several turntables released by the company in the 1990s. The first TD model, the 124, was introduced by Thorens in 1957.

Got Live If You Want It

The much-maligned MTV reinvigorated the live album genre with its *Unplugged* series. Paul McCartney was the first to immortalize his performance as an album, 1991's *Unplugged* *(The Official Bootleg)* giving him his highest US chart position since 1983. Even this paled beside Eric Clapton's *Unplugged* in 1992, whose ten million sales in the US alone truly busted open the floodgates: Neil Young, 10,000 Maniacs, Bob Dylan, Alanis Morrissette, Kiss, Jay-Z, Lauryn Hill, Bryan Adams, and Alicia Keys are among those who followed in ol' Slowhand's footsteps.

FLASHPOINT
THE ROLLING STONES (1991)

The vinyl edition of this souvenir of the Stones' Steel Wheels/Urban Jungle comeback packed fourteen songs on a single album, including the in-studio newbies "Highwire" and "Sex Drive."

WELD
NEIL YOUNG (1991)

Neil Young and Crazy Horse created one of *the* great live albums with 1979's *Live Rust*. *Weld* is a superb sequel, especially because vinyl buyers dodged the CD's unlistenable bonus disc, *Arc*.

MTV UNPLUGGED . . .
NIRVANA (1994)

If you experience Nirvana's finest hour on vinyl, flipping the disc provides respite after "Polly." It was toppled from the US top spot by another MTV live album: The Eagles' *Hell Freezes Over*.

DECADE OF AGGRESSION
SLAYER (1991)

Produced by Rick Rubin, this is a defiantly old-school double set that cherry-picks three shows to create a punishing whole. "It was kinda cool," said guitarist Kerry King. "We were proud of it."

MTV UNPLUGGED EP
MARIAH CAREY (1992)

More commonly available on CD and tape, this sneaked out on vinyl in Europe and Brazil. Its hit highlight was a last-minute addition to Carey's set: a cover of The Jackson 5's "I'll Be There."

MTV UNPLUGGED
ALICE IN CHAINS (1996)

Less revelatory than the Nirvana album—Alice had already issued two acoustic sets—this set (a double LP in its vinyl incarnation) is nonetheless a beautiful epitaph for singer Layne Staley.

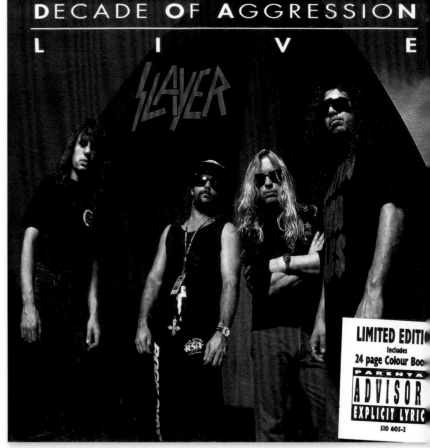

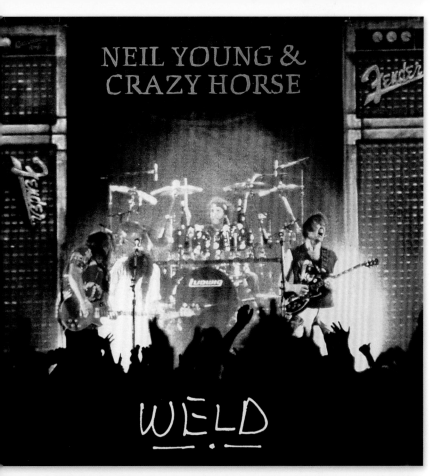

NEIL YOUNG & CRAZY HORSE

Fender

WELD

NIRVANA

MTV UNPLUGGED
IN NEW YORK

MARIAH CAREY

LIVE EP
INCLUDES THE HIT SINGLE
"I'LL BE THERE"
PLUS
6 LIVE TRACKS INCLUDING
"VISION OF LOVE"
"CAN'T LET GO"
"MAKE IT HAPPEN"
AND "EMOTIONS"
471869 1

MTV UNPLUGGED EP

ALICE IN CHAINS

MTV UNPLUGGED

2000s

Fanatical collectors, vinyl champions like Jack White, and a worldwide network of dedicated retailers from New York to New Zealand have ensured that vinyl has survived, despite the prophets of doom who predicted its demise. With the support of vinyl manufacturers who weathered the storm, the format is now enjoying its biggest boom in many years.

> Neil Young lays down a track in the Third Man Records record booth on *The Tonight Show* on May 12, 2014. The refurbished 1947 Voice-o-Graph machine records up to two minutes of audio and dispenses a one-of-a-kind six-inch phonograph disc to the user.

High Fidelity

There was a time, not so long ago, when every small town had at least one record store dedicated to selling vinyl, and later CDs, with no competition from unseen purveyors of "invisible" music via the Internet. Sadly only a fraction now survive, but those that do are in the vanguard of the vinyl revival. Here is just a small selection of some of the best disc dealers, record retailers, and vinyl vendors on the planet. In the immortal words of The Paranoids, "Come meet me at the record store / We'll scowl at the suckers in the pop rock aisle . . . "

ROUGH TRADE EAST
LONDON, UK

The first Rough Trade store opened in London in 1976. With its sister company Rough Trade Records, it was at the cutting edge of punk. Four decades later, Rough Trade East—the scene of shows by Marianne Faithfull, Blur, and Vampire Weekend—sells everything from chart titles to discs by unsigned bands, and more than one-quarter of its stock is vinyl. "Great stores like Rough Trade adapt," noted Public Enemy's Chuck D. "They understand the marketplace, and they style themselves as a specialist boutique shop."

TOWER RECORDS
TOKYO, JAPAN

The Japanese arm of the worldwide Tower Records chain went independent in 2002—so, when the empire collapsed in 2006, the stores in Japan stayed open. The flagship of eighty-five stores across the country, boasting nine floors packed with music, the Tokyo store is said to be one of world's the biggest record outlets. "The Godzilla of the world's record stores," marveled the *Los Angeles Times*. It also features a book store, café, and space for live performances, plus a video-streaming venue in the basement.

THE THING
NEW YORK, USA

With tens of thousands of records in stock, the basement of this Brooklyn store is one vast treasure trove for those prepared to scrabble through stack upon stack of vinyl. Owner Larry Fisher acquires records from auctions, estate sales, and classified ads, which are then crammed on the shelves in a haphazard order. Stock constantly shifts around the store, so each visit brings the prospect of new discoveries. Not all the records are in the best condition, but, with everything priced at $2, who's complaining?

AMOEBA MUSIC
LOS ANGELES, USA

Independent Californian chain Amoeba Music was founded in 1990 in Berkeley by a community of music lovers that wanted a better place for music than a corporate chain store. Today, the company has three stores, with the Hollywood one renowned for its sheer size. Located on Sunset Boulevard, it occupies 24,000 square feet (2,230 square meters), with more than 100,000 new and used items on vinyl, CD, and cassette. Stock changes daily and includes everything from the top forty to underground rock, hip-hop, soul, electronica, jazz, world music, roots, and experimental music. The store has hosted performances by artists ranging from Jane's Addiction and PJ Harvey to Donovan and Elvis Costello. It was the venue for Paul McCartney's live recording *Amoeba's Secret*, issued as a limited edition vinyl EP in 2007 and available as the extended *Live in Los Angeles* via his website.

12 TONAR
REYKJAVÍC, ICELAND

Famous among classical music enthusiasts for possibly the best classical selection of any record shop in the world, the modestly sized store also caters for rock, jazz, and other tastes. The back room features a cozy listening lounge, and the store regularly hosts live gigs and recitals. "People trust us to take them on a journey and steer them," cofounder Lárus Jóhannesson told *Gramaphone*. "There's so much music to explore, and we have a lot of people visit us who are really interested but don't have the time or the capacity to find what might be right next to them. That's where we come in." Catering to a mix of students, skateboarders, lecturers, musicians, politicians, and Iceland Symphony Orchestra subscribers, 12 Tonar also serves as a label for local Icelandic bands, and counts artists such as Bjork among its clientele.

MABU VINYL
CAPE TOWN, SOUTH AFRICA

Established in 2001 by Jacques Vosloo, Mabu Vinyl is renowned as the launchpad for 2012's Academy Award-winning movie *Searching for Sugar Man*, about co-owner Stephen Segerman's quest to track down singer-songwriter Sixto Diaz Rodriguez. Mabu's huge selection of vinyl of all genres—on LPs, seven-inch and twelve-inch singles, and even 78s—is complemented by a stock of music magazines, CDs, cassettes, DVDs, videos, and books. Another of the store's wondrous aspects is its entirely incongruous location in Cape Town's otherwise cosmopolitan and touristy Gardens—hardly the most obvious place, even in this hipster era, for a repository of vintage vinyl. One of the editors of this book, however, has spent happy hours trawling its racks and is forever grateful for it selling him cut-price Sarah McLachlan tapes for a road trip in a car equipped only with a cassette deck.

∧ Zero Freitas looking at one of the records stored on the shelves of his personal collection in his house in São Paulo.

⌐ Freitas stands on a pile of records in one of the warehouses he uses to store more than three million records in São Paulo.

〉 A selection of records from Freitas's personal collection.

Brazilian businessman Zero Freitas has taken obsessive vinyl collecting to a new extreme: his ongoing mission is to buy all the vinyl in the world. At more than six million records by early 2015, his collection is the largest of its kind.

Freitas first caught the record bug when his father bought him a record player and two hundred discs for his birthday. By the time he left high school, he had three thousand records, and before he was thirty that total had expanded tenfold.

As the bus business he inherited from his father boomed, so his collecting intensified. He ran an anonymous advertisement in *Billboard* magazine that read: "We BUY any record collection. Any style of music. We pay HIGHER prices than anyone else." Soon collectors were getting in touch via the network of agents who acted on his behalf.

Freitas's next move was to target record retailers who were going out of business. In 2012, he bought up the stock of 200,000 records from Colony Records in New York's Times Square. The following year, he bought the entire collection of Murray Gershenz, proprietor of the Music Man Murray store in Los Angeles, after Gershenz died at the age of ninety-one.

Zero Freitas

227

One record store owner-turned-collector was Paul Mawhinney, who, for more than forty years, had accumulated three million LPs and 45s. He chanced upon Freitas's advertisement in *Billboard* and in the fall of 2013, eight 53-feet (16-meter) semitrailers collected the vinyl from Mawhinney's warehouse for shipment to Brazil.

Freitas now maintains a team of agents around the world. He recently acquired 100,000 albums of Cuban music, which he believes is almost everything ever recorded there. The range of music is limitless and dates back to the earliest days of 78s. Interns are cleaning, photographing, and cataloging each item at a rate of about 500 records a day—it would take more than thirty years to cover the collection as it currently stands, disregarding the 20,000 new records that arrive each month.

Inspired by music archivist Bob George's ARChive of Contemporary Music in New York—a nonprofit research facility with more than two million records—Freitas has started a similar venture called Emporium Musical. He plans to convert his warehouse into a public listening library and make records that are duplicated (up to thirty percent of the collection) available for patrons to borrow and listen to at home.

One of vinyl's greatest champions, Jack White excelled even his own demanding standards with the landmark LP *Lazaretto*, released on CD and vinyl in June 2014. It was the second solo studio album from the White Stripes front man on his Third Man label, following 2012's *Blunderbuss*.

Although *Lazaretto* was also available on CD and as a download, it was on the vinyl format that White pulled out all the stops. The Ultra LP edition of the release on 180-gram vinyl featured some audacious technical tricks: two tracks were hidden under the inner label on each side of the record, one playing at 78 rpm and the other at 45 rpm, making it a 3-speed album; the A side of the LP played from the inside outward; dual-groove technology allowed for an acoustic or electric intro on "Just One Drink," depending on where the needle was placed, with the grooves meeting for the main song; both sides ended with continuous locked grooves; side B was pressed with a matte finish, giving the appearance of an unplayed 78; and a dead wax area on side A featured a hand-etched hologram that appeared on the record's surface when it was being played.

Lazaretto

For the opener, "Three Women," White harked back to "Three Women Blues" (1928) by the legendary Georgia bluesman Blind Willie McTell, to whom he gave a cowriting credit. The influence of the blues figured throughout, from the instrumental grunge of "High Ball Stepper" to the scorching mandolin and fiddle on "That Black Bat Licorice," via the sparse bar-room piano of "Would You Fight for My Love?," the teen-angst yearning of "Alone in My Home," and the black-humored hip-hop parody of the title track.

The album was universally acclaimed and a huge commercial success. It debuted at number one in the *Billboard* chart, selling nearly 140,000 copies in the first week. With 40,000 of those copies on vinyl, it set the record for most vinyl albums sold in a week since comparisons were first tracked in 1991. The album was nominated for Best Alternative Music Album, and "Lazaretto" was nominated for Best Rock Song at the 2015 Grammy Awards, where White won Best Rock Performance. With sales of 87,000 by the end of 2014, *Lazaretto* was the top-selling vinyl LP in the United States that year. A key milestone in the renaissance of vinyl, its success is a definite indicator that the vinyl revival is here to stay.

‹ The songs on *Lazaretto* were inspired in part by short stories and plays that White wrote when he was nineteen and rediscovered while making the record.

« White had previously covered songs by Blind Willie McTell with the White Stripes, whose 2000 album *De Stijl* was dedicated to the bluesman.

∨ The album's cover is reflected in the hologram of two angels that appears when the Ultra LP is being played.

Keepers of the Flame

Many saw the huge impact of the CD in the 1990s as heralding the death of vinyl. But although vinyl's market share decreased, it was still around in significant quantities. Jukebox sales hardly changed, with the majority of machines still playing seven-inch singles, while most radio stations played twelve-inch singles and almost every turntable DJ used vinyl. There were also numerous music fans who simply preferred the vinyl format over CD. For them, small record companies were set up to produce good-quality pressings of both vintage classics and new releases. These specialized labels kept the vinyl flame alive before the mainstream companies began regularly releasing vinyl again.

MOBILE FIDELITY
CALIFORNIA, USA (1977)

The American company was established in 1977 by a group of dedicated audiophiles, with the aim of faithfully reproducing high-fidelity recordings in the context of whatever changes came about in audio delivery systems. They made their name with an ultrahigh-quality version of Pink Floyd's *Dark Side of the Moon* in 1979. The label's development of lines, such as Ultra-analog vinyl and Silver LPs, has enhanced its catalog across all genres.

SPEAKERS CORNER
GETTORF, GERMANY (1993)

A vinyl-only label, Speakers Corner prides itself on its releases of vintage LPs that sound better than the original pressings. This is partly because, unlike some transfers back to vinyl, pressings are never taken from a digital file. The company's motto is "Pure Analog," and they view it as a matter of principle that no digital delay processing is used on their releases. Some of their records are even cut by the same engineer who cut the original lacquers of the first release.

THE VINYL FACTORY
LONDON, UK (2001)

The Vinyl Factory is housed in a former EMI pressing plant in west London, which in its heyday in the 1960s and 1970s produced up to twenty million discs a year. Today, it presses about two million discs per annum, but figures are increasing as the major labels want vinyl as a regular item on their release schedules. The Vinyl Factory is also a limited edition label in its own right, making customized editions for the likes of the Pet Shop Boys and Massive Attack.

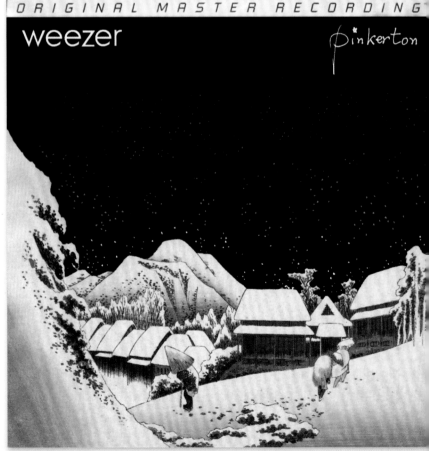

STEREO — Verve Records — MG VS - 6062 — Living Sound Fidelity

SPEAKERS CORNER RECORDS
WWW.SPEAKERSCORNERRECORDS.COM
• 180g Virgin Vinyl
• High Quality Pressing
• Pure Analogue Audiophile Mastering

LOUIS ARMSTRONG meets OSCAR PETERSON

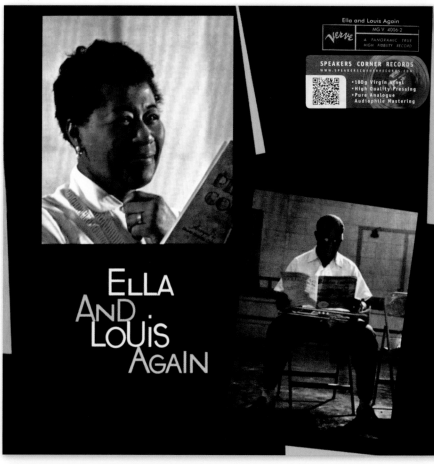

Ella and Louis Again — Verve — MG V 4006-2 — A PANORAMIC TRUE HIGH FIDELITY RECORD

SPEAKERS CORNER RECORDS
WWW.SPEAKERSCORNERRECORDS.COM
• 180g Virgin Vinyl
• High Quality Pressing
• Pure Analogue Audiophile Mastering

ELLA AND LOUIS AGAIN

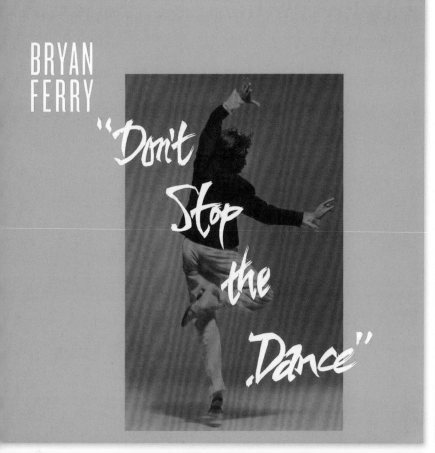

BRYAN FERRY

"Don't Stop the Dance"

MASSIVE ATTACK

HELIGOLAND

PRELUDE to
HEART IS A LOTUS

MICHAEL GARRICK SEXTET
WITH DON RENDELL AND IAN CARR

RONNIE SCOTT
QUINTET

PHIL SEAMEN
QUINTET

A FUTURE WITHOUT
BRISTOL, UK (2006)

Although it began in 2006 as a digital label, the aim of Bristol-based Will Plowman and Ross Stone was always to launch a vinyl operation. The success of their digital releases enabled them in 2012 to produce their first vinyl product: a limited run of forty vinyl postcards by With Joyful Lips, which sold out within two days. Both Plowman and Stone are musicians, and the label's ethos is to give its acts full creative freedom and encourage collaborations with other artists and labels. "This comes from a strong belief that if our artists are happy and in a comfortable creative environment/headspace they will create great music," Plowman told *The Vinyl Factory*. Plowman himself appears on the label from time to time; his latest project, *Ahamay Grove*, is a four-track ten-inch EP of experimental piano, with a spectacular origami sleeve that opens out to reveal a plain, white label record.

GEARBOX
LONDON, UK (2009)

Founded in 2009 by musician Darrel Sheinman, Gearbox is a vinyl-led label that specializes in (mainly British) jazz and jazz-related music. The company's commitment to "put the ritual back into music listening" is a reminder that listening to and playing vinyl is a dedicated activity in itself. The label puts this into practice by holding Jazz Kissaten evenings at its studio in King's Cross, taking inspiration from Japanese jazz cafés where customers can share the experience of listening to the finest jazz recordings on state-of-the-art sound systems. Gearbox's small but growing catalog includes vintage UK jazz from the likes of Ronnie Scott and Tubby Hayes, and more esoteric recent items like the poetry-and-jazz SuperJam collaboration of poet Michael Horovitz and musicians Damon Albarn, Graham Coxon, and Paul Weller.

MUSIC ON VINYL
HAARLEM, NETHERLANDS (2009)

Dutch label Music On Vinyl releases high quality 180-gram LPs and seven-inch pressings of a wide range of titles licensed from record companies, or from artists who control their own rights. Launched in 2009, it took only three years for the company to reach its five hundredth th LP pressing. Today, there are more than one thousand issues on its catalog, which is a mix of classic albums and new vinyl. Labels that they work with include Sony, Warner, Universal, Silvertone, and Cooking Vinyl. Their plant in Haarlem pressed millions of records for CBS in the 1970s and 1980s and some members of staff boast more than forty years' experience. Not all their product is cut from the analog source, with some of it taken instead from high resolution digital files supplied by the original labels, but the quality is high and the label's commitment to vinyl is unquestionable.

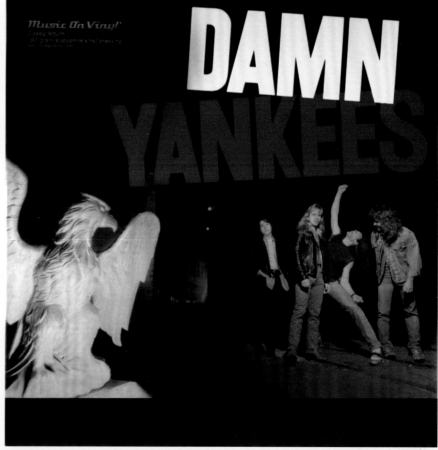

VLEK
BRUSSELS, BELGIUM (2010)

Vlek Records was started by music enthisiasts Julien Fournier, Thomas Van De Velde, and Dimitri Runkkari in Brussels in 2010. Each had been involved in different areas of the record business, so the trio decided to pool their skills and found a label to promote Belgian artists. Inspired by the opportuniy afforded by vinyl to create a "complete" physical object, all of the cover artwork for their releases is produced in-house. The design is overseen by Runkkari, who ensures that the label's small catalog maintains a consistent style. Producing every cover themselves has its disadvantages, however, because it means that the label is unable to press more than a limited edition for each release. Musically, Vlek's catalog contains everything from instumental hip-hop and pure techno to proto-house, collages, and atmocore.

SUPERIOR VIADUCT
SAN FRANCISCO, USA (2011)

The archival label Superior Viaduct was established by Steve Viaduct in San Francisco in 2011, with the simple aim of making available either out-of-print or never-released music. Initially concentrating on the local punk scene of the late 1970s, the label's first release was *Love God, Love One Another* by Black Humor. Today, the catalog includes records by Devo, The Residents, and Brigitte Fontaine, as well as first albums by Alice Coltrane, Martin Rev, and Phill Niblock and soundtracks to movies, such as *Solaris* and *La Planète Sauvage*. While the recent vinyl explosion has seen Superior Viaduct's business boom, it has brought with it one problem: where once a record was taking less than a couple of months to be pressed and delivered, it's now more like a three-month process due to the major labels overstretching the pressing plants.

BOKHARI
LONDON, UK (2012)

Created as an outlet for unknown producers around the world, Bokhari (meaning "unknown tribe") was formed in 2012 by Angus Paterson and Paul Crognale. The pair, from Oxford, England, were increasingly concerned that as the vinyl revival became a mainstream trend, major labels were jumping on the bandwagon and ignoring unknown producers in the process. "We are all for the trend for vinyl," said Paterson, "as long as the music retains its quality." Great care is taken on the presentation side, with customized sleeve artwork commissioned from a new illustrator or artist for each of the strictly limited runs. Bokhari's fourth release by Mark E had a limited edition of fifty individual covers, all with a completely different design, and release number seven had ten special editions with customized wooden covers, in reference to the track "Prototype."

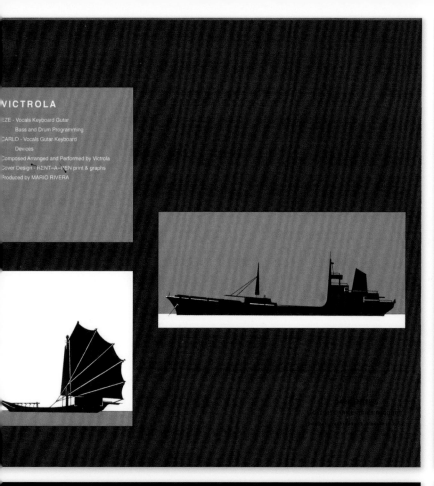

VICTROLA

EZE - Vocals Keyboard Guitar
Bass and Drum Programming
CARLO - Vocals Guitar Keyboard
Devices
Composed Arranged and Performed by Victrola
Cover Design - RENT–A–PEN print & graphs
Produced by MARIO RIVERA

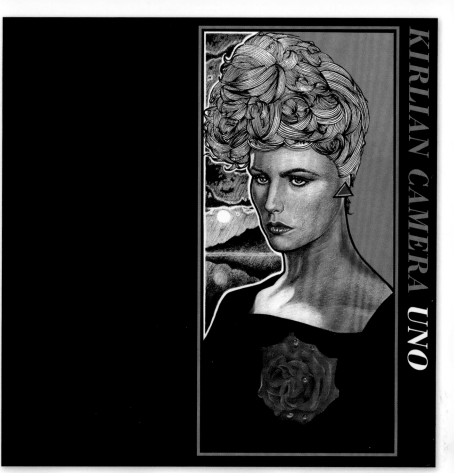

KIRLIAN CAMERA UNO

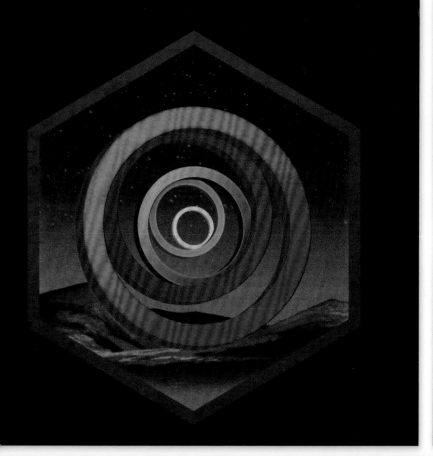

Turntable Treasures

With the postmillennial rise of digital audio came USB turntables that allowed vinyl recordings to be downloaded onto a computer, tablet, or smartphone. At the high end of the market, turntable designs took inspiration from the iPod and other digital devices in their use of clean lines and smooth surfaces.

> A 2011 update of Rega's classic P3 turntable, the RP3 features a hand assembled RB303 tone arm, a precision main bearing, and a plinth that incorporates Rega's Double Brace Technology.

> Described by VPI as "The Muscle Car of Audio," the Classic turntable has won several awards for the manufacturer since its launch in 2009.

> The plinth of the Clearaudio Ovation (2011) is made from a layer of Panzerholz ply sandwiched between aluminum layers, which is claimed to offer considerable sonic gains over alternatives.

> Released in 2012, Pro-Ject's Debut Carbon updated the Debut model with a carbon fiber tone arm, twelve-inch platter, and rear-mounted junction box.

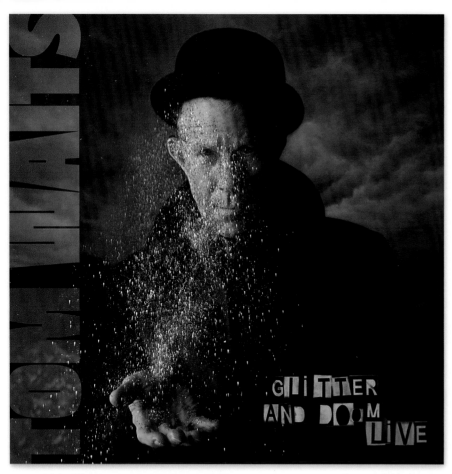

TOM WAITS
GLITTER AND DOOM LIVE

THE CURE
PLUS ENTREAT PLUS ENTREAT PLUS ENTREAT
ENTREAT

THE WHITE STRIPES UNDER GREAT WHITE NORTHERN LIGHTS

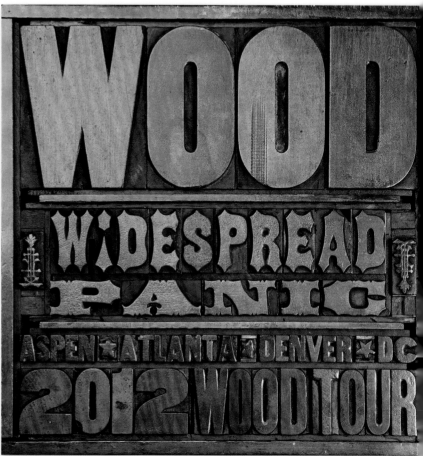

WOOD
WIDESPREAD PANIC
ASPEN ★ ATLANTA ★ DENVER ★ DC
2012 WOOD TOUR

Got Live If You Want It

The vinyl revival of the past few years has brought the live album back into vogue. In the vanguard, unsurprisingly, is Jack White, whose own label has issued Live at Third Man Records sets by himself, his bands The Raconteurs and The Dead Weather, and his former wife Karen Elson, plus the Melvins, Willie Nelson, The Kills, Mudhoney, The Shins, Jack Johnson, Seasick Steve, Jenny Lewis, the Cold War Kids, Jerry Lee Lewis, The 5.6.7.8.s, White Denim, Reggie Watts, The Black Lips, Jeff the Brotherhood, Nobunny, White Denim, King Tuff, and Ted Leo.

GLITTER AND DOOM LIVE
TOM WAITS (2009)

The vinyl version of Waits's previous live set, *Big Time* (1988), had suffered the indignity of fewer tracks than the CD and tape versions. *Glitter and Doom* restored him to double LP, gatefold glory.

. . . NORTHERN LIGHTS
THE WHITE STRIPES (2010)

This red-sleeved double LP variant was part of a lavish vinyl-CD-DVD set on Jack White's Third Man label. A bonus seven-inch single featured a cover of the kids song "The Wheels on the Bus."

ENTREAT PLUS
THE CURE (2012)

Issued as the promotional Entreat in 1990, this expanded version—taped in London in 1989—graced a deluxe CD set of *Disintegration* in 2010 and appeared in its own right on vinyl in 2012.

WOOD
WIDESPREAD PANIC (2012)

Half of Georgia jam band Widespread Panic's catalog is comprised of live albums. This double set from their twentieth-anniversary tour opens with a cover of "The Ballad of John and Yoko."

LIVE AT THE GREEK
JIMMY PAGE/BLACK CROWES (2013)

First released in 2000 and belatedly on vinyl in 2013, this titanic team-up—packed with covers of Page's old band—was a better live Zeppelin LP than their own *The Song Remains the Same*.

TOKYO DOME IN CONCERT
VAN HALEN (2015)

Van Halen's first live album with David Lee Roth (1993's *Right Here, Right Now* featured Sammy Hagar), this appropriately over-the-top set, from Japan in 2013, runs to four vinyl LPs.

JIMMY PAGE & THE BLACK CROWES
LIVE AT THE GREEK

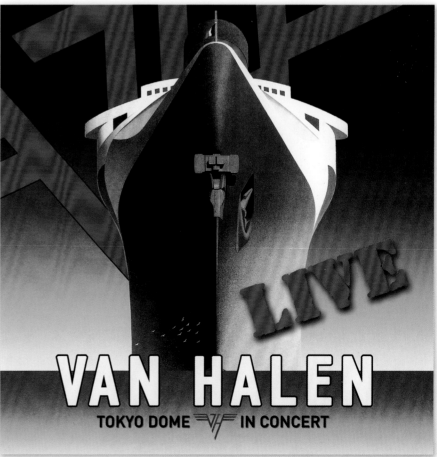

VAN HALEN
TOKYO DOME IN CONCERT

And
Vinally

Customers crowd the vinyl
section of Rough Trade
Records in London as part
of the Record Store Day
celebrations on April 18, 2015.

Run Out Grooves

The dead wax between the final grooves and the label of vinyl records is customarily occupied by nothing more than a matrix number. However, some imaginative engineers and recording artists—notably Morrissey and Johnny Marr of The Smiths—have taken the opportunity to place messages in the empty space. These can contain anything from inside jokes and funny comments to, in the case of Led Zeppelin, scary quotes from occultist Aleister Crowley.

One of the most infamous run-out messages appeared on side A of Elvis Costello's second album, *This Year's Model* (1978). It read: "Special pressing No. 003. Ring Moira on 434 3232 for your special prize." The telephone number was a real one and connected to the increasingly unamused Moira, who was Costello's press agent at the label WEA.

All grammar and spelling of the following run-out messages is attributed to the artists or engineers responsible.

SO MOTE BE IT /
DO WHAT THOU WILT

LED ZEPPELIN,
LED ZEPPELIN III (1970)

DO WHAT THOU
WILT SHALL BE
THE WHOLE OF
THE LAW

LED ZEPPELIN,
"IMMIGRANT SONG" (1970)

IF LOVE IS
THE ANSWER,
YOU'RE HOME

PAUL MCCARTNEY,
RAM (1971)

DON'T WORRY /
NOTHING WILL BE O.K!

EAGLES, *ONE OF THESE*
NIGHTS (1975)

TEAR... /
DOWN... /
THE... /
WALLS!

THE CLASH,
LONDON CALLING (1979)

I'VE BEEN LOOKING
FOR A GUIDE

JOY DIVISION
UNKNOWN PLEASURES (1979)

ANTMUSIC /
. . . FOR SEX PEOPLE

ADAM AND THE ANTS,
*KINGS OF THE WILD
FRONTIER* (1980)

THERE ARE NOT
ENOUGH PEOPLE /
WITH FLOWERS IN
THEIR HAIR

ECHO AND THE BUNNYMEN,
CROCODILES (1980)

IN SPACE... /
NO ONE... /
CAN... /
HEAR... /
YOU... /
CLASH!

THE CLASH,
SANDANISTA! (1980)

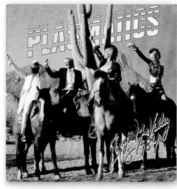

HEADBANGER
YOU'VE GOT
YOUR BRAINS
FRENCH FRIED

PLASMATICS,
*BEYOND THE VALLEY
OF 1984* (1981)

AFTER 15 YEARS,
I STILL CAN'T
SPELL SZYMCZYK /
IS IT ONE "L", OR TWO?

JOE WALSH, *THERE GOES THE
NEIGHBORHOOD* (1981)

. . . WITHIN THE
CIRCUTS THAT
MAKE PAC-MEN
DIE AND VESSELS
DISINTEGRATE...

HÜSKER DÜ,
ZEN ARCADE (1984)

THERES ONLY ONE
UM /

IRON MAIDEN,
POWERSLAVE (1984)

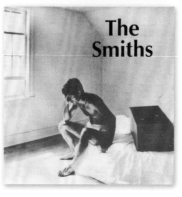

THE IMPOTENCE
OF ERNEST /
ROMANTIC AND
SQUARE IS HIP
AND AWARE

THE SMITHS, "WILLIAM,
IT WAS REALLY NOTHING" (1984)

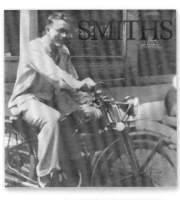

BEWARE THE
WRATH TO COME /
TALENT BORROWS,
GENIUS STEALS

THE SMITHS,
"BIGMOUTH STRIKES AGAIN" (1986)

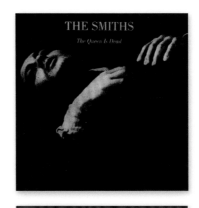

FEAR OF
MANCHESTER /
THEM WAS
ROTTEN DAYS

THE SMITHS,
THE QUEEN IS DEAD (1986)

ARE YOU
LOATHESOME
TONIGHT? /
TOMB IT
MAY CONCERN

THE SMITHS,
"ASK" (1986)

WE LOVE YOU
DINASOUR /
SST'S GOTTA
LOTTA NERVE

SONIC YOUTH,
SONIC YOUTH (1987, REISSUE)

IT WAS
SCREAMING BUT
I COULDNT TELL
WHERE THE
MOUTH WAS

DINOSAUR, *YOU'RE LIVING
ALL OVER ME* (1987)

I TRIED TO
LOVE LIFE... /
BUT IT
WANTED TO BE
"JUST FRIENDS"

GREEN RIVER,
DRY AS A BONE (1987)

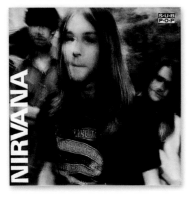

WHY DON'T
YOU TRADE
THOSE GUITARS
FOR SHOVELS?

NIRVANA,
"LOVE BUZZ" (1988)

NUDISM

PIXIES,
SURFER ROSA (1988)

HOW THE END/
ALWAYS IS
THE CURE,
DISINTEGRATION (1989)

TINY LITTLE
BUNNIES, PLAYING IN
THE GRASS /
TINY LITTLE
BUNNIES KICK YOUR
FUCKIN ASS
HAPPY FLOWERS,
OOF (1989)

FREE SLY
STONE NOW! /
FREE JAMES BROWN
PRIMAL SCREAM,
"LOADED" (1990)

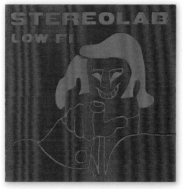

GO BOIL AN EGG!
STEREOLAB,
LOW FI (1992)

PIGS ON COKE
HUGGY BEAR,
"HER JAZZ" (1993)

YOU'RE VERY
CLEVER, YOUNG MAN,
VERY CLEVER . . .
TURTLES ALL
THE WAY DOWN...
TORTOISE, *MILLIONS NOW LIVING*
WILL NEVER DIE (1996)

I'M AN
IMPORTANT
PERSON. WOULD
YOU LIKE TO
COME HOME
WITH ME?
RADIOHEAD,
OK COMPUTER (1997)

VINYL MAKES
EARS HAPPY!
EL-P,
FANTASTIC DAMAGE (2002)

Record Manufacturers

With the resurgence of vinyl over the past few years, there has been a sharp increase in business for the many pressing plants around the world. The list here is just a selection of vinyl record manufacturers who do pressing at their own facilities. The list is meant as a guide, and does not constitute an endorsement of any particular company or their services. All details are accurate at the time of going to press.

AUSTRALIA

IMPLANT MEDIA
Suite 1, 11-13 Lygon St.
Brunswick, VIC 3056
(+61) 03 9387 5433

ZENITH RECORD PRESSING
Factory 5
155 Donald St.
East Brunswick VIC 3057
(+61) 03 9383 6572

BELGIUM

DISCOMAT
Houwijkerstraat 2
3540 Herk-de-Stad
(+32) 13 55 31 11

BRAZIL

POLYSOM
Areia Branca
Belford Roxo
Rio de Janeiro

CZECH REP.

GZ VINYL
Tovární 340
267 12 Loděnice
Czech Republic
(+420) 311 673 675

FRANCE

MAGNETIC MASTERING
magneticmastering@
yahoo.fr

MPO INTERNATIONAL
Domaine de la Lorgerie
5700 Averton (France)
(+33) 2 43 08 36 00

GERMANY

AMEISE
Sukale
Medientechnik,
Schneisenstr. 10
22145 Hamburg
(+49) 40 22618012

CELEBRATE RECORDS
Am Birkenwaeldchen 2
D-09366 Stollberg
(+49) 37296 9201 60

FLIGHT13 DUPLICATION
Sophienstrasse 232
D-761 85
Kalsruhe
(+49) 721 8315415

MASTER MEDIA PRODUCTIONS
Humboldtstrasse 6
D-53819
Neunkirchen-Seelscheid
(+49) 2247 916810

MY45
Andreas Bauer
Hauptstrasse 30
84184 Tiefenbach
(+49) 8709 2695016

OPTIMAL MEDIA
Glienholzweg 7
17207 Röbel/ Müritz
(+49) 39931 56 500

ITALY

PALLAS GROUP
Schallplattenfabrik
Pallas GmbH
Auf dem Esch 8
49356 Diepholz
(+49) 5441 977 0

R.A.N.D. MUZIK
Göschenstr. 2-4
D-04317 Leipzig
(+49) 341 688 439 1

PHONOPRESS INTERNATIONAL
Via Cesare Battisti, 1
20090 Settala (MI)
(+39) 2 95307058

JAMAICA

TUFF GONG
RMF Jamaica
56 Hope Rd.
Kingston 6
(+1 876) 978 2929

JAPAN

TOYOKASEI CO. LTD
1-1-1, West 7th Floor
Shin-Aoyama Building
Minami-Aoyama
Minato-ku
Tokyo

MEXICO

RETROACTIVE RECORDS
Jalapa 125, Col. Roma
Norte
Mexico City DF
(+52) 5555 642565

NETHERLANDS

RECORD INDUSTRY
Izaak Enschedeweg 13
2031 CR Haarlem
Netherlands
(+31) 23 551 11 15

RUSSIA

VINYL RECORDS
Народного Ополчения,
д. 39, корп
People's Militia Str. 39,
Bldg. 2
Moscow
(+7) 495 925 04 49

SWEDEN

TAIL RECORDS VINYL
Enekullegatan 5 D
418 75 Göteborg
(+46) 707 499817

VIC-TONE RECORDS
Kanalvägen 7
360 13 Urshult
(+46) 477 20089

USA

A&R RECORD MANUFACTURING
902 N. Riverfront Blvd.
Dallas, TX 75207
(+1) 214 741 2027

ARCHER RECORD PRESSING
7401 E. Davison
Detroit,
MI 48212
(+1) 313 365 9545

BILL SMITH CUSTOM RECORDS
127 Penn St
El Segundo,
CA 90245
(+1) 310 322 6386

BROOKLYN PHONO
270 42nd St.
Brooklyn,
New York City
NY 11232,
(+1) 718 788 5777

CAPSULE LABS
2415 Eads St.
Los Angeles,
CA 90031
(+1) 323 362 6049

ERIKA RECORDS
6300 Caballero Blvd.
Bueno Park, CA 90620
(+1) 714 228 5420

FURNACE RECORD PRESSING
PO Box 3268
Merrifield, VA 22116
(+1) 703 205 0007

GOTTA GROOVE RECORDS
3615 Superior Ave.
Cleveland,
OH 44114
(+1) 216 431 7373

HIT-BOUND MANUFACTURING INC
89 North 4th St.
Brooklyn,
New York City, NY 11249
(+1) 718 486 6080

MORPHIUS DISC MANUFACTURING
100 East 23rd St.
Baltimore, MD 21218
(+1) 410 662 0112

MUSICOL RECORDING
780 Oakland Park Ave.
Columbus,
OH 43224
(+1) 614 267 3133

PALOMINO RECORDS PRESSING
2818 KY-44
Shepherdsville,
KY 40165
(+1) 502 543 1521

QUALITY RECORD PRESSINGS
543 N. 10th St.
Salina, Kansas
KS 67401
(+1) 785 820 2931

RAINBO RECORDS
8960 Eton Ave.
Canoga Park, CA 91304
(+1) 818 280 1100

RECORD TECHNOLOGY INC
486 Dawson Dr.
Camarillo, CA 93012
(+1) 805 484 2747

UNITED RECORD PRESSING
453 Chestnut St.
Nashville, TN 37203
(+1) 615 259 9396

AGR MANUFACTURING
The Old Exchange
Mill Lane
Great Dunmow
Essex, CM6 1BG
(+44) (0)1371 859 393

CURVED PRESSINGS
The Green House
49 Green Lanes
London, N16 9BU
(+44) 333 0119106

HDC MEDIA
Bracken House
Broad Lane
Bradford,
BD4 8PA
(+44) (0)1274 656565

SOUND PERFORMANCE
3 Greenwich Quay
Clarence Road
London, SE8 3EY
(+44) (0)208 691 2121

VINYL FACTORY
Units 3-5, Enterprise House
133 Blyth Rd.
Middlesex,
UB3 1DD
(+44) (0)20 8756 7704

Record Shop Directory

Maniac Records
Av. Cabildo 2040 Local 90
Galeria Boluevard
Los Andes
Buenos Aires 1428
(+54) 11 4782 5307

Minton's
Local 26
Galería Apolo
Av Corrientes 1382
Buenos Aires,
C1043ABN
(+54) 11 4371 2216

Rockaway Records
Westfield Carindale
Shopping Centre,
1151 Creek Rd.
Brisbane,
Queensland 4152
(+61) 7 3395 4707

Atlantis Music
78 Scarborough St.
Southport,
Queensland 4215
(+61) 7 552 71816

Goodwax
35 York St.
Adelaide,
South Australia 5000

Quality Records... plus
269 Glenferrie Rd.
Malvern,
Melbourne, Victoria 3124
(+61) 3 9500 9902

Vinyl Solution
Shop 5/10 Park Rd.
Cheltenham,
Melbourne, Victoria 3192
(+61) 3 9585 0133

Dr. Disc Records
471 Ouellette Ave.
Windsor,
Ontario N9A 6Y4
(+1) 519 253 9744

Remember Vinyl Records
428 Main St, Penticton,
British Columbia V2A 5C5
(+1) 778 476 5838

Rotate This
801 Queen St. W.
Toronto, Ontario M6J 1G1
(+1) 416 504 8447

Sound Central Store
4486 Coloniale Ave
Montreal,
Quebec H2W 2C7,
(+1) 514 393 4495

Underground Music
Unit 4-1331,
Ellis St
Kelowna,
British Columbia V1Y1Z9,
(+1) 778 478 0215

Black Light
Fredensgade 31,
Aarhus, Jylland 8000
(+45) 8620 2320

Mazeeka Samir Fouad
Ismail Mohamed St.
Zamalek, Cairo

Terminal
Gonsiori 2
Tallinn,
Harjumaa 10143,
(+372) 622 9258

Aikakone
Kyttalankatu 14
Tampere 33100
(+35) 840 083 4838

Deep End Records
16 rue Porte Basse,
Bordeaux
33000
(+33) 6 24 33 82 82

Monster Melodies
9 rue des
Dechargeurs,
Paris 75001
(+33) 1 40 28 09 39

Toolbox Records
30 rue St Ambroise,
Paris 75011
(+33) 1 48 05 80 16

Vicious Circle
7 rue des Puits Clos
Toulouse, 31000
(+33) 5 61 23 82 83

12inch
Marktstr. 60a
Stuttgart,
Baden-Württemberg
70372
(+49) 711 763565

Cheap Trash Records
Forststr. 166
Stuttgart,
Baden-Württemberg
70193

**Coast to Coast
Records**
Danziger Straße 21
Berlin 10435
(+49) 30 54776168

DEEJAYS Tonträger
Vertriebs GmbH
Knochenhauerstr. 27
Bremen 28195
(+49) 421 1692166

Mythos Records
Höhenstraße 20
Frankfurt am Main,
Hessen 60385
(+49) 69 49085244

Spacehall Records
Zossener Straße 33
Berlin 10961
(+49) 30 6947664

Schallplanet
Boxhagener Str. 34
Friedrichshain
Berlin, 10245

12 Tónar,
Skólavörðustígur 15
Reykjavik
(+354) 5115656

MusicCircle
V Mall, Shop No. 40,
Ground Floor Thakur
Complex
Kandivali (East)
Mumbai,
Maharashtra 400101
(+91) 9820365979

**Backflip
Record Store**
Via Nino Bixio 37
Milan 20129
(+39) 02 8706 9095

Tower Records
1-22-14 Jinnan
Shibuya-ku, Tokyo
(+81) 03 3496 3661

Retroactive Records
Jalapa 125
Col. Roma Norte
Mexico City 06700
(+52) 5555 642565

The Jazzhole,
Shop No. 168
Awolowo Rd., Lagos
(+234) 706 064 8580

My Music Taupo
79 Tongariro St.
Taupo 3377
(+64) 7 378 2844

Real Groovy
438 Queen St.
Auckland 1010
(+64) 9 302 3940

Southbound Records
69 Mount Eden Rd.
Grafton, Auckland 1023
(+64) 9 302 0769

Vinyl Destination
64-66 Mokoia Rd,
Birkenhead, Auckland 0626

**Strømsø
Plateforretning**
Schultzgate
Drammen, Buskerud 3044
(+47) 46641549

Grubanuta.pl
ul. Lowicka 50
02-531 Warsaw
(+48) 509793339

Mabu Vinyl
2 Rheede Street Gardens,
Cape Town 8001
(+27) 21 423 7635

Funk Soul Records
Ronda Sant Pau 17/19,
Tienda 8, Barcelona 08015

Plattfon
Feldbergstrasse 48
Basel
4057
(+41) 61 681 34 73

**Jammin's
Vinyl Records**
Sıracevizler Cd. No.92/B
Sisli, Istanbul 34381

Velvet Indieground
Firuzaga Mh., Bostanbasi,
Cd No:2A, Beyoglu,
Istanbul 34425
(+90) 5350121416

Ohm Records
Trade Centre Rd.
Dubai
(+971) 4 397 3728

Action Records
46 Church St.
Preston,
Lancashire, PR1 3DH
(+44) (0)1772 252255

Astral Vinyl
11 Marsh Street,
Hanley, Stoke-on-Trent,
Staffordshire, ST1 1JA
(+44) (0)7704 300304

Audio Gold
308-310 Park Rd.
Crouch End
London, N8 0QA
(+44) (0)20 8341 9007

Banquet Records
52 Eden St.
Kingston upon Thames,
Surrey, KT1 1EE
(+44) (0)20 8549 5871

Barefoot Records
19 Claremont
America Ground
Hastings, TN34 1HA
(+44) (0)7989 408122

Camden Lock Vinyl
35c Middle Yard
Camden Lock Place
London, NW1 8AL
(+44) (0)7759 156227

Carnival Records
83 Church St.
Malvern, WR14 2AE
(+44) (0)7435 963894

Circular Sound
5 St Benedicts St.
Norwich, Norfolk, NR2 4PE
(+44) (0)7990 618293

CounterCulture
130 Desborough Rd.
High Wycombe,
Buckinghamshire,
HP11 2PU
(+44) (0)1494 463366

Crash Records
35 The Headrow
Leeds, LS1 6PU
(+44) (0)113 243 6743

Custard Cube
Custard Cube Music
28 Blackburn Rd.
Accrington, Lancashire,
BB5 1HD
(+44) (0)1254 399669

Disc Covery Records
3 Kingsway
Huncoat, Accrington,
Lancashire, BB5 6LA
(+44) (0)1254 231 387

**The Drift
Records Shop**
103 High St.
Totnes, TQ9 5SN
(+44) (0)1803 866828

Flashback
50 Essex Rd.
Islington, London, N1 8LR
(+44) (0)20 7354 9356

Groucho's Record Store
132 Nethergate
Dundee, DD1 4ED
(+44) (0)1382 228496

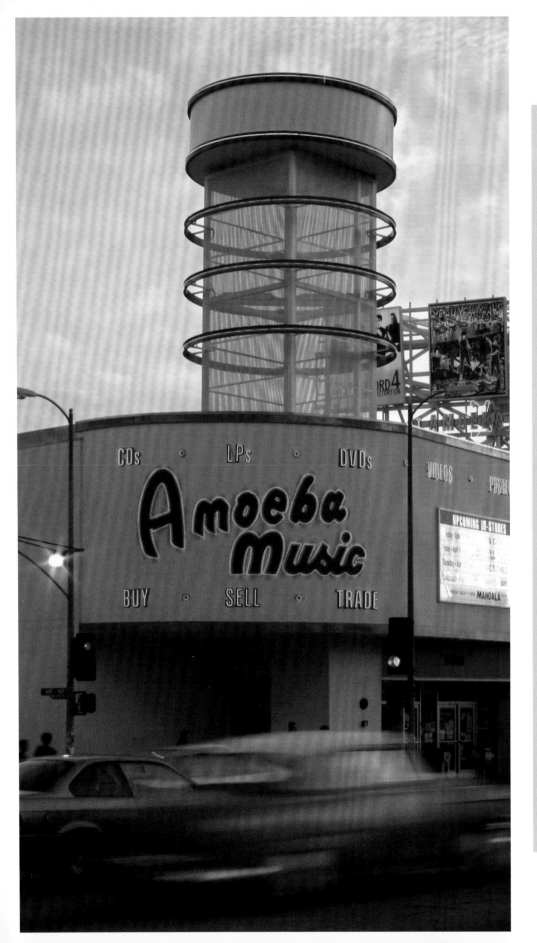

Haggle Vinyl
114-116 Essex Rd.
Islington, London, N1 8LX
(+44) (0)20 7704 3101

Hot Salvation
29 Rendezvous St.
Folkestone, CT20 1EY
(+44) (0)1303 487657

Jumbo Records
5-6 St Johns Centre
Leeds, LS2 8LQ
(+44) (0)113 245 5570

Love Music
34 Dundas St.
Glasgow, G1 2AQ
(+44) (0)141 332 2099

Monorail
12 Kings Court
Glasgow, G1 5RB
(+44) (0)141 552 9458

The Music Exchange
2 Stoney St.
Nottingham, NG1 1LG
(+44) (0)115 958 3274

Piccadilly Records
53 Oldham St.
Manchester, M1 1JR
(+44) (0)161 839 8008

Pop Recs Ltd
50 Fawcett St.
Sunderland, SR1 1RF
(+44) (0)7783 975 660

Probe Records
Retail Unit 1, The Bluecoat
School Lane
Liverpool, L1 3BX
(+44) (0)151 708 8815

Red House Records
21-23 Faringdon Rd.
Swindon,
Wiltshire, SN1 5AR
(+44) (0)1793 526393

Rise Music
70 Queens Rd.
Bristol, BS8 1QU
(+44) (0)117 929 7511

Rough Trade East
Dray Walk
Old Truman Brewery
91 Brick Lane
London, E1 6QL
(+44) (0)20 7392 7788

RPM Records
4 Old George Yard
Newcastle-upon-Tyne,
NE1 1EZ
(+44) (0)191 221 0201

Rude Not To
12 Bond Street
Weymouth,
Dorset, DT4 8HE
(+44) (0)1305 785770

Skeleton Records
1st Floor, 11 Oxton Rd.
Birkenhead, Merseyside,
CH41 2QQ
(+44) (0)151 653 9003

Soundclash
28 St Benedicts St.
Norwich, NR2 4AQ
(+44) (0)1603 761004

Sound It Out Records
Yarm Street, Stockton-on-
Tees, TS18 3DR
(+44) (0)1642 860068

Spillers Records
27 The Morgan Arcade
Cardiff, CF10 1AF
(+44) (0)29 20224905

Tangled Parrot
32 King St.
Carmarthen, SA31 1BS
(+44) (0)1267 235511

Underground
Solu'shn
9 Cockburn St.
Edinburgh, EH1 1BP
(+44) (0)131 226 2242

Unknown Pleasures
110 Canongate
Edinburgh, EH8 8DD
(+44) (0)131 652 3537

Vinyl-Junction 42
194 Barnsley Rd.
Moorthorpe
Pontefract,
West Yorkshire,
WF9 2AL
(+44) (0)7947 141727

Vinyl Tap
42 John William St.
Huddersfield,
HD1 1ER
(+44) (0)1484 845999

VoxBox Music
21 St. Stephen St.
Stockbridge
Edinburgh, EH3 5AN
(+44) (0)131 6296775

US

Amoeba Music
6400 Sunset Blvd.
Los Angeles, CA 90028
(+1) 323 245 6400

Aquarius Records
1055 Valencia St.
San Francisco, CA 94110
(+1) 415 647 2272

Arkansas Record
& CD Exchange
4212 MacArthur Dr.
North Little Rock,
AR 72118
(+1) 501 753 7877

Big Oomp
2668 Campbellton Rd SW
Atlanta, GA 30311
(+1) 404 349 0620

Black
Pancake Records
593 Haight St.
San Francisco,
CA 94117
(+1) 415 626 6995

The Business
402 Commercial Ave.
Anacortes,
WA 98221
(+1) 360 293 9788

Earwax Records
167 North 9th St.
Store #2,
Brooklyn, NY 11211
(+1) 718 486 3771

Ernest Tubbs
417 Broadway
Nashville, TN 37203
(+1) 615 255 7503

Gramophone Records
2843 N. Clark St.
Chicago, IL 60657
(+1) 773 472 3683

Groovy Records
3749 Park Blvd.
San Diego, CA 92103
(+1) 619 542 0597

Headline Record
7706 Melrose Ave.
Los Angeles, CA 90046
(+1) 323 655 2125

Hello Records
1459 Bagley St.
Detroit, MI 48216
(+1) 313 300 5654

In Your Ear Records
957 Commonwealth Ave.
Boston, MA 02215
(+1) 617 787 9755

Last Vestige
Music Shop
173 Quail St.
Albany, NY 12203
(+1) 518 432 7736

Louisiana Music Factory
210 Decatur St.
New Orleans, LA 70130
(+1) 504 586 1094

Mobile Records
140B S. Sage Ave.
Mobile, AL 36606
(+1) 251 479 0096

Nuggets
486 Commonwealth Ave.
Boston, MA 02215
(+1) 617 536 0679

Peoples Records
4100 Woodward Ave.
Detroit, MI 48201
(+1) 313 831 0864

Record Runner
5 Jones St.
New York, NY 10014
(+1) 212 255 4280

Rockzone Records
2155 E. University #104
Tempe, AZ 85281
(+1) 480 964 6301

Shangri-La,
1916 Madison Ave.
Memphis, TN 38104
(+1) 901 274 1916

Sound Exchange
805 W. Bloomingdale Ave.
Brandon, FL 33511
(+1) 813 651 9316

Submerge
3000 East Grand Blvd.
Detroit, MI 48202

Telegraph
19 Golden St.
New London,
CT 06320
(+1) 860 701 0506

The Thing
1001 Manhattan Ave.
Brooklyn, NY 11222
(+1) 718 349 8234

Third Man Records
623 7th Ave. S.
Nashville, TN 37203
(+1) 615 891 4393

UHF
512 S, Washington Ave.
Royal Oak, Detroit,
MI 48067
(+1) 248 545 5955

Used Kids Records
1980 North High St.
Columbus, OH 43210
(+1) 614 294 3833

Vintage Vinyl
925 Davis St.
Evanston,
IL 60201
(+1) 847 328 2899

The Vinyl Destination
2050 Clark Ave.
Raleigh,
NC 27605
(+1) 919 631 1403

The Vinyl Room
3333 Midway Dr.
Suite 105
San Diego, CA 92110
(+1) 858 740 6030

Virginia's Memory
Lane Records
6114 Lakeside Ave.
Richmond, VA 23228
(+1) 804 261 1511

Weirdo Records
844 Massachusetts Ave.
Cambridge, MA 02139
(+1) 857 413 0154

Who Shot
Ya Records
3442 Emerson Ave. N.
Minneapolis,
MN 55412
(+1) 612 267 7045

Wuxtry Records
197 E Clayton St.
Athens, GA 30601,
(+1) 706 369 9428

Index

Picture Credits

Every effort has been made to trace all copyright owners, but if any have been inadvertently overlooked, the publishers would be pleased to make the necessary corrections at the first opportunity.

Key t top; c center; b bottom; l left; r right; tl top left; tc top centre; tr top right; cl center left; cr center right; bl bottom left; bc bottom centre; br bottom right

2 © Neal Preston/Corbis 6 Tim Roney/Getty Images 7 Sipa Press/REX 9 Keystone/Getty Images 10 tl Frederic Lewis/Getty Images tc SSPL/Getty Images tr Stock Montage/Getty Images bl Universal History Archive/Getty Images bc Science & Society Picture Library/SSPL/Getty Images br SSPL/Getty Images 11 tl Jay Paull/Getty Images tc Universal History Archive/UIG via Getty images tr Blank Archives/Getty Images bl SSPL/Getty Images bc Bain News Service/Buyenlarge/Getty Images br Fox Photos/Hulton Archive/Getty Images 12 tl Stock Montage/Getty Images tc Buyenlarge/Getty Images tr Henry Groskinsky/The LIFE Images Collection/Getty Images bl Stock Montage/Getty Images br Apic/Getty Images 13 tl Universal History Archive/UIG via Getty images tr Lipnitzki/Roger Viollet/Getty Images 16 Murray Garrett/Getty Images 17 tl ullstein bild/ullstein bild via Getty Images 18 Dan Kitwood/Getty Images 19 t Universal History Archive/Getty Images 20 APIC/Getty Images 21 t DeAgostini/Getty Images bl Archive Photos/Getty Images 22 tl Cornell Capa/The LIFE Picture Collection/Getty Images br Metronome/Getty Images 23 Gilles Petard/Redferns 24 CBS via Getty Images 25 tr CBS via Getty Images br CBS via Getty Images 26 Martin Divisek/Bloomberg via Getty Images 27 tl Tomas Benedikovic/isifa/Getty Images tr David Redfern/Redferns b Tomas Benedikovic/isifa/Getty Images 28 Martin Divisek/Bloomberg via Getty Images 29 r Martin Divisek/Bloomberg via Getty Images 30 tr Scott Eells/Bloomberg via Getty Images l Martin Divisek/Bloomberg via Getty Images cr Adam Berry/Getty Images br Tomas Benedikovic/isifa/Getty Images 31 Patrick T. Fallon/Bloomberg via Getty Images 32 Erich Auerbach/Getty Images 36 Eric Schaal/Time Magazine/The LIFE Picture Collection/Getty Images 37 bl Fox Photos/Getty Images tr CBS Photo Archive/Getty Images 38 tr Archive Photos/Getty Images 41 William P. Gottlieb Collection (Library of Congress) 43 t Charles Hewitt/Picture Post/Hulton Archive/Getty Images cl Silver Screen Collection/Getty Images bl Mark and Colleen Hayward/Redferns br Archive Photos/Getty Images 46 t Topical Press Agency/Getty Images bl Metronome/Getty Images br Keystone/Hulton Archive/Getty Images 47 tl Michael Ochs Archives/Getty Images tr ARCHIVE/AFP/Getty Images b Michael Ochs Archives/Getty Images 48 Archivio Cameraphoto Epoche/Getty Images 55 bl © Pictorial Press Ltd/Alamy 56 tl Michael Ochs Archives/Getty Images 59 tl Michael Ochs Archives/Getty Images tc Michael Ochs Archives/Getty Images tr Michael Ochs Archives/Getty Images bl Michael Ochs Archive/Getty Images 60 Michael Ochs Archives/Getty Images 62 b Topical Press Agency/Getty Images 63 tr Michael Ochs Archives/Getty Images 67 t Earl leaf/Michael Ochs Archives/Getty Images cl John D. Kisch/Separate Cinema Archive/Getty Images bl Michael Ochs Archives/Getty Images br Burton Berinsky/Timepix/The LIFE Images Collection/Getty Images 70 akg-images/Interfoto/TV-yesterday 71 bl akg-images/Interfoto br © Pictorial Press Ltd/Alamy 83 Michael Ochs Archives/Getty Images 85 tl Eliot Elisofon/The LIFE Picture Collection/Getty Images tr Gilles Petard/Redferns bl Paul Hoeffler/Redferns 88 tl Metronome/Getty Images bl FPG/Getty Images

br Michael Ochs Archives/Getty Images 89 tl Metronome/Getty Images tr PoPsie Randolph/Michael Ochs Archives/Getty Images br William Gottlieb/Redferns 90 Popperfoto/Getty Images 92 VisitBritain/Eric Nathan/Getty Images 93 l Archive Photos/Getty Images r ChicagoHistoryMus/UIG/Lebrecht Music & Arts 95 tr Michael Ochs Archives/Getty Images 99 Petra Niemeier - K & K/Redferns 101 bl RB/Redferns br Jim Britt/Michael Ochs Archives/Getty Images 102 tl Michael Ochs Archives/Getty Images 104 t KPA/ullstein bild via Getty Images b David Redfern/Redferns 105 t David Redfern/Redferns b RB/Redferns 106 Michael Ochs Archives/Getty Images 107 Michael Putland/Getty Images 110 BIPs/Getty Images 111 tc GAB Archive/Redferns 113 John Downing/Getty Images 116 bl SSPL/Getty Images br akg-images/Interfoto/Günter Höhne 121 tl Peter Macdiarmid/Getty Images for NARAS tr John D. Kisch/Separate Cinema Archive/Getty Images bl Gus Stewart/Redferns br Chris Walter/WireImage 125 © Martyn Goddard/Corbis 132 Bleddyn Butcher/REX 133 b David Corio/Michael Ochs Archives/Getty Images 136 b Chris Ratcliffe/Bloomberg via Getty Images 137 Michael Ochs Archives/Getty Images 143 bl akg-images/Interfoto 151 Evening Standard/Getty Images 156 Richard E. Aaron/Redferns) 157 t Blank Archives/Getty Images 159 tr GAB Archive/Redferns bl Michael Ochs Archives/Getty Images br Fin Costello/Redferns 166 NASA/JPL 167 tl NASA/Hulton Archive/Getty Images tr Space Frontiers/Archive Photos/Getty Images bl NASA/JPL br Space Frontiers/Archive Photos/Getty Images 168 Ray Stevenson/REX 169 b Brian Cooke/Redferns 173 REX 174 t Terry Lott/Sony Music Archive/Getty Images 175 © Photos 12/Alamy 177 tr Paul Natkin/WireImage b Jack Mitchell/Getty Images 180 t Ebet Roberts/Redferns bl Michael Ochs Archives/Getty Images 181 t KMazur/WireImage b Ed Molinari/NY Daily News Archive via Getty Images 184 © Michael S. Yamashita/Corbis 187 t Mick Hutson/Redferns bl © Peter Anderson/Corbis br Rob Verhorst/Redferns 190 t ITV/REX bl Matthew Lewis/Getty Images br ITV/REX 191 tl Clive Hunte/Redferns 195 Normski/PYMCA REX 197 t Kristy Sparow/Getty Images 197 b Nick Cunard/PYMCA/REX 200 l Martyn Goodacre/Getty Images r PYMCA/UIG via Getty Images 201 t Andy Paradise/The Independent/REX b Chelsea Lauren/WireImage 203 b ITV/REX 204 l Tristan O'Neill/PYMCA/REX r Patrick Barth/REX 205 tr Peter J Walsh/PYMCA/REX br Peter J Walsh/PYMCA/REX 206 tl Jay Brooks/PYMCA/REX bl PYMCA/UIG via Getty Images r Nick Pickles/WireImage 207 r PYMCA/UIG via Getty Images 209 t © Charles Peterson/Retna Ltd./Corbis br David Tonge/Getty Images 212 tl Stuart Mostyn/Redferns/Getty Images b Martyn Goodacre/Getty Images 214 © Neal Preston/Corbis 215 br Ron Galella, Ltd./WireImage 221 Douglas Gorenstein/NBC/NBCU Photo Bank via Getty Images 223 tl © age fotostock/Alamy tr © dpa picture alliance/Alamy 224 t Sebastian Artz/Getty Images 226 tl Sebastian Liste/NOOR. tr Sebastian Liste/NOOR. br Sebastian Liste/NOOR. 228 JazzArchivHamburg/ullstein bild via Getty Images 229 tr GAB Archive/Redferns